Dear unity

Overdue Love Letters to Heal a Divided Church

General Editor

PHILIP RYALL

WHITAKER HOUSE

Boldface type in the Scripture quotations indicates the author's emphasis.

Dear Unity
Overdue Love Letters to Heal a Divided Church

dearunity.com
hello@dearunity.com
Dear Unity
PO Box 165
Surry Hills NSW 2010
Australia

ISBN: 979-8-88769-397-2
eBook ISBN: 979-8-88769-398-9

Printed in the United States of America

Whitaker House
1030 Hunt Valley Circle
New Kensington, PA 15068
www.whitakerhouse.com

Library of Congress Control Number: 2025935740

1 2 3 4 5 6 7 8 9 10 11 **W** 32 31 30 29 28 27 26 25

CONTENTS

INTRODUCTION

Philip Ryall

As in the days of old, where heartfelt apostolic love letters were written to encourage and challenge the early Christian communities with words of life not death, we are reminded by the apostle Paul:

> *You yourselves are our letter, written on our hearts, known and read by everyone. You show that you are a letter from Christ, the result of our ministry, written not with ink but with the Spirit of the living God, not on tablets of stone but on tablets of human hearts.* (2 Corinthians 3:2–3 NIV)

The time has come for believers to drag Christian unity out of the Dark Ages and into the glorious light of a new global connectivity. Could it be that the world is too quickly dividing into chaos because the church is too slowly uniting in peace? The forgotten truth is that by our baptism, we have all been wired by God for unity, to be conduits of His light and power. There is an urgent need for shepherds of the faith to rise up and show the way forward by loving and honoring each other through radical words and works of breathtaking solidarity. The church calls all the faithful to courageously exhibit the beauty of an undivided Jesus into a divided world. On such a journey toward oneness, we must be prepared to come across various forks in the road that may challenge our long-held views. Our heart posture here will determine whether we take the path that leads to a slow understanding of the other … or a quick misunderstanding. While we are clearly called to speak the truth in love, let's make sure that we are acting in love before we speak the truth.

MY STORY TOWARD A DEEPENING GRATITUDE

As the vision bearer of this project, I'm not exactly sure how I came to carry the responsibility of orchestrating a cross-denominational book on Christian unity. I am not a learned theologian but more of a foolish lover who yearns for oneness in God's family, warts and all. I take great comfort in Jesus's words in

Matthew 11:25: *"I thank you, Father, Lord of heaven and earth, that you have hidden these things from the wise and understanding and revealed them to little children."*

To share something of my own faith background, my mother's father was a Polish Jew who married my Irish Catholic grandmother. My devout Catholic mother went on to marry my Anglican-born father. After being raised a Catholic and even serving faithfully as a young altar boy, I soon found myself at a teenage horseback riding camp, where Baptist Church leaders inspired me to commit my life to Jesus in a deeply personal way. On returning from a trail ride the very next afternoon, I encountered an outpouring of God's love on the back of a horse that would change my life forever. Sometime later, back at my Jesuit Catholic secondary college, I affectionately became known as "Father Phil" after my school headmaster priest insisted I take over his personal column in the college magazine for a season in order to share my ecumenical faith discoveries with parents, teachers, and students. Looking back upon that stunning gesture, it was clear that the earliest seeds were being sown in me to write courageous love letters for God that might awaken and soften the hearts of the faithful. And as to my continuing faith experiences, as hard as I tried to ward off the advances of the Pentecostal movement in later years, I failed miserably after encountering the undeniable power of the Holy Spirit when hands were laid on me in prayer. I guess, after all this, one might best describe me today as a committed Catholic with a Pentecostal style and a Baptist smile!

Is it any wonder why my life compass was so predisposed to building bridges of vulnerable unity between the missing family members of my Christian faith? I discovered that by accepting random opportunities to learn, worship, and serve alongside these passionate followers, the cataracts of prejudice and judgmentalism would soon start falling from our eyes. It honestly caused me to wonder what we could all be missing out on—and indeed, what my life may have otherwise become if I had politely closed myself off from these amazing sisters and brothers in my wider church community. Instead, my heart filled with gratitude and gave me the desire to steward ways of showcasing expressions of heroic love and reconciliation across the separated family of Christianity. I believe God is yearning for us all to highlight these expressions of beauty in each other as we rebuild a *culture of honor* together with a new and courageous vigor.

DAY ONE IN HEAVEN: PLEASE FORGIVE ME!

I fancy that Christians today would unanimously accept that in heaven, there will be no division whatsoever. Jesus reminds us: *"People will come from east and west, and from north and south, and recline at table in the kingdom of God. And behold, some are last who will be first, and some are first who will be last"* (Luke 13:29–30).

Now, with this in mind, may I boldly suggest that we do not want to have these types of conversations as we mingle in heaven with those of differing expressions:

"Oh, it's you! Welcome, my brother! But please forgive me, for I knew not who I was ignoring on earth. I didn't know what a man of God I had living so nearby in a neighboring church. I apologize for turning down your dinner invitations. I was closed to the hidden mysteries I now see your church tradition so beautifully carried. I had no idea what passionate love you poured out to God in your Spirit-led worship."

"Forgive me for scoffing at your consecrated Eucharist. I knew not what grace you were carrying for me and what grace I was carrying for you that would have purified our missions."

"I'm sorry, I quite honestly didn't even think you and your church were saved! And yet here I see that God has honored you greatly in a higher place than me. Please accept my humble apologies."

"Although it so wonderful to be here in heaven today, I am troubled that I didn't recognize who you were on earth as I do now in heaven. You are glorious and beautiful. What light of Christ we could have shone if we had only drawn closer together in deeper trust and unity. Please, please forgive me!"

WE ALREADY AGREE ON ENOUGH!

We have just celebrated the momentous 1700-year anniversary of the first ecumenical Council of Nicaea (in modern-day Turkey), where the Roman Emperor Constantine invited more than three hundred bishops of all persuasions to pray and resolve disputes over the divinity of Jesus Christ while forming a common creed on the fundamental theological doctrines of the church. This was a significant foundational milestone.

The easily forgotten truth is that most of today's Christians are now in agreement on nearly all of the primary beliefs of our faith. While we still must work through various secondary issues and interpretations in a humble posture of loving mystery and patience, the gospel remains our clear and common guide as we navigate both the truth of love and the love of truth. Surely we already agree on enough and can no longer afford to find excuses to delay our love one moment longer! My simple spirit tells me that if we can just set out together with a new resolve to listen and pray more than we speak, the Lord will join us on our road to Emmaus and begin to teach us together what we could not discover apart. While perfect agreement must wait, love and unity need not.

THE BACKSTORY OF A MIRACULOUS JOURNEY

Over these past five years, it hasn't always been easy stepping out as an unknown entity—a nobody really—to ask all the somebodies of the church to believe in and get behind the sacred vision of this book. Thankfully, it didn't take very long for others to recognize that this good idea was more like a God idea! One after the other, replies to my invitations started coming back thick and fast. Cardinal P. Raniero Cantalamessa, the appointed preacher to the papal household for three popes over four decades, suggested that this vision came straight from the heart of the Father. To him, he wasn't saying yes to me, but yes to God. Then Heidi Baker took it to prayer with her Spirit-filled community in Africa, only to report back with a sense of excitement for the grace they believed this book was destined to release. Randy Clark only took twenty minutes to say yes. Others took months.

The general secretary of the World Council of Churches, Jerry Pillay, graciously agreed to take part. Some said no; some said yes but later retracted for reasons unknown. Francis Chan initially said no as he was only willing to share if God gave him a clear message on what to write. Thankfully after I boldly reapproached him several months later, he had an inspiration from prayer and agreed to write his beautiful chapter on Communion.

There were so many other signs and stories that helped me to see this book as a miracle in the making. Even the unexpected challenges in finding a strong and willing publisher became a testing, two-year process despite the impressive gallery of devout authors from diverse backgrounds. I think the words of C. S. Lewis (from *Out of the Silent Planet*) best sum up my privileged experience in all this: "The journey you go on is your pain, and perhaps your cure: for you must be either mad or brave before it is ended."

OPENING WIDE THE DOORS OF WELCOME

Perhaps it's not surprising to discover that *hospitality* derives from the root word *hospital* (*hospes* in Latin), where weary guests would be readily welcomed, fed, and given healing respite from their often-treacherous journey.

So it was in the story of the Good Samaritan in Luke 10:30–37, in which the beaten robbery victim is treated and taken to the hospital-like inn at Jericho by the caring stranger of another religious expression.

As a broken church, we must come as both the healer and the afflicted. We each carry the oil and wine of the other's healing when it comes to unity. They have mine and I have theirs. The Good Samaritan gave up his time, gave up the comfort of riding his donkey so it bore the wounded stranger instead, and gave up his finances to pay for the stranger's care. And he made plans to return to oversee the ongoing recovery of his newfound brother.

Unity is expensive—*dear* in every sense of the word. Just as Jesus paid the ultimate price by dying for us while we were still sinners, are we not equally called to go out of our way to love and forgive our neighbor well before we think they meet our standards? We're never really loved until we are loved and accepted unconditionally. The long-standing sickness of division in the church is in dire need of a hospital of new, merciful love and hospitality from those of another expression. The front doors of our churches and family homes must be flung wide open to become new places of a radical welcome where healing, honor, and tenderness are not limited by any set opening or closing times.

UNITY DINNER—OH, WHAT A NIGHT!

For me, it started out as a simple idea when I bravely suggested to my wife Jennie that we host a sit-down dinner party in our family home for more than sixty guests to celebrate the global week of prayer for Christian unity. Like any initiative that promotes God's pet subject of unity, we were soon to encounter heaven's favor as we cleared out all of our furniture and made room for dear unity. As with a great wedding banquet, we intentionally set out to do everything with a spirit of excellence, from the dining experience to the table settings to the quality of musicians and the colorful speeches given by the many leaders who represented the various expressions of Christianity across our city. Guests included pastors, bishops, a Salvation Army major, priests and religious sisters, Indigenous pastors and elders, family, and friends.

A beloved Greek Orthodox bishop wore his majestic black garments as we celebrated both unity and his birthday. Other guests included Mozambique missionary Dr. Heidi Baker, a former Australian prime minister, and the worship legend Darlene Zschech, who led us in the singing of "Amazing Grace." And I cannot forget to mention the brilliant rapping Pentecostal pastor who spontaneously sung his ecumenical rhymes from table to table, drawing bouts of laughter from all. Oh, what a night!

As I later welcomed everyone into our home, I reminded them that this was not merely a gathering of distant cousins but a gathering of close family members because we all share the same Father. When we come to appreciate this fact, we are then ready to pray the "Our Father" together with the true conviction Jesus so desired. Late into the night, we finished with holy songs and an exchange of contact information. Many of us left anticipating the likely blessing that falls over entire cities whose believers learn to befriend the strangers in their midst, only to find the richness of their unmet family while doing so. (See documentary of this night at www.dearunity.com/dinner.)

THE COMMANDED BLESSING AWAITS

Psalm 133 speaks of this great grace of unity as the commanded blessing of God, which is likened to the precious oil poured over the head of Aaron, the first high priest, before running down his beard and descending onto the whole body. May I boldly suggest that this *Dear Unity* vision is less about a book of unity and more about a movement of unity—a downward movement from heaven to earth. It begins with the heads of many church expressions who have deemed the oil of unity to be far too precious or *dear* to hold only for themselves. We too are being inspired as members of the body of Christ to take new opportunities to come under this offered grace and be strangely saturated by the blessed contributions of so many of our leading brothers and sisters gathered here in this book of unity. Each share a common passion to see the prayer that Jesus so fervently expressed in John 17 finally come about on our watch.

As each chapter unfolds, please do not run for shelter should any sacred downpour start raining on your long-held views or valid concerns. Seek less to understand but rather to stand under the potential grace that each author brings so that the precious oil from these pages may flow into any wounds of division being revealed in your own heart. I pray that any unknown pride or prejudice is exposed, challenged, softened, and ultimately healed so that we find ourselves able to love and accept others at a whole new level.

Let us pray as David did: "*Search me, God, and know my heart; test me and know my anxious thoughts. See if there is any offensive way in me, and lead me in the way everlasting*" (Psalm 139:23–24 NIV).

"MAKE US ONE" PRAYER

(Adapted from John 17 for all to pray with Jesus for unity)

Dear Father,

We join with Jesus in His final prayer for unity, asking first that You protect us as Your disciples here on earth by the power of Your name, the name You gave Your Son Jesus, so that we may be one as You and He are one. May You not take us out of the world but protect us from the evil one. Please sanctify us by the truth because Your Word is truth.

We pray too for *all* our brothers and sisters who believe in Your Son Jesus through their testimony. That we all may be one, just as You, Father, are in Jesus and He is in You. May we also together be in Your oneness of love so that the world may believe that You sent Your only Son.

Father, You have given Your church the same glory that You gave Jesus, so that we may be one as You are one—Jesus in us and You, Father, in Jesus—so that we together may be brought to complete unity. Then the world will know that You sent Jesus and have loved us even as You have loved Him.

Father, make us one! We pray this prayer now with renewed confidence in the power of Jesus's name. Amen.

Philip Ryall is the general editor of ***Dear Unity*** *and the visionary behind this global movement. To connect with Philip, visit www.dearunity.com.*

JOIN THE MOVEMENT!

Share your own online postcard of love and unity to another Christian expression at dearunity.com/post.

1

HOW BEAUTIFUL IT IS TO DWELL IN UNITY

Nicky Gumbel
| Anglican |

How good and pleasant it is when God's people live together in unity! . . .
For there the Lord *bestows his blessing, even life forevermore.*
—Psalm 133:1, 3 (NIV)

There is something amazingly powerful about unity. Unity is not simply the work of the Holy Spirit but the very instrument through which the Holy Spirit works.

Unity is not easy. Saint Paul writes, "*Make every **effort** to keep the unity of the Spirit*" (Ephesians 4:3 NIV). Paul was writing to people who probably knew people who'd actually seen the risen Jesus—and yet they were struggling with unity. So if you're struggling with unity, you're not alone! Unity is hard and has been from the earliest days.

Why is that? Well, Adam and Eve fell out. Cain and Abel fell out. Unity is really hard. No couple in marriage are completely compatible. Marriage is about how you deal with your incompatibilities. And that's true of every relationship. In business, no working relationships are 100 percent compatible. It's hard to have unity in a business. It's hard to have unity in a charity. It's hard to have unity in a local church.

We are so blessed that at Holy Trinity Brompton (HTB) Church, our church in London, God has blessed us with unity for so many years all through the leadership of my predecessors John Collins and Sandy Millar. I was so blessed to inherit that unity, and I don't take it for granted. I value it so much. But it's not easy to maintain the unity. We have to make an effort every single day.

Some people think it *is* easy for us at HTB. They say, "It's okay for you, Nicky, to have unity at HTB, but you don't understand what I'm facing in my church. We have Fred; Fred is impossible to work with! If *you* had Fred, *you* couldn't work with him." Let me tell you something: we've got lots of Freds in our church—and I'm one of them! It's not easy. None of us are easy to work with.

And in the denominations, we're struggling with unity. It is a challenge for the global church. Look at the struggles over women bishops, over baptism, over contraception, over issues of sexuality. It's easy to argue. It's really easy to split. It's easy to start our own group with everyone who agrees with us. But Paul says, "*Make every effort.*" We are to be zealous, be eager, spare no effort, and take pains to keep the unity of the Holy Spirit.

How do we do that? Well, he says, we need the right attitude. What's the right attitude?

- *Be completely humble.* Because pride causes division. People are struggling for power, and it leads to division.
- *Be gentle.* That's the opposite of arrogance. Jesus was humble and He was gentle, the model for us.
- *Be patient, long-suffering, "bearing with one another in love"* (Ephesians 4:2 NIV). I looked up the word for "*bearing with one another.*" It means *enduring* one another, putting up with one another!
- And it can only be done in *love*. Love is what binds it all together. That's why Jesus said, "*By this all people will know that you are my disciples, if you have* ***love*** *for one another*" (John 13:35).

If all that sounds like too much hard work, you might say, "Why bother? It's so hard making all that effort."

We're living in extraordinary times; in some ways, they are times of great crisis. There's a crisis of *faith*. And in a time of crisis, we can split and run, or we can stand together. And I believe that this crisis is a massive opportunity for us as a church to stand together and fight together.

So what's the key to unity?

First, unity is *relational*. Unity is around the Trinity. The best model for unity you'll find in the universe is the model of the Trinity: Father, Son, and Holy Spirit—one God, united.

And unity around *Jesus* is the key to the evangelisation of a nation. Paul says in Ephesians 4:5 that there is *"one Lord,"* Jesus, and *"one faith,"* faith in Jesus. It's the risen Jesus who is alive today. It's all about Him.

There's one Lord. There's one faith. There's one hope: Jesus. And that's why, as Cardinal Raniero Cantalamessa, the preacher to the papal household, has often said, "What unites us is infinitely greater than what divides us." If the world sees us divided, they're never going to believe.

I have a friend who's not a Christian. He said to me, "You Protestants and Catholics look exactly the same to me. You both have churches, you both say the Lord's Prayer, you do services that look similar to me. Whatever it is that divides you—and I have absolutely no idea what it is—it's got nothing to do with my life. But while you're fighting each other, I'm not interested."

That's why Jesus prayed, *"That they may all be one ... so that the world may believe"* (John 17:21). Because He saw that my friend was not going to believe unless we *are* united.

Unity's not an *option*. It was Jesus's last prayer. He's still praying it. What's He praying for? He's praying for our unity, *so that the world will believe*. Because the world is desperate!

That's why we've been hosting the Alpha Course for many years. My wife Pippa and I absolutely love it because at every course, we see people coming to know Jesus Christ, having their lives changed.

There is such a hunger out there for the truth. Some people don't even believe Jesus existed. They don't realize He existed in spite of all the evidence. But the majority of people have a Christian friend, and they admire their Christian friend. What an opportunity this is to bring people the good news about Jesus. It's the only hope for the world.

Jesus died on a cross for *you*. You're forgiven. You're free. Jesus has died for you. He's risen from the dead. He's alive! There's hope for *you*.

This is the most amazing message: God *loves* you. Jesus died for you. What an amazing message we have for the world! Why would we be fighting each other instead of telling the world the good news about Jesus? What a waste of time when there's such an urgent message for the world!

Second, unity of the Holy Spirit is key to the *revitalization of the church*. We are one body, Paul says, one Spirit. Jesus only has one body on earth! He doesn't have lots of bodies! He has *one* body. And we are all part of it.

But unity does not mean unanimity. It doesn't mean that we have to agree on everything. Disagreement is healthy. We have a rule in our church called the *obligation to dissent*. I say to everyone, "If you disagree, please say so. It's *good* to disagree."

I was a barrister for several years, and I believe in the English legal system, which is that you have a strong statement of two opposite points of view, and that's how you get at the truth. So it's good to have disagreement. Meetings are really boring if you don't have disagreement; it makes them interesting.

But it is within a relationship of love that we disagree. And when a decision's made, we have to back the leader.

So unity does not mean unanimity ... nor does it mean uniformity. It doesn't mean that we all have to look alike, sound alike, dress alike, think alike. In 1 Corinthians 12, Paul says there is this huge variety in any body, and there are different parts. I used to think that if some part of the church was different from me, they must be wrong. Now I think, "Wow, if they're different from me, I must have so much to learn from them."

And I've come to love the Catholic Church. We did the first Alpha for Catholics conference in 1996, and we saw the most amazing outpouring of the Holy Spirit at that conference. That night, I went home, and I again read Acts 11:17, where God says that if He has given the same Spirit to others, *who are we to oppose God?*

The same Spirit lives in the Catholics and the Orthodox and the Pentecostals and the Protestants... even the Anglicans have the same Holy Spirit living within them. That's what makes us one.

This doesn't mean we're not interested in the truth. Paul speaks of "*speaking the truth in love*" (Ephesians 4:15). We need truth. John Stott said, "Love becomes weak if it's not strengthened by truth. Truth becomes hard if it's not softened by love." I think this is so true.

You know the church's history. The Donatists in the fourth century thought they were the only true Christians, and they separated. And there was a debate with Saint Augustine who said, "No, you haven't got the truth because you only have truth if you have unity."

If you lose one part of the body of Christ, you lose a part of the truth, because that part will see things in a different way. And the only way that we'll get the truth is through unity. The more we have the whole body of Christ, who see different aspects of the truth, the closer we get to the truth. Unity and truth are not opposed; they're complementary.

And so, Paul says, *"Speaking the truth in love, we will grow to become in every respect the mature body of him who is the head, that is, Christ. From him the whole body, joined and held together by every supporting ligament, grows and builds itself up in love, as each part does its work"* (Ephesians 4:15–16 NIV).

Could we resolve to love one another, to learn from one another, to honor one another, to speak well of one another, to stop hating each other, and to stop fighting each other?

You know, in a body, it's absurd, isn't it? The hand and the eye are one body. Paul said if someone's attacking my eye, what does the hand do? It comes to its defense.

If someone's attacking another part of the body of Christ, let's go to their defense, even if it's not *our* part. What damage we do when we start punching ourselves and attacking another part of the body of Christ—because there's *one body*! So let's defend one another. Let's fight for one another and stop criticizing one another.

As the late Pope Francis once said, "Let's trust the Holy Spirit, who can heal and reconcile us and accomplish what humanly does not seem possible."

Unity comes around Jesus. Unity comes from the Holy Spirit. Unity comes from the Father, who is the key to the transformation of society.

We live in a divided world, and a divided world demands a united church. What is the root of all the problems in the world? Division and the breakdown of relationships: breakdown of marriage, breakdown of family life, breakdown internally in nations, and between nations. This is at the root of all the problems in the world. And we have the answer! What is the answer? Paul gives the answer in Ephesians 4:6: *"One God and Father of all, who is over all and through all and in all."* The answer is in relationships.

Third, we have the model of unity as *the family*: the family of God, with God as our Father. We are brothers and sisters, one family, united around the Father. Whatever part of the body of Christ you belong to, you love Jesus, and I love Jesus. Whatever part of the body of Christ you belong to, you have the

Holy Spirit living in you, and I have the Holy Spirit living in me. But more than that, God is your Father, and God is my Father. That's why we're brothers and sisters, together in one family. And that's why this is all relational.

In a family, we don't exclude people we disagree with. You can disagree vehemently with someone's views in a family but they're still part of the *family*.

The devil is prowling around trying to divide us. I saw a program on BBC entitled *Wildlife on One*. And they filmed a lion waiting to kill a springbok. What the lion does is it waits and waits until two springboks start fighting each other—and at that moment, their attention is diverted, and the lion pounces.

"The devil prowls around like a roaring lion" (1 Peter 5:8), waiting for the church to fight each other, and at that moment, he pounces. We have to resist the devil. We have to say, "We're not going to fight each other. We're not going to allow you to pounce and to destroy the church. We are going to unite. We're going to keep attentive. We're going to keep vigilant. And we're going to ensure that we resist you."

We need a new perspective on the issues in the world. What are we fighting about as churches? The issues may be *significant*; I am not saying they are not. There are big issues in the church. Let's discuss them. They're important. But how important are they compared to the fact that ISIS beheads Christians?

Before they behead a Christian, do they ask, "Could you tell me, are you a Coptic Christian, Catholic, Pentecostal, Protestant?"

"Oh, I'm a Protestant."

"Okay. Well, are you conservative or liberal?"

They don't ask those questions; they just behead them because they're *Christian*. *They* think we're united. *They* think we're just one body. Well, why are we thinking we're not?! We *are* one body! Let's get perspective.

This is my *longing*: that our children and our grandchildren will look back at this generation of the church and they *won't* say, "They just kept splitting. They kept fighting each other about issues that they thought were important at the time, but now we see with a little bit of perspective that they weren't *that* important." I am passionate that we won't see that happen.

My dream, my longing, is that they'll look back and they'll say, "This generation, they got together. They united. They decided they were going to lay aside their personal agendas, the political agendas, all the *stuff* that could get in the way of unity, and they resolved to unite around Jesus. They resolved that they would so seek the Holy Spirit and be filled with the Holy Spirit that the Spirit would bring about this unity, the unity of the Holy Spirit. And that they would see each other, whatever parts of the body of Christ they were—rather than criticizing them, rather than fighting with them—they would see each other as brothers and sisters with the same Father. They resolved that they would do everything in their power, make every effort. And from that, a movement spread that brought a unity to the church. They saw the evangelization of their nations. They saw the revitalization of the church. They saw the transformation of their society."

If that is your dream too, will you join me in praying for it and making every effort to see it happen in our lifetimes?

DEAR BROTHERS AND SISTERS:

If the world sees us divided, they are never going to believe. We need to stand together, in unity, as one church, lifting high the name of Jesus so that all will see and believe.

Father, our prayer today is that the name of Jesus will be honored in our nations and our world. Lord, we thank You that denominational barriers are coming down. We pray that there will be such a unity in the churches that people outside would be astonished and say, "What is it that all these people are agreed about?" And they will believe in You as a result. We pray that our societies will be transformed by the love and the power of Jesus Christ. And, Lord, we pray for an outpouring of Your Spirit, that You would fill each one of us with Your Holy Spirit. Give us a big vision, like You gave to Saint Paul, of what You could do with each of our lives. Help us to work together, fixing our eyes on Jesus, so that Your name will be glorified and Your kingdom come. Amen.

Nicky Gumbel is an Anglican priest and pioneer of the Alpha Movement. You may connect with him at alpha.org.

2

MY JOURNEY TOWARD LOVE FOR CHRISTIAN UNITY

Cardinal P. Raniero Cantalamessa
| Catholic |

I did my theological studies in Loreto, Italy, from 1954 to 1959. I still have many of my course notes and every so often, I glance at them again. The lessons almost always followed the same pattern: the proposed position, what the adversaries hold, and the proof that always crowned the Catholic position. In a few instances, the adversaries holding opposing views were the Orthodox, but in the great majority of cases, our adversaries were Protestant. I suspect that, within the other denominations, things were pretty much the same, except that the adversaries—or heretics—were us Catholics. I not only accepted this *esprit de corps,* but in my own youthful enthusiasm, at times felt the need to add my own voice to the chorus, like a child who yells at someone when he hears one of his parents yelling at him.

I pursued a doctorate in theology in Fribourg, Switzerland, from 1959 to 1962, but not much had changed by then. Although it was during the years of the Second Vatican Council, all our study texts and manuals were the ones previously in print. Without a doubt, the council was a definitive turning point inaugurating a new era for the Catholic Church in ecumenical concerns. From *adversaries,* the other Christians came to be known first as *our separated brothers,* and then simply as *our brothers.*

The council created a doctrinal basis for this change to occur, but the council was not, at least for myself, the determining factor. For myself, the precipitating factor was my contact with the Catholic Charismatic Renewal and receiving the baptism of the Holy Spirit in the United States in 1977. I will not recount all the circumstances of that event here. There was, however, one specific moment that had a deep impact on me. It was at a Charismatic Ecumenical Conference taking place in Kansas City in July 1977, with about 40,000 people—about half of them Catholic, and the other half of various Christian denominations. We were in the stadium one evening, and one of the leaders approached the microphone and began speaking in a way totally unknown to me at that time: "Cry and mourn, because the body of My Son is broken!" Little by little, I saw the people around me fall to their knees, sobbing and praying. While all this was going on in the stadium, the words, "Jesus is Lord" appeared in bright lights written overhead, which struck me as a living prophecy. I said to myself, "This is exactly how it would be if one day, Christians were to be reunited in a single body: we would all be on our knees, shedding tears of repentance, under Christ's overarching lordship."

It wasn't any theological discourse or argumentation that changed my attitude toward Christians of other churches, but rather, that change happened spontaneously as part and parcel of my baptism in the Holy Spirit, without any effort on my part. The grace of unity came with the gift of the Spirit.

I later realized that what I had experienced in the Charismatic movement exactly replicated the experience of the church at its beginning. How was it that the risen Lord moved the primitive Jewish community to open itself to the gentiles and to accept them into the one church? Simply by filling the gentiles with the Holy Spirit and by gifting them with the same Spirit in all its myriad forms and manifestations with which He had filled the Jewish believers at Pentecost. Peter came to the inescapable conclusion: *"If then God gave them the same gift he gave to us when we came to believe in the Lord Jesus Christ, who was I to be able to hinder God?"* (Acts 11:17 NAB).

The same thing has happened over the last century. The risen Lord has lavished His Spirit on Christians of various denominations—often with the same, identical manifestations, precisely to eliminate any cause for doubt—and we have no choice but to accept the same conclusion that Peter came to. Who are we to say that those who have received the Spirit of Christ are not members of the body of Christ? No one church has a monopoly on the Holy Spirit!

The first opportunity I had of manifesting my new attitude toward the brothers and sisters of other churches was at the international conference of the leaders of the Catholic Charismatic Renewal held in Rome in 1984. I was asked to give a teaching on "The Church as a Sacrament of Unity." Among other things, I remember sharing this reflection of mine: "The question many today are beginning to raise is this: should the communion I feel as a Catholic be deeper with those many people who were baptized in my own church but have completely disassociated themselves from Christ and are Christian in name only? Or with those many others who, despite belonging to other denominations, believe in the same fundamental truths that I believe in, truly love Jesus Christ to the point of giving their lives for Him, and work in the power of the same Holy Spirit? We cannot evade this issue for long; we must give some response. To continue giving precedence to institutional communion over spiritual communion—in those instances where, unfortunately, the two do not coincide—goes against a very traditional principle, by placing a communion based on external signs (in traditional terminology *communio sacramentorum*) above a communion based on the reality of the signs (*societas sanctorum*), which is the Holy Spirit."

One of the guest participants at that conference was a man I had never met before and, unfortunately, never had the pleasure of meeting again, the Pentecostal pastor David du Plessis. It was he who, following my talk, suggested the Vatican's Secretariat for Christian Unity (now the Pontifical Council for Christian Unity) should invite me to become a member of the Catholic delegation participating in the dialogue with the Pentecostal churches. (He was the organizer and the first chairman of the Pentecostal delegation.) And that's how I found myself to be part of the Catholic delegation, through the good offices of a Pentecostal brother!

This experience was a true blessing in my life. Sitting down together, one week a year, for over a decade, around the same table, sharing prayer and our thoughts, we developed close human relationships—not just academic or operational relationships, but real ones. It was there, when I was able to listen to them face-to-face, that I became aware of how dissimilar the various viewpoints of the other Christians were in comparison to what I had read about them in books, and how much more difficult it was to always come out a winner in our discussions.

The divergence of doctrinal positions and structures between the Catholic Church and the Pentecostal churches was no barrier to creating deep, spiritual bonds and authentic friendships, which are the underpinning of any true reconciliation among Christians. I saw something extremely interesting happening in those dialogues. When we were around a table asking and answering what we called *hard questions*, we couldn't be more divided between us; after discussion, however, when we went to the chapel, sharing the Word of God and praying together (often in tongues), nobody could tell who was a Catholic or a Pentecostal.

In the meantime, I was involved in a project for the "decade of evangelization in preparation for the coming of the Third Millennium of the birth of Christ," sponsored by the Catholic Tom Forrest, the Lutheran Larry Christenson, and the Anglican Michael Harper. The heart and soul of this project was expressed in the form of a question. "Until now, Christians of diverse denominations have proclaimed the gospel in competition with one another, thus compromising the effectiveness of the proclamation itself. Why not use this extraordinary occasion to finally proclaim to the world that Jesus Christ alone is the Lord and Savior, in a spirit of reconciliation and in fraternal unanimity, respecting the traditions of the respective churches and the directives of each one's hierarchy?" Based on that challenge, a European meeting took place in Bern in 1990, followed by another international meeting in Brighton in 1991, and subsequently other continental ones such as that in Orlando, Florida, in the United States, in 1995. All of them focused on three facets: renewal, unity, and evangelization.

The Brighton rally in 1991, in my view, proved to be the most significant. I started my talk, just as we Catholics begin the holy Mass, namely by confessing my sins against unity and my love of Christians of other denominations. Then I quoted Ephesians 2:14–18 (NAB):

> *For he is our peace, he who made both one and broke down the dividing wall of enmity, through his flesh, abolishing the law with its commandments and legal claims, that he might create in himself one new person in place of the two, thus establishing peace, and might reconcile both with God, in one body, through the cross, putting that enmity to death by it. He came and preached peace to you who were far off and peace to those who were near, for through him we both have access in one Spirit to the Father.*

"This passage from Scripture," I said, "has come true among us today. We too can proclaim to the world: Jesus Christ is our peace. He has made us one people by breaking down the dividing wall of hostility. Through Him, in one Spirit, we, Christians of different denominations, have access to the Father."

I ended my talk with a prayer: "Just like on the day of Pentecost, here we are, men and women *from every nation under the sun*, gathered in Your presence, summoned by You. Renew the wonder of that first Pentecost. Make us, too, *one heart and one Spirit, so that the world may believe.*"

Never had I witnessed a response like the one that followed. There was a standing ovation (I am sure to the Word of God, not to me), followed by a prolonged singing in tongues.

My ecumenical openness has not remained limited to the Pentecostal and Charismatic churches. Once the Lord asked me to leave my university teaching position to dedicate myself full time to evangelization, I soon discovered the power behind the thought of Luther; his works are among the books I always have at hand. His name has been pronounced on more than one occasion in my preaching to the papal household in the pope's presence, and certainly not in a context of repudiation. In May 2003, I was invited to the *Ökumenischer Kirchentag* (Ecumenical Church Congress) in Berlin, sponsored by both the Lutheran and Catholic churches. In my talk, among other things, I remember saying, "I am a Catholic—and in addition an Italian one!—but I have to say that there are times when I wish that Germany would give another Luther to the world of today, because certain particular doctrines and controversial points aside, Luther for me is the man whose faith in Jesus Christ was more rock-solid than granite. But we must move ahead together; our present situation is no longer the same as that of his time. In the tales of medieval battles, there always comes a moment when the orderly ranks of archers and cavalry and all the rest are broken and the fighting concentrates around the king. That is where the outcome of the battle will be decided. For us too, the battle today is taking place around the King. … It is the person of Jesus Christ Himself that is the real point at issue, no longer a particular doctrine."

In 2017, for the fifth centenary of the Protestant Reformation, I delivered a sermon in the pontifical household on "Justification by Faith," which was published in Germany in *Stimmen der Zeit* (*Voices of the Time*) and in the United States in the *Journal of Ecumenical Studies*. This is how I concluded my bird's-eye view of the five centuries since the beginning of the Protestant Reformation: "It is vital for the centenary of the Reformation not to be wasted and for us not to remain prisoners of the past, in trying to determine rights and wrongs, even if that is done in a more irenic tone than in the past. Instead, we need to take a leap forward, just as a ship reaching a river lock resumes its course at a higher level. The situation has changed since then. This does not mean ignoring the enrichment brought by the Reformation and wanting to restore the state of things prior to it. Rather, it means allowing all of Christianity to benefit from its many important achievements once they have been freed from certain distortions and excesses resulting from the overheated climate of the time and major abuses have been duly corrected."

I also had wonderful and encouraging experiences with the Anglican Church. In November 2015, the Archbishop of Canterbury Justin Welby invited me to preach at Westminster during the Mass for the inauguration of the General Synod of the Anglican Communion, in the queen's presence. It was an incredible sign of the shared quest for unity among Christians, as Queen Elizabeth II herself remarked in the meeting that followed the Mass. The main message of my homily was this:

> Unity needs to start among the big historical churches, those that are well structured, putting together that which unites them, which is vastly more important than what divides them; not imposing uniformity but aiming at what Pope Francis calls *reconciled diversities*. Nothing is more important than fulfilling Christ's own heart's desire for unity. In many parts of the world, people are killed and churches burned down not because they are Catholic, or Anglican, or Pentecostal, but because they are Christians. In their eyes, we are already one! Let us be one also in our eyes and in the eyes of God. The Anglican Church has a special role in all of this. It has often defined itself as a *via media*, a middle way, between Roman Catholicism and Reformed Christianity. From being a via media in a *static* sense, it must now become more and more a via media in a *dynamic* sense, exercising an active function as a bridge between the churches. The presence among you of a priest of the Catholic Church, in circumstances of such special significance, is a sign that something of the kind is already happening.

Besides this event, I had the privilege of collaborating on many occasions with Nicky Gumbel at Alpha Course. One of the dearest memories of my ministry with other Christian denominations was the leaders conference sponsored by Alpha Course that took place at the Royal Albert Hall in London in 2015, on "Proclaiming Together the Joy of the Gospel to a Troubled World."

I can't conclude the story of my *conversion* to love for unity without mentioning another healing the Lord has worked in me, one that I believe must accompany the healing of relationships among all Christian denominations. I am referring to a reconciliation with the people of Israel. I will never forget the first moment of my conversion in this regard. I was on an airplane, returning from my first pilgrimage to the Holy Land. I was reading the Bible and a phrase from Ephesians 5:29 (NAB) struck me: *"No one hates his own flesh."* I understood that this also applied to Jesus's own relationship with His people, those of His flesh. And with that, I recognized that my prejudices towards the Jewish people, which had been unwittingly instilled in me during my formative years, were offensive to Jesus Himself. I understood that I needed a conversion toward Israel, *"the Israel of God,"* in the apostle's own words in Galatians 6:16.

This new attitude found concrete expression in the homilies I have been preaching for forty years in St. Peter's Basilica during the Good Friday liturgy of the passion, in the presence of the pope. For centuries, this day of the year was the day the Jews were most afraid of because of hostile representations and even popular mobilization against them. Whenever the dates of the celebration coincided, in my homily, I tried to send a greeting or highlight the connection between the Jewish Passover and the Christian Easter in positive terms.

The Good Friday homily of 1998, entitled "He Broke Down the Wall of Separation," was entirely dedicated to this issue. The text was translated and circulated in various languages and was commented on positively in some Jewish magazines. In it, I tried to get to the spiritual root of Christian anti-Semitism, showing that the latter was not born out of *fidelity* to the Christian Scriptures, as some had recently suggested, but out of *infidelity* to them. Jesus, the apostles, and Stephen the deacon (see Acts 7) all spoke out against the Jewish leaders, and at times very harshly. But in what spirit did they do this? Jesus wept when he foretold the destruction of Jerusalem, just as he did at the death of Lazarus, his friend. Stephen died crying out, *"Lord, do not hold this sin against them"* (Acts 7:60 NAB). Paul, who is most often blamed for all of this, said something that surely must make us shudder:

> *I speak the truth in Christ, I do not lie; my conscience joins with the holy Spirit in bearing me witness, that I have great sorrow and constant anguish in my heart. For I could wish that I myself were accursed and separated from Christ for the sake of my brothers, my kin according to the flesh.* (Romans 9:1–3 NAB)

These men were speaking as members of the Jewish people; they identified themselves as Jews and were one with their people, members of the same religious and human family. They could say, *"Are they Hebrews? So am I. Are they Israelites? So am I. Are they descendants of Abraham? So am I"* (2 Corinthians 11:22 NAB). When you love someone, you can talk like that. Were the prophets and Moses any less harsh in confronting Israel? At times, they were even harsher. But did the Jewish people take offense at Moses and the prophets for saying such things to them or accuse them of anti-Semitism? No, because they knew they were speaking out of love. Dante Alighieri, in his *Divine Comedy,* uttered terrible words against Italy, Florence, and the Catholic Church of his time, but we Italians are not offended by them; we know that he was one of us; he did not rejoice, but suffered in denouncing evil.

What happened in the transition from the primitive Judeo-Christian church to the church of the gentiles? The gentiles picked up from Jesus and the apostles the arguments leveled against some Jews of His time, but none of the love for the Jews. The polemic was passed on, but the love was not. When the church fathers later speak of the accomplished destruction of Jerusalem, they do not shed tears. On the contrary! It is here that we discover the root of the problem, in our lack of love, in our infidelity to the central precept of the gospel. From this point we should start, and, on this ground, we should also build, a real (not just a formal or doctrinal) Judeo-Christian dialogue and reconciliation.

As a result of these mutual relationships, when in the consistory of November 2020, I was made cardinal by the late Pope Francis, some of the very first people who sent congratulations to me were Dr. Alon Goshen-Gottstein, director of the Elijah Interfaith Institute in Jerusalem, and Marco Cassuto Morselli, president of the Association for Hebrew-Christian Friendship in Italy.

Let me end the account of my ecumenical pilgrimage on a lighter tone, like Beethoven's Ninth Symphony. There's a Black spiritual entitled "There Is a Balm in Gilead" that I like very much. The words are accompanied by a music that is heartrending in its simplicity:

There is a balm in Gilead
To make the wounded whole;
There is a balm in Gilead
To heal the sin-sick soul.
Sometimes I feel discouraged
And think my work's in vain,
But then the Holy Spirit
Revives my soul again.

Gilead, or Galaad, is mentioned in the Old Testament as a place famous for its perfumes and ointments. (See Jeremiah 8:22.) As the song progresses, it becomes clear that the real balm—of which the balm of Gilead is just a symbol—is the Holy Spirit.

The Spirit is the great *remedy* for the wounds of the church and love for the unity of Christians is the clearest sign of His presence in us today. In Sermon 269, Saint Augustine beautifully expresses this truth: "As at the beginning of the Church, the fact that one person was able to speak various languages was a sign of the presence of the Holy Spirit, so now *the love of unity* that makes many people one, is a sign of his presence. ... Know, therefore, that you have the Holy Spirit when you adhere to unity by the sincerity of your love."

There is, however, a Christian church with which I have had very few occasions to work with and to share our common love for unity, the Eastern Orthodox Church. During Lent 2015, I gave a series of meditations to the papal household on Catholic and Orthodox relationships; it was entitled, "Two Lungs, One Breath." My intention was to contribute to the present efforts of the leaders of both churches, Pope Francis and Patriarch Bartholomew, in view of a full communion between the two *sister churches*. Following the publication of these meditations, I had the joy of being asked by an Orthodox publisher to publish a series of my meditations on the Holy Spirit in Greek. But this is still minimal and indirect and does not satisfy my great love and admiration for the Orthodox tradition and spirituality. This is why I would like to make up for the omission by writing to them a kind of "love letter," much in the spirit of the other contributions of the present collection:

DEAR ORTHODOX PATRIARCHS, METROPOLITANS, BISHOPS, PRIESTS, MONKS AND MONIALES, LAY BROTHERS AND SISTERS,

Peace be with you!

I have just finished reading the monumental work on *The Christian Tradition* by Jaroslav Pelikan—who incidentally ended his religious pilgrimage by joining the Orthodox Church—and I am still under the impression of the immense debt of gratitude we Christians of every other denomination owe to you. The incredible intellectual effort to establish the fundamental truth of our religion—the Trinity, the perfect divinity and humanity of the unique person of Christ—has been primarily the work of your forefathers. The close connection between theology and spirituality, doctrine and life, which should characterize every expression of Christian faith, shines most especially in your tradition. During my studies and ministry, I fell in love with the Cappadocian Fathers, Maximus the Confessor, Simeon the New Theologian, Nicolas Cabasilas, Silvanus of Mount Athos, and Seraphim of Sarov, and never cease drawing on them.

I know that one of the principal obstacles to a full communion between our own churches is not theological in nature, but historical. In the past, especially in the events leading to the fall of Constantinople, the western Christian world did terrible wrongs to your church that did not take place without some responsibility of the Catholic Church and the popes of the time.

What I dare suggest is the same I dared say to our Protestant brothers and sisters on the above-mentioned occasion: "Let us not remain prisoners of the past, in trying to determine rights and wrongs. Instead, we need to take a leap forward, just as a ship reaching a river lock resumes its course at a higher level." The gospel needs all our joint forces to be proclaimed to the modern post-Christian world. Let us repeat with the apostle Paul: *"Forgetting what lies behind but straining forward to what lies ahead, I continue my pursuit toward the goal, the prize of God's upward calling, in Christ Jesus"* (Philippians 3:13–14 NAB).

Cardinal P. Raniero Cantalamessa is a Capuchin Franciscan, the preacher emeritus to the papal household, and the author of numerous books. He may be reached at www.cantalamessa.org.

3

ONENESS OF HEART CREATED BY THE SPIRIT

Randy Clark
| Charismatic |

As the proud father of four adult children and a growing number of amazing grandchildren, I look back and recall how my spirit was always so joyous on the days when my children played well together, loved each other, spoke words of life, and expressed acts of affection toward each other. On other days, my spirit was actually grieved when they were cruel and spoke ill of each other and didn't play well together. I believe my fatherly experience of both the loving, joyous spirit and the grieving spirit points to the fact that we are indeed created in the same image and likeness of a loving Father, who feels the depth of both our unity and our division in the wider church family of God.

As I've often observed with my own children and grandchildren, there can be such a variety of personalities, interests, and giftings within one nuclear family. This diversity is true of the church family as well. Paul's discussion of the one body with the many parts that need to honor each other (see 1 Corinthians 12) is not only applicable to the local congregational level but in the church universal as well. Failure to realize this causes us to compare others in light of our own personalities, preferences, and interests. This unfair comparison fails to see God's wisdom in creating people differently and the Holy Spirit's action of gifting people with the fullness of diversity for a divine purpose. Different people have different giftings and abilities but so do different movements and denominations and different orders within the Roman

Catholic and Orthodox churches. Here we see some who focus on education, others on ministry to the poor, others on preaching, others on intercessory prayer, and others on health care or serving in hospitals.

MY RELIGIOUS CULTURAL HERITAGE

When I was a small child, we attended a general Baptist church in the country with an average attendance of forty members. I would ask my mother why the other small general Baptist church just down the road didn't join together with us to form a larger church. It seems that unity was not of high value, even when it was within the same denomination between those who shared the same beliefs!

As a young boy, I recall attending a grade school with about eighty students overall. There was one Roman Catholic child surrounded by all of us Protestants, who generally believed that Catholics did not have salvation. They too felt the same about us. Furthermore, my Baptist background didn't believe one had salvation unless they were born again; this would result in our errant belief that Lutherans, Episcopalians, and most Presbyterians did not have salvation either.

In my teenage years, I was raised on a farm in Illinois, seven miles from the county seat, with a population of three thousand. The next largest town in the county had about four hundred people. There was great religious prejudice in that area. Pastors taught their people to make judgments based on name, mode of baptism, understanding of Communion, the government of the church, and various doctrinal issues. This all fostered a growing unease within my spirit.

TURNING TOWARD GOD'S HEART FOR ECUMENISM

When I entered college, I began learning about the charismatic movement. On my first day in college, I received a powerful impression from the Holy Spirit that revealed, "The focus of your life will be the Holy Spirit." Based upon this word, I tried to take all the courses I could in college and later in seminary that dealt with the Holy Spirit, His gifts, or baptism in the Spirit. In seminary, I became aware of a renewal movement within the Southern Baptist denomination called *Fullness*, with a magazine under the same name. Jack Taylor would be one of the key leaders in this movement, and through his writings, he became a hero of mine. Later we would meet and become close friends. Eventually, he became a spiritual father to me.

Two other things happened in the seminary that opened me up to other denominations. I learned that in the ten years from 1967 to 1977, over fifty million Roman Catholics had been touched by God through the grace of the charismatic movement. I learned about many other denominations that were impacted by the charismatic renewal. Now I was not only believing non-Baptists were experiencing salvation, but I was finding some of my new heroes of the faith coming from other denominations, and surprisingly from the Episcopalian and Roman Catholic churches.

At age twenty-five, I graduated from seminary and began a pursuit of healing. I participated in a seminar on healing where the power of God would change my wife and my life. This experience of being filled by the Spirit resulted in my becoming involved in planting churches, which would be the context of my next turning point.

Later, my wife DeAnne and I would join the Vineyard Movement led by John Wimber. Our exposure to Wimber would impact us significantly due to John's love for the whole church. He would tell his pastors, "I want you to love the entire church, from the bells and the smells to the holy rollers." John would experience great favor with the Anglican and Roman Catholic churches. I loved John's emphasis and was in full agreement with his approach. I came to believe that this serving and honoring other churches was essential to the heart of God.

DeAnne and I moved to St. Louis and started a church. I met monthly with other pastors in my area from several denominations, including Missouri Synod Lutheran, United Church of Christ, and Baptist. Through these relationships, I was learning to honor and love the whole church, which was much larger than what I had believed. My *remnant few* was becoming *"a great multitude that no one could number, from every nation, from all tribes and peoples and languages"* (Revelation 7:9).

Eight years into the church plant, desperate for more of God in my life, I was touched by the power of God and became involved in a global revival at Toronto Airport Vineyard that would last for over twelve years and see more than four million people come to Jesus.

During the first few years after the revival broke out, I witnessed a Catholic woman from Louisville, Kentucky, who was awaiting a heart transplant. A friend drove her to our meeting which was cosponsored by a Catholic church in Indiana. I saw her receive her healing instantly and watched her run all over the sanctuary, out the door and around the parking lot, and then back into the church sanctuary, running up and down the stairs. When she returned home, her doctor said, "This is not the heart you had; you have had a heart transplant from God."

At about this same time, Pastor Tommy Reid invited me to speak at his large Assemblies of God church in Buffalo, New York. He asked me if I realized that Pentecostals have more in common with Roman Catholics than they do with many mainline Protestants. I had never heard that and asked him to explain. Pastor Reid said, "It's all about presence. Both Roman Catholics and Pentecostals have a high value on the presence of God in their worship. Roman Catholics, unlike Protestants, have never been cessationists regarding the gifts of the Spirit." Over time, I too found that the Catholic Church was more open to the gifts and healing than many Protestant denominations.

Another turning point for me was a supernatural divine appointment with Keith and Iwona Major. Keith was then an Assemblies of God minister and Iwona was a Polish Roman Catholic. They became missionaries to Russia from my church and later became a powerful force for Christian unity within the Catholic Church of America. We began a long relationship, and they helped me with my first two large meetings in Moscow. On one occasion there, I spoke with an Anglican missionary who shared with me about the martyrdom and imprisonment the Orthodox suffered for their faith there under Communism. He told me the Orthodox had more martyrs than any other part of the church. This information on the Orthodox loving Jesus unto death changed my perspective on the Orthodox part of God's family which I was discovering was much larger than I had ever imagined.

My next turning point occurred in Australia, when a local parish priest invited me to St. Thomas Roman Catholic Church in Canberra. We stayed up most of the night, discussing issues related to the Eucharist, the level of commitment in the local parish, and worship. One of the eye-openers for me was when he said that about 80 percent of the work and the giving came from 20 percent of the membership, with 20 percent of the work and donations coming from 80 percent of the parishioners! I was shocked. I realized these were the same percentages that were characteristic of the four denominations I had pastored. This *aha moment* caused me to wonder whether we all too easily make the fatal mistake of judging other churches and denominations on the 80 percent of their less committed members—who we are more likely to come across—rather than the passionate 20 percent who beautifully represent the thriving grace of their rich expression!

In the nineties, I read a book by Ralph Martin, a Catholic leader, entitled *The Catholic Church at the End of the Age: What Is the Spirit Saying?* This book touched me profoundly. I sold it at my meetings, highly recommended it, and told people that if the Protestant denominations had someone who spoke to them with the same prophetic insights as Ralph Martin had to the Catholics, we would see revival break out.

Several Catholics who knew me wanted me to connect with Dr. Mary Healy, a Sacred Heart Seminary professor in Detroit, Michigan, who later volunteered to read a portion of my doctoral thesis that pertained to Catholicism. We became friends. She came to Brazil on one of my teams and later wrote a book on healing in which she included a whole chapter on what she learned in Brazil. God has since opened up several opportunities for Dr. Healy and me to minister together in Poland, France, Croatia, and other countries. The fruits of unity can bring great friendships, and friendships lead us to powerful opportunities for mission together.

At a Voice of the Apostles conference in Orlando, a young priest and his lay friend asked if I would pray for Catholics. I prayed for them with the laying on of hands but there were no noticeable manifestations. Sometime after this, however, word came to me that both of them began to pray for healing for others. This young priest turned out to be an adjunct professor at Sacred Heart Seminary. He began taking seminarians out to the streets and sidewalks to pray for people for healing. Today, Father Mathias Thelen and his friend, Patrick Reis, conduct powerful healing seminars in Catholic churches around America. I have a love in my heart for these young men of God and the way God uses their zeal to touch the downhearted.

MY TRANSFORMED VIEW OF COMMUNION

Being raised in a Baptist church, the Lord's Supper or Communion was something we received about four times a year and only because we were told to do so. It was not a sacrament to us and had no saving grace and no strength to really bless you with. It was more of a symbol that represented the lowest view of Communion one could have. My understanding soon began to change in college as I studied the church fathers from the first century, who were literally the disciples of the first disciples. They helped me to see things in

Scripture I had never seen before. I came to understand that when the church gathered in those early days, taking Communion was the highlight of their meetings. It was, for them, the great moment of unity.

Not long after I was appointed to my first church in full-time ministry, I sought a meeting with the deacon board to share my heart for Communion and my desire that we offer it at every Sunday service. They said no! Unperturbed, I would venture out on every fifth Sunday of the month (when we had no service) to visit other churches in the region—Catholic, Orthodox, and the like—to closely observe their services and liturgy and in particular how they celebrated Communion as a sacrament that carried grace. It wasn't until much later when I planted my own church in Saint Louis, Missouri, made up of mainly non-churchgoing believers, that I had the freedom to implement my long-awaited dream for weekly Sunday Communion. I recall not wanting this to just be a ritual, but for each member to tarry at the altar and not to rush things. I would instruct my flock to prepare by repenting and forgiving under the blood of Jesus. As they approached the Communion table, I would tell them to pray like this: "O Lord, as I partake of Your body and blood, may it be a grace to me. May it strengthen me that I sin less this coming week. May it cause me to be transformed into Your very nature." After praying a blessing over the elements, what was previously bread and grape juice, we humbly believed they had become the body and the blood of Jesus.

Now while I understand that in the minds of the traditional churches, I was not in apostolic succession and therefore unable to consecrate the elements as such, our congregation nevertheless grew to believe in the real presence here in our service. We threw nothing away and learned to clean up every crumb of His body and every spill of His blood with the greatest care and respect. Those who did not accept this higher view of the Eucharist chose to lovingly honor those who did. Before long, it seemed that all of our views began to get higher, with many subsequent healings taking place as we partook in Communion. This gave testimony to our united faith and in our mutual conviction that something very powerful was at work beyond the logic of our naked eye.

Scripture reminds us, *"The one who receives a prophet because he is a prophet will receive a prophet's reward, and the one who receives a righteous person because he is a righteous person will receive a righteous person's reward"* (Matthew 10:41). So when it comes to Communion, if you receive merely bread or a cracker in the name of the bread or a cracker, what are you going to get? But if you receive the blood of Jesus, shed for the remission of sins, and you receive the body of Christ, which bore our sins, our sicknesses, and our diseases (see Isaiah 53:4–5 and Matthew 8:17), then Communion becomes the high point of both our cleansing and our healing. This is what we began to see as we moved into this grace; salvations and healings were truly happening when we took Communion. Therefore, the Lord's Supper has become a lot more meaningful to me. With the higher view of Communion, you expect grace, you expect power, you expect healing, and you expect mercy. I pray that one day, the barriers that make it difficult for all of us to do this together will no longer be there. I am certain that we are going to see much more power in the church when we are able to receive Communion together and in the splendor of our diverse unity.

THE CALL TO A LONG OVERDUE MATURITY

The challenge of unity is loving and honoring people who don't agree with everything you believe and how you walk that out together. Perhaps we start by praying more diligently for God to create an ecumenism of the Spirit in our hearts, one that's reflected in honor, genuine love for each other, and a willingness to cooperate at a whole new level of maturity. I would like to think that the church has had its infancy, and we've been through our teenage years where we just cut each other down all the time. But when we become mature adults, we stop this kind of behavior. I believe God is now bringing us forth and calling us into a long-awaited maturity together as never before.

TAKE-AWAYS

First, we live in a new day, thank God, when there is a greater openness to Christian unity than at almost any time in church history in the last five hundred years. My prejudices as a boy and a teenager were wrong, and I believe I grieved the Holy Spirit.

Second, it is essential to want to honor other Christian churches, denominations, and movements when possible. This honor allows the Holy Spirit to build a bridge to other groups different from one's own group.

Third, spending time with people of other churches can often lead to truly having a love for different groups of Christians that you didn't anticipate.

Fourth, there is a tendency for us to create a false perception by comparing the best 20 percent of our group with the worst 80 percent of other groups.

Remember, these percentages of those who did the most/gave the most and did the least/gave the least in St. Thomas Roman Catholic Church were the same as had been my experience in Baptist churches and my Vineyard church.

Fifth, it is crucial to apply Paul's analogy of the body in 1 Corinthians 12 with the local congregation to many congregations in a city, in a region, and in the world.

Sixth, there are different ways people come to have a personal relationship with God through the Holy Spirit. Depending upon the church or denomination, they may have a different language to talk about this relationship.

Seventh, we know it is the will of God for unity among Christians. Jesus prayed in John 17:21–23 for such unity. Until it is possible to have any form of ecclesial unity, let us strive for a unity of heart and spirit rooted in love, honor, and respect for the Christ living in our brothers and sisters who are in Christ.

DEAR BRAZILIAN BAPTISTS,

I want to express my thanks to you for your warm welcome of my ministry in your churches. Realizing you are one of the largest denominations in Brazil, it is a great privilege to serve some of your churches. I have been deeply impressed by the servant leader model of some of the pastors of some of your largest churches. The hunger for the presence of God among your people has been very impressive. Your openness to the power of God to regenerate the nonbeliever by grace, your excitement about the power of God to heal and deliver people from sickness and demonic bondage, and your openness to the gifts of the Spirit has given me much hope that God would move among the Baptist denominations of North America as He is now doing in Brazil.

Being raised in a Baptist denomination and called to preach in a Baptist church at eighteen, then over the next several years licensed and ordained in the Baptist denomination, receiving my bachelor's degree in religious studies in a Baptist college and my Master of Divinity degree in a Baptist seminary, I have much to thank the Baptists for in my life. Thirty-eight years ago, I was led to work outside the Baptist denominations and have since seen my calling from God as one of His servants to bless the whole church—to be used as an agent of renewal for all denominations. He opened the doors for me to minister in the largest Baptist churches in Brazil, Argentina, and South Africa. I celebrate what God is doing by His divine grace in your midst. He is raising up very strong pastors as servant leaders with vision beyond their local churches, inspiring many other pastors to develop better systems of discipleship and better strategies to nurture the members of their churches. I thank God for your strong servant leaders who have a sense of God's call as a "sent one" to strengthen the churches in their states and nations. Other pastors are being gathered around these leaders who want to gain wisdom, strategies, and activation in the graces of the Holy Spirit for themselves and for the members of their churches. It is a privilege to have opportunities to be part of the renewing of the churches in Brazil, especially the Baptist churches.

I want to honor the Baptist heritage God allowed me to have with its commitment to the Word of God as the final basis for all beliefs. I want to honor the heritage of pastors and churches praying and participating in revivals who have a heart for evangelism. These are precious deposits into my life.

One of my personal commitments is to work among the Baptists in Brazil with some of your servant leaders whom God has raised up to lead revival in their cities. Though I still am committed to minister to the whole church, a major commitment of my time in Brazil since 2016 has been among Baptists of both the traditional Baptist convention and the charismatic Baptist convention. I have talked about your hunger all over the world and how God is utilizing you to evangelize the lost, heal the sick, equip the saints, and deliver the demonized, all while working for justice among the poor and the marginalized of your cities and states. Thank you for your obedience to the leading of the Holy Spirit, who has enabled you to do this kingdom work for the glory of the name of Jesus and the delight of His Father.

Dr. Randy Clark is the overseer of the Apostolic Network of Global Awakening in Mechanicsburg, Pennsylvania, USA, and president of Global Awakening Theological Seminary of Family of Faith Christian University. Connect with him at globalawakening.com.

4

IN CHRIST WE ARE ONE

Archbishop Elpidophoros of America

| Eastern Orthodox |

For the peace of the whole world, for the stability of the holy churches of God, and for the unity of all, let us pray to the Lord.
—*The Divine Liturgy of St. John Chrysostom*

This petition speaks to the heart of the ecumenist and the ecumenical mission we are all called to enliven. This year, we held our archdiocese's 47th Biennial Clergy-Laity Congress with the theme "In Christ We Are One." Indeed, the reminder to our clergy and laity alike is that we are all a part of the one body of Christ. The only divisions that exist among us are those that we, fallen human beings, create with one another.

I was born in Bakirköy, Istanbul, to a Greek father and a Syrian mother. Being an Orthodox Christian in a historically Orthodox land, yet now as a religious minority, gave me tremendous insight into the struggles of those who are not able to worship freely. This experience left an indelible mark on my soul, one that would lead my trajectory of service to the church, to our sisters and brothers who struggle for freedom spiritually, physically, or geographically, and for actualizing the prayer of Christ, "*That they may all be one*" (John 17:21). I learned at a tender age to appreciate the limited freedoms we had within our patriarchate, while learning to work across religious and political boundaries for peace. His All-Holiness Ecumenical Patriarch Bartholomew, archbishop of Constantinople, continues to be one of my biggest inspirations for serving Christ and His church.

I studied at Aristotle University in Thessaloniki, specifically in the School of Pastoral and Social Theology, from which I graduated in 1991. My training opened my eyes to the deeper needs and suffering of those around us. I am reminded of three of the petitions throughout the beginning of the Divine Liturgy (*enarxis*):

- For favorable weather, for an abundance of the fruits of the earth, and for peaceful times, let us pray to the Lord.
- For those who travel by land, sea, and air, for the sick, the suffering, the captives, and for their salvation, let us pray to the Lord.
- For our deliverance from all affliction, wrath, danger, and distress, let us pray to the Lord.

Our theology must be pastoral, or we will not follow Christ's example of caring for His sheep. Our theology must be social, or we are not relating to our sister and brother, which strongly contradicts Jesus's golden rules: "'*You shall love the Lord your God with all your heart and with all your soul and with all your mind and with all your strength.' The second is this: 'You shall love your neighbor as yourself.' There is no other commandment greater than these*" (Mark 12:30–31).

In 1993, I completed postgraduate studies at the Philosophical School of the University of Bonn, Germany, submitting a dissertation entitled "The Brothers Nicholas and John Mesarites: Defenders of Orthodoxy in the Union Negotiations from 1204 to 1214 (in the historical and theological framework of the era)."

This was a sensitive time in history wherein the Orthodoxy was subjected to the Fourth Crusade sacking the city of Constantinople, pillaging, and plundering. This, rather unfortunately, was like added salt to the still bleeding wound of the schism that had taken place one hundred and fifty years prior, along with centuries of strenuous ties. Nevertheless, we are grateful to our almighty Father that our relationship with the Roman Catholic Church is as close, or in many ways closer, than it was in the first millennium. We are blessed to have the past three ecumenical patriarchs and four pontiffs who have toiled for unity as *sister churches*.

I was ordained shortly thereafter to the diaconate in 1994, at the Patriarchal Cathedral in Constantinople. I was appointed by His All Holiness as the codecographer of the Holy and Sacred Synod of the Ecumenical Patriarchate. This position afforded me yet another opportunity to engage and learn from our synod of hierarchs and have a deeper insight into the inner workings of our church and the pastoral/social struggles that our people are facing. The Orthodox hierarchy is not bureaucratic; its very heart is pastoral. We endeavor to meet the needs of our flocks and our clergymen who are on the front lines of our parishes with arch-pastoral guidance and support. In 1995, I was further honored with the appointment of deputy secretary of the Holy and Sacred Synod. I later was given the honor of chief secretary of the Holy Synod. Our synod exists for the promotion and example of unity within the leadership of our church, exemplified par excellence by the Holy Trinity. We are called, in our diversity, to be unified. This comes by way of thought, action, and belief. Having been gifted with such an honorable position, I received firsthand insight by some of our church's most profound thinkers and doers when it comes to unity within the Orthodox Church and unity at large within the *oikoumene* (inhabited earth).

One of my great joys during these years was studying at the world-renowned Theological School of St. John the Damascene in Balamand, Lebanon, where I was able to enhance my knowledge of the Arabic language, my mother's native tongue. To this day, my experience with the Church of Antioch has aided in fostering greater ties with our sister archdiocese here in the United States. No cultural immersion is ever wasted; rather, it strengthens our core values, polishes our perceptions, and permanently opens our eyes.

Inter-Orthodox relations were something I have been striving for my entire ordained life. I firmly believe that unity as Orthodox is among the most pressing issues of our day, including the mending of the fracture between the Eastern and Oriental Churches. In 2001, I defended my doctoral dissertation in the Theological School of the Aristotle University of Thessaloniki under the title, "The Opposing Stance of Severus of Antioch at the Council of Chalcedon." Our struggles have theologically been overcome by the joint efforts in dialogue throughout the past six decades. It is time to move forward as brothers and sisters in Christ to restore communion. Intercommunion is the result of an agreement between churches, such as it exists between our sisters and brothers in the Middle East, especially in the See of Antioch. This exists because, especially in the Middle East, Christians are a minority. Out of pastoral care for the people, the churches have agreed, in their own jurisdictions, to accept the other by way of the sacramental life of the church. As in other times in history, the church responds to a particular context with a specific remedy for the pain and suffering of the people, without creating precedence elsewhere. It is true *oikonomia* (pastoral care). Clergy and laity have often asked, "How much more should we have in the land of the free, especially with the gift of religious freedom?" This is one issue to think about, and with guidance of the Holy Spirit, move forward in wisdom and love.

Shortly thereafter, I had the joyful opportunity of teaching for a semester at our theological seminary, Holy Cross Greek Orthodox School of Theology, in Brookline, Massachusetts. Little did I know that fourteen years later, I would return to the school as the board and archbishop of America chairman. God truly works in wondrous and mysterious ways.

In March 2005, at the proposal of His All-Holiness Ecumenical Patriarch Bartholomew, I was promoted by the Holy and Sacred Synod to the position of chief secretary. He ordained me to the priesthood in the Patriarchal Cathedral. In 2009, I submitted two dissertations to the Aristotle University of Thessaloniki – School of Pastoral and Social Theology. I was unanimously elected assistant professor of Symbolics, Inter-Orthodox Relations, and the Ecumenical Movement. The dissertations are entitled: "The Synaxes of the Hierarchy of the Ecumenical Throne (1951-2004)" and "Luther's Ninety-Five Theses: Historical and Theological Aspects. Text – Translation – Commentary." I was fortunate to serve the faculty for roughly thirteen years, and in 2018, I was elected full professor.

During this time, I was tremendously blessed to serve as the Orthodox secretary of the Joint International Commission for the Theological Dialogue between the Orthodox Church and the Lutheran World Federation and as a member of the patriarchal delegations to the General Assemblies of the Conference of European Churches (CEC) and the World Council of Churches (WCC). My experience within the Orthodox-Lutheran Dialogue continues to have a profound impact on my life now as archbishop of America. This was enhanced by the encounters of mind and spirit that I shared with convening members of the CEC. While involved with the WCC, I met a dear friend and inspiration through the humility and zeal of Fr. Jean-Marie Roger Tillard.

On May 11, 2019, I had the overwhelmingly humbling honor of being elected archbishop of America by the Holy and Sacred Synod of the Ecumenical Patriarchate. I was enthroned at the Archdiocesan Cathedral of the Holy Trinity in New York City on June 22. This chapter of my pastoral life has been both edifying and insightful. I have come to understand the everyday needs of the Greek Orthodox community and the greater necessities and desires of the communities in which we live. Certainly, leading through my first full year as archbishop within a global pandemic was not easy, as it wasn't for all of humankind. We tirelessly worked not only to preserve and assist the communities of our faithful but also lent time and helping hands to our brethren in the direst straits. Ecclesial consistency was a challenge because of the divided politics of our great nation. However, we overcame with the love and support of my brother bishops, the priests, deacons, and laity that comprise our communities.

The Eastern Orthodox Church has ecumenism running through its veins. After all, the church of the first millennium strove to reconcile continuously, even though not always possible. This focus on unity answers the prayer of Christ but also demonstrates to us that we are all a part of the body of Christ. The Eastern Orthodox Church—speaking experientially and jurisdictionally of the Ecumenical Patriarch—has been a driving force for modern ecumenism since the turn of the twentieth century. The Patriarchal Encyclical of 1902 by Ecumenical Patriarch Joachim III first demonstrated the need for Orthodox unity and then the need to be open to our Christian sisters and brothers. He reminds his brother hierarchs, "It is, indeed, necessary that those who are set over the faithful for their spiritual government should pay attention to the greater good of all Christians so that the most precious crown of love might be enabled to bear more fruit according to the divine will."

Following this encyclical, Ecumenical Patriarch Germanos in 1920 issued a letter "Unto all the Churches of Christ Wheresoever They Be." Within this outpouring of love to all Christian bodies, rallying camaraderie after the worst tragedy the world had seen then (World War I), His All-Holiness charged Christian heads of the church by stating, "Even if in this case, owing to antiquated prejudices, practices or pretensions, the difficulties which have so often jeopardized attempts at reunion in the past may arise or be brought up, nevertheless, in our view, since we are concerned at this initial stage only with contacts and rapprochement, these difficulties are of less importance. If there is goodwill and intention, they cannot and should not create an invincible and insuperable obstacle." This goodwill and intention continue to be two of the most important ingredients for ecumenical dialogue. Love, faith, and Christ are necessary to have an authentically Christian dialogue.

One of my greatest influences outside the Orthodox Church came through Rev. Fr. Jean-Marie Roger Tillard, a Dominican priest. He was a man of charisma, deep theological insight, and openness to dialogue. He was a conduit for breaking through dialogical barriers and encouraged me to dig deeper into how we may overcome historical divisions. He used his church role for efforts related to unification and encouraged me to do the same. He once said, "This huge change of Roman Catholic mentality is certainly largely due to the high quality of the work done by the World Council of Churches, and especially Faith and Order. It is mainly the seriousness and commitment of the Faith and Order documents which helped reticent or perplexed Catholic people to understand that the Holy Spirit was there at work, particularly after the World Conference of Montreal."

The International Orthodox-Lutheran dialogue has been one of my personal joys, both as an observer and a developer. I am so proud of the work that has been accomplished and the unique friendships and colleagues that have been formed through this admirable effort. Even recently, the work of the dialogue has impressed me with its theological aptitude and efforts toward unity. The dialogue recently came out with a statement on the *Filioque* (and the Son) clause, similar to statements previously produced by the Orthodox Catholic North American Consultation. And in May 2025, the Lutheran and Orthodox churches jointly celebrated the 1,700th anniversary of the first Ecumenical Council of Nicaea. With great fervor, I pray all of our advancements in dialogue move to the grassroots level and do not remain theoretical, permanently present only on paper.

Since arriving in the United States, I have understood the intricacies and difficulties of racial tension, even within the church. That is to say, people in the church, across denominations, have to be introspective about how a particular denomination or community is (or is not) spreading Christ's love through reconciliation with our brethren. I have been moved by and committed to racial reconciliation since walking the streets of New York in June 2020 as a participant in the Black Lives Matter march with Mayor Eric Adams in Brooklyn, honoring the memory of Breonna Taylor. The Greek Orthodox Archdiocese of America has created a racial reconciliation resource page to help engage conversations to bridge racial gaps and provide resources for those seeking to learn more. We have the guidance of several African American priests in our archdiocese who are aiding our understanding and action steps. We have a legacy of this type of action as a church, dating back to the walk in Selma, wherein Archbishop Iakovos of blessed memory walked with Dr. Martin Luther King Jr. in unity.

One of our greatest demonstrations of pride and joy comes from the St. Nicholas Greek Orthodox Church and National Shrine at the site of the World Trade Center Memorial at Ground Zero. As an archdiocese and as a city, we rose from the ashes of the tragedy of 9/11 and have come together not only to rebuild with the intentions of defying those who attempted to shake our freedom but also to demonstrate to the world that religious freedom is a beacon of the United States.

The shrine is used as a house of worship for Greek Orthodox Christians and all Orthodox visitors of other faiths in the non-denominational chapel. Furthermore, it has been the center of ecumenical and interfaith prayer, including, most recently, our first annual Juneteenth commemoration. Gatherings like this indicate the strong bonds we are building in this archdiocese across denominational, faith-based, ethnic, and racial lines. A new dear friend of mine, Bishop Vashti Murphy McKenzie, whom I have the great pleasure of working with on the National Council of Churches of Christ USA, offered the following words at the gathering: "Forgetting history is to forget who you are. … It is to put a different benediction on what happened. … History gives us a chance to review lessons learned and lessons lost and this helps us to see the pits and the pitfalls so we don't fall into the pit again."

How true it is that we need to reflect on the past to learn and forge ahead! How fitting to come together for such a cause at the site of this greatest tragedy.

A LETTER OF FILIA TO MY SISTERS AND BROTHERS IN THE LORD

My dear sisters and brothers in the Lord:

Peace be to all! With heartfelt greetings, I approach our brothers and sisters in Christ in the household of God, as did Patriarchs Joachim III and Germanus V, with faith, love, and the desire to be closer to one another. How has it happened that the course of human history has created divides in the most sacred establishment, the church? Furthermore, we have somehow neglected to do our best to take care of the body of Christ, which we are all called to be a part of. We have experienced wars for religion, politics, and power. We have attacked one another verbally, physically, intellectually, and spiritually. We compare ourselves theologically and liturgically. We allow for the secular and profane to mar the sacred and holy. This includes our brother and sister, the true human icon made in the image and likeness of God.

I approach you all with humility, respect, and, most of all, love. With our forms of technology, communications, and resources, we have no excuse not to draw closer to one another. We may join in action for those most in need: the impoverished, the hungry, those with disabilities, those in lands that do not have the basic needs for a humane life, and those ravaged by war, genocide, oppression, and intolerance. Let us band together to accomplish these things; moreover, in doing so to help our brethren, we follow the teachings of the apostle Paul: *"Bear one another's burdens, and so fulfill the law of Christ"* (Galatians 6:2).

His Eminence Archbishop Elpidophoros (Lambriniadis) of America is the eighth Archbishop of America elected since the establishment of the Greek Orthodox Archdiocese in 1922. For more information on the archdiocese, please visit www.goarch.org.

5

UNITY THROUGH FORGIVENESS—OUR WAY OF THE CROSS

Daniel Abdallah
| Maronite Catholic |

Father, forgive them, for they know not what they do.
—Luke 23:34

My family hears these powerful words each Holy Week as we gather at our local Maronite Catholic Church, reminding us of the way Jesus prayed for His tormentors during His agonizing passion on Mount Calvary. So, it was again for us on Good Friday in April 2019 when my wife Leila and I and our six remarkable children—Antony, Angelina, Liana, Sienna, Alex, and Michael—prayed together with our community and recalled how Jesus made the ultimate sacrifice of love and forgiveness for the sake of the world. We remembered too how Mary, His mother, looked on and prayed in her anguish while remaining with her son until the very end. How excruciating, we thought, that moment must have been! What grace from heaven must have been operating as they helplessly watched?

Our family has always been so close-knit and fun-loving. People used to ask me what I did for a living, and I would say I was a full-time father and a part-time worker. And Leila has always been an incredible mother, nurturing and protective like a hen with her little chicks. Her love wraps around them like a shelter, always present, always strong.

Despite our love for each other and being a God-fearing family, nothing would quite prepare us for the approaching darkness that would demand our entire strength. Soon we would be asked to climb our own hill of Calvary. To carry our own heavy cross—four of them, in fact.

As you hear our story unfold, our deepest personal hope is that it might bring about a powerful Easter rising within you. A rising inspired by the ultimate Good Friday-like sacrifice paid by our darling little ones: Antony, age thirteen; Angelina, twelve; and Sienna, eight; as well as their beautiful cousin Veronique, eleven, whose lives carry a great message of forgiveness and unity for those with ears to hear. We know too that they would be praying for your personal blessing now from the heavenly places where God has promised to turn all of our *"mourning into dancing"* (Psalm 30:11).

OUT OF TRAGEDY TO UNITY

The day that would ultimately change our lives forever was the first of February 2020. It was a very hot and sticky summer's day with ongoing drought and devastating bushfires raging around Australia at the time. In preparation to attend our relative's birthday that Saturday evening, the younger cousins decided to come to our house to play in the late afternoon. There were ten children in all and with the stifling heat, I suggested they take a walk down the street together to the local store to get some ice creams to cool down and then come back home. Four of my children and three of their cousins, ages eight to thirteen, decided to go. They were all innocently walking and talking together along the road when a young driver, intoxicated with drugs and alcohol, sped through a red light at 150 kph (over 90 mph). He continued down the hill and swerved around the corner out of control before mounting the curb and plowing directly into the seven children on the footpath along the side of the road. The local police commissioner said that it was one of the most horrific accidents he had ever witnessed in his twenty-five years in the job.

On my frantic arrival at the scene, I remember, as a father, looking at the kids lying there and praying, "Oh, God, I surrender them to You." But I didn't know which child to go to first. I was running around in circles trying to resuscitate one and feeling guilty about not attending to the others. When Leila arrived, she started praying. Everyone was screaming around her, but she was just hovering and praying and flagging everyone down to join her in prayer. And then the paramedics came and pushed us lovingly out of the way. Soon enough, I saw them placing covers over four of the bodies, and I knew then the stark truth that they had died and had gone to heaven. I then had to go and tell Leila this most painful news. Now this just happened to be the day in which our church commemorated the feast of the presentation of Jesus at the temple when Joseph and Mary dedicated their child over to God's service. Even more surreal for my wife were the words of Simeon in the gospel that day as he ominously turned to Mary and proclaimed, *"And a sword will pierce through your own soul also"* (Luke 2:35).

Over the next day or so, the police were trying to navigate the traffic caused by the huge crowds that had gathered, both at the scene of the tragedy and also at the overwhelmed hospital, where Leila was attending to the recovery of our other daughter Liana. Our nephew too was in a coma there, fighting for his life, so we didn't stop praying all through the night. During these days, Leila could be heard saying to those around her, "Everyone must come together for prayer. And not just for our children who are already in heaven but pray for your children that they may come to truly believe in God." When we look back over these painful hours, we recognize that this was a great moment of unity; we were one together with the crowd in our grief and in our prayers. There were Catholics, Orthodox, and Protestants, even Muslims and atheists joining us in praying our Rosary together at various times. We could find no words, only our traditional prayers, which brought us together as they all joined along and lifted their hearts for us and with us to the same Jesus. It's funny how you learn in the darkest times of grief that trying to work out and fight for the perfect theological truth or method just fizzles out and makes way for love to come shining through. Love just saturates you when you have no choice but to surrender together as one body, in order to be covered by the glorious prayer of unity!

THE DAY OF FORGIVENESS

C. S. Lewis says it so well: "To be Christian means to forgive the inexcusable, because God has forgiven the inexcusable in you."

On Monday morning, they took my daughter Liana into surgery. Leila went back to the scene of the accident, and the television reporters approached her. She was about to show the world the possibilities of a love born of surrendered suffering. Fighting back their own tears, the reporters did not know what questions to ask her. They simply held their microphones up to Leila, and one of them murmured, "Just say whatever you want, Leila."

And she just spoke from her heart: "I am sad. I am heartbroken, but I'm at peace because I know my kids are in a better place. My kids are angels. I have goosebumps even now as I can feel them touching me and hugging me as I speak with you. The reality is that I still keep feeling that it can't be true. I'm still waiting for them to come home. When it comes to the driver, right now, I can't hate him. I think in my heart I forgive him, but I want the court to be fair. But I do forgive him. This is a cross we are all carrying."

Everyone was stunned by Leila's words and act of forgiveness. In that moment, she was a pure instrument of God for the world. It was like a stone had just hit the water, and it began rippling out from our local community across Sydney and quickly throughout Australia. Overnight, the news went viral around the world and we began receiving innumerable messages of love and prayers from San Francisco, Ecuador, Lebanon, Iraq, and London—from politicians, church leaders of every expression, rabbis, and sheiks. Upon later reflection, we wondered if it all had to happen this way in order for the family's powerful message of forgiveness to reach and penetrate the farthest corners of the world.

We have learned through the years that an unforgiving heart is the devil's playground, and it starts with just a little crack of pride or unforgiveness, whether it seems justified or not. And when it comes to the revenge business, we all face *the hour of the devil,* as we say in Arabic. He comes knocking with the temptation that demands we take offense before taking matters then into our own hands. Here, right at this point, we get the choice to focus our attention on God's grace or someone else's disgrace. It's safe to say that Leila's words of forgiveness were a grace that just came out of her. I think we all have the gift of forgiveness deep within us from our baptism, but our pride and anger can obscure our better judgment. In the end, to forgive the inexcusable is not about experiencing a great feeling but making a great choice. A choice of life, not death. Not just for the sake of ourselves, but to change the very culture of our divided world.

A FUNERAL ORCHESTRATED FROM HEAVEN

While the day of our family's triple funeral was always going to require our complete dependence on God's strength, we were also determined that it would be a celebration of our children's lives as we looked ahead to the mission at hand and not back. Antony's school generously led the way with marching drummers. Colorful balloons and white doves were released into the air over their three little white coffins. Not only was it a visible celebration of life but a visible celebration of Christian unity for all the world to see. Over 20 million mourners from all walks of life and expressions of faith flooded the Internet to watch.

We will never forget the feeling as our family walked into the crowded Maronite church and gazed upon what appeared to be Christianity's *coat of many colors* patched together delicately in such a diverse splendor. It was both covering and comforting to us in our painful and yet beautiful moment of agony. Just picture Darlene Zschech, known from her Hillsong days, singing "Shout to the Lord" and being joined by Catholic musicians. Add to the mix an Anglican minister reading the Prayers of the Faithful, with Orthodox and Melkite priests, Baptist pastors, Pentecostal leaders, rabbis, sheiks, and Muslims all singing, praying, and mourning together as one body in one heart surrounded by our fervent Maronite Catholic community.

The painful reality was that while all of this harmony surrounded us, we were seated right in front of the three coffins cradling the bodies of Antony, Angelina, and Sienna. We were literally in so much pain. We just kept thinking, "These are our kids!" We were supposed to be organizing Sienna's first Holy Communion and other future celebrations, not their funerals. Strangely, it is hard to explain, but the peace amid the sorrow we felt at that moment was so deep that we actually experienced heaven on earth. In fact, the closest I have ever felt to God was when I buried my kids. His merciful presence was just that near to us in this place of surrendered unity.

Now here's the main point I want to make: When we are willing to go together to the places of shared sorrow and shared joy, unafraid to celebrate our diversity, the walls of division that were built up in our heads will begin to miraculously drop away. During this funeral, just for those one or two hours of glory together, no one cared anymore about our differences. It was as though our departed children had taken charge of the ceremony and wanted to give us a foretaste of heaven's amazing oneness so that we too might desire and pray for this same oneness *"on earth as it is in heaven"* (Matthew 6:10).

LET THE LITTLE CHILDREN COME UNTO ME

Going back some five years before the accident, Antony, then eight, had a vivid dream that he needed to share with his mother the very next day. In that dream, Jesus said to him, "Antony, what would you like to be?" And Antony said, "I'd like to be a saint." In response, he heard Jesus saying clearly to him, "I am going to take you early." Well, as you can imagine, Leila was horrified. I remember she called me at work and insisted I come home immediately to process this and pray with her. Later, she went to church and prayed repeatedly, "Lord Jesus, take this cup away from me." Looking back, she now recognizes that through this and other hardships she has faced, God was preparing her to become a woman of deepening prayer. This would soon become the solid foundation of her amazing faith and strength in order to fully endure all that was to come.

As incredible as this all may sound, our then four-year-old son Alex also had a dream only six months before the accident. In this dream, the Lord was planting a mission in his heart to be a future ambassador of forgiveness. Alex told us that Jesus said to him, "You are the voice of *no smacking*." In processing this dream, we soon came to understand that Jesus was speaking to Alex in the language of a child, knowing that he wouldn't understand forgiveness at his young age but would clearly get the message of "no smacking." Little did I know, of course, that our family was not only going to become a powerful voice of forgiveness and begin a global foundation called *i4Give*, but that we would one day be forgiving and befriending the very man responsible for the death of three of our children! Through all of this, our amazing son Alex was fast becoming a wise young man with a special anointing over his life to share the message of forgiveness to everyone with boldness. Yes, even in Rome, when we were invited to speak in front of tens of thousands in Saint Peter's Square, our now eight-year-old Alex was later included in a television interview during which he spoke honestly about his vulnerable process to forgive. "When I heard that my mother and father had decided to forgive the driver," he said, "I wasn't that happy because it was too quick. I have forgiven him now, but I didn't say that to him. Just in my heart I know." When a reporter later asked him how it felt to forgive, he said, "It felt very good." When it comes to this no-smacking message given to our child, we adult Christians must equally work hard to avoid the trap of offense within the body of Christ as we remember Jesus's words: *"If anyone slaps you on the right cheek, turn to them the other cheek also"* (Matthew 5:39 NIV). Now when you do this, don't be surprised if it feels very good!

WE MUST DRAW CLOSER TO SEE CHRIST IN EACH OTHER

About six months after the tragedy, it was apparent that the devil hadn't quite finished with our family yet. We were overjoyed that Leila was pregnant, and we were just looking forward to moving into this next chapter of our life. Sadly, it wasn't too long before Leila suffered a heartbreaking miscarriage, which truly felt like we'd been hit by a baseball bat. Leila took the baby and buried it next to Antony, Angelina, and Sienna. Not long after this, our house was broken into and robbed while some of the family was in the front room. It was all over the news that night, and the police investigators seemed to be more upset for us than we were ourselves. Although the thieves took many of our material possessions, this was of low importance to us now. Soon after the police left, I played with the kids in the backyard, determined not to allow these setbacks to get the better of us or, more importantly, rob us of the much greater treasure of our family life.

Leila and I are just an ordinary couple. We fight, we make up, we hate each other, we love each other. That's all part of life. The truth back then was that our marriage was heavily rocked during this time; Leila wasn't okay, and I wasn't okay. It's been said that 65 to 70 percent of marriages fail after the couple loses a child, and we were clearly struggling to stay in the minority. Now, with the latest loss of our unborn baby, everything had become magnified again, but we tried to just persevere by grace. One day, out of the blue, Leila started to cry. I said, "Are you okay?" She said, "Danny, I can't leave you, and I will never leave you. I love you, and I can't live without you." When I took her in my arms to hug her, she said something I will never forget: "Danny, I can't leave you because you look like Antony, you act like Angelina, and you remind me of Sienna. Our kids came to the world as a result of our love, and they are a piece of you. I see them in you. How can I ever leave you? I love you. And I can't live without you." Leila could see her children in me, her husband, and that caused her to remain.

Now, I humbly put this question to you: Is Leila's cry here not the same cry of Jesus in John 17 that we might be "so one" that we can no longer be separated? As we begin to draw near, will the world not begin to recognize Jesus by the way we see and love each other? Perhaps, in a new humility, we too need to return to the ancient truth that we cannot live in God's fullness without rediscovering His image in each other. We all must surely begin to say to the separated members of the church who inspire our faith, "I can't leave you because you look like Jesus, you act like the Holy Spirit, and you remind me of the Father."

LOVE SMASHING THROUGH THE PRISON WALLS

Soon after the driver, thirty-year-old Samuel Davidson, was convicted and sent to prison, I received a random message one night from a fellow inmate who informed me of his intention to kill Samuel inside the prison for causing the accident that killed four children. He said, "Danny, we're going to get him. He's a dead man." I immediately sent the inmate a copy of an article on the importance of forgiveness that Leila and I had written for a newspaper. After a few minutes' delay, he responded with a crying emoji that said, "You've broken me." I said, "Yes, leave him alone. No one touch him. We have forgiven him." And the prisoners soon backed away. Samuel had been under police protection for a long time.

The day came when I finally mustered the strength to visit him in prison, accompanied by my dear priest friend. When we met, Samuel began to tell me why he had decided to become a Christian. He said, "Danny, I want what you have. Yours and Leila's one act of forgiveness changed my life undeservingly. Everyone wanted to come after me. When my fellow inmates heard of your decision to forgive me, everyone left me alone." Upon hearing all of this, I began to think not only of the powerful impact forgiveness had on Samuel, but also on the contagious effect it had on the hardest of hearts in that prison environment. And you've just got to see this guy today. He gets up at 4:30 every morning and starts with an act of contrition, confession of sins, traditional rosary prayers for the grieving families, and then an hour's personal prayer, followed by ten chapters of the Bible, among other devotions. This is Samuel's daily morning routine! He has literally become like a monk in a prison cell and yet he's probably freer than most people living on the outside who sadly do not know the merciful heart of Christ.

When I left the prison that afternoon, there was something going on in my heart, and I was a total mess in tears trying to understand it. As my dear priest friend and I made the long car trip back to Sydney, I confided that I needed to tell him something but wasn't sure how to express it. He told me, "Say it anyway." I said, "I saw a glow on Samuel's face today. I saw God's face shine on him." The priest said, "I saw it too." I replied, "Yes, but how can I say this about the man that took my children? How?" And he helped me to understand that God had made all of us in His glorious image despite our many imperfections. But more so, we had been looking upon a man who was a completely new creation in Christ. His past had just been washed away by another's forgiveness and by his sincere and contrite heart. This showed me the depths of God's grace. If we choose to embrace Christ's suffering on the cross with Him, He can work the impossible inside of us and then begin to change the world.

Jesus didn't ask us to tolerate our enemies or merely to forgive them. He challenges us to love them, where and when that is possible. When it comes to the careless drunk driver who took our kids, we now speak of him as Samuel our friend. He is not just a friend; he is our brother. We do not just forgive him; we actually love him. My kids get on their knees regularly at night and have made the decision to pray for him. When Leila eventually gave birth to our new daughter Selina, Samuel was one of the first to call and congratulate us from prison. He calls us freely because he feels safe in the knowledge that we freely forgive and truly love him.

As a result of my visits to those behind bars, I have now discovered a newfound ministry in sharing the power of forgiveness with prisoners. More significantly, Samuel and I have a future dream that one day soon, we might minister together side by side through prison ministry as we put purpose to our pain and bring life from every death. Could this also be our dream as a reconciled church whose members learn to walk side by side in a fresh love for each other? This is the love that sets the captives free and messes with the hearts of a world so desperate to see Christ in the way that we love each other.

There is no more fitting conclusion than to repeat the words of a dear friend who summed up our story this way: "Danny, that night, God was playing chess with the devil. And the devil took out four pawns and said, 'Check' to God. And then Leila said, 'I forgive.' And God then moved the queen and said to the devil, 'Checkmate!'"

DEAREST FAMILY OF GOD (BY LEILA ABDALLAH):

In a world that often values pride and position, may we instead choose humility—a humility that kneels in prayer and rises in compassion. It is in this quiet surrender that true unity is found. Unity begins not when we all think the same, but when we choose to love one another despite our differences.

As a mother, I've learned the power of loving unconditionally. Motherhood has taught me to give without expecting, to love without limits, and to forgive without end. It is through this kind of love that I've found strength—not a loud strength, but a gentle, enduring strength that holds families together and reflects the heart of God.

I have also learned to carry suffering with dignity. When heartbreak came, I chose not to let it define me, but to let it refine me. Through prayer, I was able to hold my pain with grace—not by my own strength, but by the strength God gave me in each moment. Suffering, when offered with love, becomes a sacred act of unity and peace.

We all have it in us—this same strength, this same courage, this same capacity to forgive and love. Because we all have access to the same God. No matter where we come from or what we've been through, we can draw from the same well of grace, the same source of hope, and the same divine love that binds us all together in Christ.

With all my love and prayers,
Leila Abdallah

Daniel and Leila Abdallah founded the i4Give Foundation to help others learn how to forgive those who have hurt them. They may be reached at www.i4give.com.

6

ECUMENISM: UNITY IN A RECONCILED DIVERSITY

Bishop Dr. Munib A. Younan
| Lutheran |

The grace of our Lord Jesus Christ, the love of God, and the communion of the Holy Spirit be with you all.

I grew up in the Old City of Jerusalem, which is the cradle and center of Christianity. Although I grew up in the Lutheran Church, which molded and shaped my identity and way of thinking, I was in constant contact with Christians of various denominations. My family was Lutheran, but one of my uncles was Roman Catholic and other relatives were Greek Orthodox. There was no luxury to think that your confession was better than others. Instead, we were taught to seek the commonality of our shared faith in Christ, although it was expressed in different ways.

As I visited Rome, one of the Catholic cardinals told us, "Bishop, be aware, if ecumenism succeeds in Rome, it will succeed in the whole world." My response was, "Your Eminence, I have always thought that if ecumenism succeeds in Jerusalem, it will succeed in the whole world." This discussion helped us to understand the difficulties of the quest of unity, but at the same time the blessings that the search for unity offers to all Christians. Indeed, we are joined by the high priestly prayer of Jesus, who prayed, *"Holy Father, protect them by the power of your name, the name you gave me, so that they may be one as we are one"* (John 17:11 NIV).

ECUMENISM AS INTEGRATION OF FAITH AND LIFE

We consider the life of the church in relation to our common human life with the perspective of the inner unity of the Holy Trinity, into which we are included by grace and faith. Just as the Triune God is the all-encompassing One—a differentiated, divine unity—human life is shared life in the setting of divine reconciliation. The community of the church, which is human life in a complex God-given unity, is not only a unity in diversity, but a unity in reconciled diversity.

Ecumenism happens when, and only when, there are partners who intentionally seek to establish or further pursue relationship aimed at increased mutual communication and understanding. Such a process presupposes:

- A certain level of commonality between the partners.
- The existence of difference. These differences normally constitute the focus of dialogue and the challenges in relations.
- The motivation to pursue an ecumenical process with a view to overcoming divisive factors, i.e. with a view to reconciliation.
- The ecumenical dialogue is led by the Holy Spirit, who works in us.

Thus, as noted by the Lutheran World Federation (LWF) in the document "Commitments on the Ecumenical Way of Ecclesial Communion" in 2018, "Ecumenism is anchored in truthfulness. This means seeking accuracy in our understanding of our ecumenical partners and readiness to be corrected when we fail. It also means being truthful to our tradition and identity while recognizing the potential to change and grow. Ecumenism is costly. It requires active sensitivity to various issues that are of importance for the well-being of the global Christian Community."

Ecumenism is an essential part of the nature and mission of the church itself. The unity for which ecumenism strives is not apart from the unity that is sought by the church—the unity by which the church wishes to be recognized. The unity established in Word and sacrament within a single congregation is the same as that which unites the congregations of a church body, and the same as that which drives the pursuit of unity among churches of differing traditions and confessions.

As such, ecumenism can be likened to the image of ever-expanding rings in water. Ecumenism on the local level is a God-given gift in Christ by the Holy Spirit. More often, it grows naturally between the churches of a community. It is neither the result of dialogue, nor negotiations, but the result of lives lived together in community, overlapping and interconnected.

Ecumenism on a broader level necessarily enters deeper into issues of theology and doctrine. We praise God for the ecumenical work and agreements that church bodies have come to, especially the reciprocal recognition of baptism in the name of the Triune God. The holy sacrament of baptism is an expression of God's grace received in faith. It is not a product of human theological endeavors. However, baptism is certainly an appropriate subject for ecumenical theological reflection.

I am pleased that the document, "From Conflict to Communion: Lutheran-Catholic Common Commemoration of the Reformation in 2017," considers baptism as the basis for unity and common communication. It states, "The church is the body of Christ. As there is only one Christ, so also he has only one body. Through baptism, human beings are made members of this body. ... Since Catholics and Lutherans are bound together in the body of Christ as members of it, then it is true of them what Paul says in 1 Corinthians 12:26: '*If one member suffers, all suffer together. If one member is honored, all rejoice together.*' What affects one member of the body affects all others. For this reason, when Lutheran Christians remember the events that led to the particular formation of their churches, they do not wish to do so without their Catholic fellow Christians. In remembering with each other the beginning of the Reformation, they are taking their baptisms seriously." What is true between Catholics and Lutherans is also true between all other Christian confessions.

UNITY IN RECONCILED DIVERSITY

With Christianity worldwide, as a Lutheran, I confess that the church is one, holy, catholic (universal) and apostolic. However, I also recognize that the one body of Christ is manifested in a plurality of churches. Ecumenism does not work for unity in uniformity but unity in a reconciled diversity.

The official proceedings of the LWF Sixth Assembly in Dar es Salaam, Tanzania, in 1977 describes unity in a reconciled diversity this way:

> This way to unity is a way of living encounter, spiritual experience together, theological dialogue and mutual correction, a way in which the distinctiveness of each partner is not lost sight of but rings out, is transformed and renewed and in this way becomes visible and

> palpable to the other partner as a legitimate form of Christian existence and of the one Christian faith. There is no glossing over differences. Nor are the differences simply preserved and maintained unaltered. On the contrary, they lose their divisive character and are reconciled to each other.

As the LWF noted in 2018, "All churches refer back to the one truth of the gospel which precedes faith and gives rise to it. Unity is therefore based on our common participation of the churches in this truth of the Gospel. ... For ecclesial communion the two necessary criteria are those which also constitute the church in general: Word and Sacraments (Augsburg Confession article VIII). Since both are given by God, the ecclesial communion is also God's doing and can never be brought about by the churches themselves. The churches are called to be that communion."

FROM CONFLICT TO UNITY IN RECONCILED DIVERSITY

In 1999, Catholics and Lutherans signed the Joint Declaration on the Doctrine of Justification (JDDJ). This statement was a landmark in our ongoing ecumenical dialogue, in that it was a differentiated consensus. In particular, the JDDJ outlines how our churches understand justification. For Lutherans, this was critical, as our brother Martin Luther has called justification by faith "the doctrine by which the church stands or falls." For both our churches and our members, this document has been a word of grace, for it has removed all historic condemnations of the other that had been in place for hundreds of years.

Another outcome of this fifty-year journey of Lutheran-Catholic dialogue was the 2016 worship service of Common Prayer in Lund, Sweden. As president of the Lutheran World Federation, I cohosted this event with the late Pope Francis and Rev. Dr. Martin Junge, LWF's general secretary. This Common Prayer, which took place on Reformation Day at the beginning of the 500th anniversary year, was a historic reconciliation. It was a moment that no one could have envisioned fifty years earlier. I was deeply honored to cohost and colead this event with the pope, a visible sign of Christian unity, and to sign a joint statement of ongoing reconciliation.

This historic reconciliation between the Roman Catholic Church and the Lutheran Communion has had profound significance for global ecumenism. In 2010, Anglican theologian Andrew McGowan relayed the sense that we are now in the midst of an "ecumenical winter," where the movement toward visible Christian unity had reached a low point. McGowan suggests that many Christians "find their most powerful and transformative experiences of ecumenism in experience, in shared prayer and mission." This sharing of prayer and mission is what we experienced; perhaps, alongside many other movements, what we have achieved in the last decades of Lutheran-Catholic dialogue will lead to further breakthroughs of an ecumenical spring.

The joint common prayer in Lund had three important elements. First, it was a service of thanksgiving: giving thanks for faithfulness to the gospel of Jesus Christ in both churches, Catholic and Lutheran, and for the freshness of unity we are feeling today. Second, it was a service of repentance: repenting for the mistakes of the past which both churches have committed against one another and asking for God's mercy on us. Third, it was a service of commitment: committing that the Lutheran and Catholic churches will work together through the five imperatives outlined in the document "From Conflict to Communion." Thanks be to God, as we left this common prayer in Sweden, we felt confident that our churches were committed to a future of inclusive mission, including a prophetic *diakonia* (ministry).

Historic reconciliation, as important and monumental as it is, cannot be allowed to remain only an end unto itself. Ecumenical dialogue, even on the academic level, can help us discern convergences and diversity, leading us toward common mission. These dialogues must address our common search for responding to the needs of the world. In this arena, we discussed challenges facing human communities in Syria, India, Burundi, South Sudan, and Colombia. This event showed how ecumenical engagement can propel the church into the world. The agreement between Caritas Internationalis and LWF World Service demonstrated ecumenism based on mutual friendship and trust. Through the agreement and our shared work, we show that we are working together, following Christ's command, for the sake of the world.

During the service in Lund, Pope Francis and I signed a joint declaration stating, "Through dialogue and shared witness we are no longer strangers. Rather, we have learned that our division had wounded the visible unity of the church." We rejected "all hatred and violence, past and present, especially that expressed in the name of religion." I continue looking for the Holy Spirit to guide us through issues on which we still disagree: ecclesiology, ministry, and Eucharist. Honest disagreement is the foundation of dialogue; I am confident that we will be able to find convergence on many issues.

No matter how difficult and long it is, I encourage Lutherans to continue this process because it is Christ's call: to have one baptism and one table for the Eucharist. It continues to be my conviction that the Eucharist is the table of Christ, not a Lutheran, Catholic, Reformed, Anglican, or Orthodox table. It is Christ's table of generosity. God's Word and promise makes a thing holy, not any human effort or label. In other words, the event in Lund is not yet finished. Its positive energy continues to expand, even into interreligious relations.

But I want to share with you something that caught my attention in Lund even before we had the opportunity to meet with the pope. One day earlier, during regular Reformation Day worship at Lund Cathedral, following the liturgy of Holy Communion, something very special happened. Just before the closing hymn, we suddenly saw the dean of St. Thomas Aquinas Parish in Lund entering the Lutheran cathedral with the Vatican flag, an icon of the Virgin Mary, and the entire Catholic congregation. Together, they processed to the front of this Lutheran cathedral and joined the Lutheran congregation in shared songs and prayers.

As we gathered together around the altar, I have never seen faces so elevated and happy. It was as if we were dreaming. Many in the church were amazed; it reminded me of the day of Pentecost when the disciples and the people were amazed with what was happening in front of their eyes. Many people were in tears. Later, some observed that our ecumenical celebration the next day would have meant very little if the local people had not embraced it so fully.

This, my friends, is the positive energy emanating out of Lund. Like the work of the Holy Spirit, it has not remained in that place alone. I am confident that this energy will spread throughout our churches. Each diocese and congregation has an opportunity to reach out to Catholic and Lutheran neighbors and other Christians, urging them to build on this ecumenical energy.

The energy of Lund is not only limited to Christian ecumenical relations. Al-Mayadeen television station in Lebanon interviewed me about our historic reconciliation; I was told that the interview was watched by thirty million people throughout the Arab and Muslim world. Dr. Muhammad Al-Sammak, secretary general of the Christian-Muslim Committee for Dialogue in Lebanon and copresident of Religions for Peace, has offered several comments on Catholic-Lutheran reconciliation. Sammak, who has said, "The task of Muslims today is to defend and purify our faith from the exploitation of the jihadists," has also suggested that Sunni and Shi'a Muslims must learn from the energy of Lund to explore reconciliation between their communities as well. The energy of Lund will create more energy and trust, and not just among Lutherans and Catholics. Surely, this is the ongoing work of the Holy Spirit!

If Lund only remains in Lund and does not infiltrate into the Catholic and Lutheran churches, its meaning will diminish day by day. The more we receive and implement it into our churches, the more energy will be created. While the energy continues, we must invest in it. We must build relationships with Catholics, Orthodox, Evangelical, Anglican, and Reformed churches, along with others. The more we build this energy, the more we will be reminded that we will share one mission in the world. The event is not finished; it continues, just like the ongoing reformation of the church. The energy going out from our celebration in Lund is a sign that the Holy Spirit is at work in the world, liberating us by creating trust and reconciliation in a time of fragmenting relationships. It is my sincere hope that the ecumenical winter we have been experiencing will indeed give way to an ecumenical spring.

THE AMMAN DECLARATION 2006 AS AN EXAMPLE OF UNITY IN RECONCILED DIVERSITY

The nineteenth century was a century of active mission work in the whole Middle East. The missionary societies from Germany, Britain, the United States, and Nordic countries succeeded in their mission by creating strong educational ministries that played a role in shaping the Arab world, including the translation of the whole Bible (Old and New testaments) into the Arabic language in 1864.

However, the mission created and established recognized mainline churches in the Middle East. These evangelical churches represented the Lutheran tradition in Palestine and Jordan; the Anglican tradition in Palestine, Jordan, and Cyprus; the Presbyterian tradition in Lebanon, Syria, Egypt, Kuwait, and Iran; and the Congregational tradition in the Union of the Armenian Evangelical Church in Lebanon, Syria, and Iran.

In the midst of the twentieth century, these churches started to be led by indigenous leaders and pastors. The indigenization of these mainline churches created the discussion of unity. Two main steps were taken for inter-evangelical efforts toward greater unity.

1. The Arab World Evangelical Church leaders' conference in Beirut in 1955 met to discuss the subject of "Christ calls the Churches in the Arab world to unite and evangelize."

2. The second step was the undertaking of the United Evangelical Church in the Arab World Project in 1962–1964. It aimed at creating a regional evangelical church with dioceses in Jordan, Palestine, Syria, and Lebanon.

However, these two efforts did not result in any further steps, partly due to the constantly changing regional political uncertainties as well as the lack of an effective mechanism of interpretation.

In 1974, the Fellowship of the Middle East Evangelical Churches (FMEEC) was established. The fellowship offered an appropriate forum to bring together evangelical churches of diverse ethnic, cultural, and confessional backgrounds in the Middle East and North Africa.

When I was elected as the president of FMEEC in 2004, I initiated the idea of an evangelical mutual recognition agreement among the three traditions, namely Lutheran, Reformed, and Anglican. This agreement would reflect the theological principle of unity in reconciled diversity.

All of our churches base our theology on the doctrine of justification by faith. This is the reason it was not difficult to get a mutual recognition agreement. In January 2006, six Reformed churches in the Middle East from Lebanon, Syria, Kuwait, Iran, Jordan, Palestine, and Egypt signed this agreement with the Lutheran Church in Jordan and the Holy Land.

I pray for the Holy Spirit to continue to work in our churches and the world toward unity in reconciled diversity. Ecumenism is the gift of the Holy Spirit. Let us all pray for Holy Spirit to work in and among us, that the church would be one, as Jesus and the Father are One, so that the world may believe.

God bless you.

MY DEAR SISTERS AND BROTHERS IN CHRIST,

In the name of our Lord and Savior, Jesus Christ, I greet you from Jerusalem, where the Holy Spirit was bestowed through tongues of fire upon the first disciples of Christ. The Holy Spirit qualified the disciples and every Christian to carry the gospel of love to the world. This Holy Spirit continues to create communities of love wherever the gospel Word of God is preached and the holy sacraments are celebrated. The Holy Spirit did not stop working in the 28th chapter of the Acts of the Apostles! The Spirit continues to work in every Christian, in every church, and in every city, inspiring us all to join in the mission of love that we share. We share this mission regardless of denomination, tradition, culture, theology, history, ethnicity, or any other difference. Through baptism, we are the one body of Christ, each of us an essential part of the body. Christ calls us to be one and shows us that what joins us in faith is far greater than what divides us. In the first century, the Roman world said about the Christians, "Look how much they love one another." Today, would the world say the same about us?

My sincere plea to all of us, the one body of Christ, is that we would seek to love one another not by word but by truth and in action. Our world becomes ever more broken and needs saving love more than ever. We must not allow our differences, disagreements, boundaries, and brokenness to become obstacles to our Spirit-given power to love one another. We are called to be witnesses to the love of God, a love we have seen through the cross and the empty tomb. When this love is our first priority, it will mold us, shape us, transform us, and lead us into a future of peace, justice, and reconciliation. This love has the power to convert the whole world to become, as the Rev. Dr. Martin Luther King Jr. suggested, "Extremists for love." As Jesus said, "*This is my commandment, that you love one another as I have loved you*" (John 15:12).

May the love of God, which flows from the cross of Christ and fills believers today through the Holy Spirit, be our guiding light in our churches and communities.

LET US PRAY

Our Lord and Savior Jesus Christ, forgive us for our disagreements, shortcomings, and the sin of division. Move us and guide us by the power of Your love, so that the world may believe. May the power of Jesus's expansive love embrace us, enlighten us, and guide us to love as He loves. Send Your Holy Spirit among us, that divisions in our families, churches, and communities, and between nations and peoples, would decrease. We thank You that in spite of our weaknesses, You dare to call us to be apostles of love in this broken world.

We pray all of this in the name of our Lord and Savior, Jesus Christ, who loves us on the cross, at the table, on the way, and to the end. Amen.

Your brother in Christ,
Bishop Dr. Munib A. Younan

Bishop Dr. Munib A. Younan is the Palestinian bishop emeritus of the Evangelical Lutheran Church in Jordan and the Holy Land, former president of the Lutheran World Federation, and honorary president of Religions for Peace. Connect with him at www.rfp.org.

7

A GRACE FOR THE UNITY OF CHRISTIANS

Matteo Calisi
| Catholic Charismatic |

On January 1, 1901, an outpouring of the Holy Spirit took place at Bethel Bible School in Topeka, Kansas. Directed by Rev. Charles Fox Parham, it was better known as the "Awakening of Stone's Folly," for the school was held in an unfinished mansion once owned by Erastus R. Stone.

It was an event of historical and ecumenical significance because it marked the beginning of the Pentecostal charismatic current destined to cross most of the Christian denominations in the last century. Its message speaks to us of the urgency to rediscover the Holy Spirit in our days. The world and the church are in desperate need of permanent Pentecost.

For us Italians, the Awakening of Stone's Folly was an event of great importance and significance. At the beginning of the last century in the Catholic Church, there was a certain nostalgia for the gift of the Spirit. Prayer groups sprung up, and the people called upon the Holy Spirit through the ancient hymn "Veni Creator Spiritus" (Come Creator Spirit).

This Catholic doctrine on the rediscovery of the gift of the Holy Spirit coincided with that of the sanctification of the oldest holiness movements that harkened back to the founder of Methodism, John Wesley.

A religious sister, Elena Guerra, founded the Oblates of the Holy Spirit and inspired then-Pope Leo XIII to ask God on behalf of the whole Catholic Church for the gift of the Holy Spirit on the first day of the first year of the twentieth century.

This was exactly the same day that the Holy Spirit fell on the Bethel Bible School.

This coincidence is undeniable considering the development of the enormous Pentecostal charismatic movement that arose after the Spirit's outpouring in Topeka. The spiritual phenomenon was in some respects a shock even within the Catholic Church, since no one could have foreseen or planned an injection of the Holy Spirit and power into the millions of Catholic charismatics who hungered for the Spirit in their search for God.

In Topeka, the Holy Spirit really became the protagonist, giving life to the rediscovery of the Pentecost in the church. Awakenings followed in other places spiritually connected to it, such as Wales in 1904 and Azusa Street in Los Angeles in 1906. After these came the birth of the Charismatic renewal in Protestant, Episcopal, and Catholic churches.

After twenty centuries, Pentecost once again became a lived story, no longer just told and imagined. Baptism in the Spirit became a unique and unrepeatable personal experience, the crucial moment of conversion, the turning point in a person's spiritual history.

With the birth of Pentecostalism, a new page has opened in the history of the church, not only because of the phenomenon, for its consistency and its proportions, but also because it leads to overtures to new people living at the margins of the Christian community. People in inner cities and metropolitan suburbs, crowds of poor of all kinds, find in Pentecostal communities forms of communication in keeping with their essentially oral culture. As theologian Walter Hollenweger noted, "For them the medium of communication is, just as in biblical times, not the definition but the description, not the statement but the story, not the doctrine but the testimony, not the book but the parable, not a systematic theology but a song, not the treatise but the television program, not the articulation of concepts but the celebration of banquets."

However, it should be noted that many things have changed. Today almost all the branches of the great Pentecostal tree include leaders and pastors attentive both to academic theology and the theological dialogue conducted outside the charismatic and Pentecostal world with Catholics, Reformed, and Orthodox. In recent decades, a specifically Pentecostal academic culture has also been born, worthy of note and appreciation. These are the abundant fruits that the church and the world have reaped from this Pentecostal charismatic revival initiated by Stone's Folly.

THE "ITALIAN CASE"

It is well-known that global ecumenical dialogue with Pentecostals, who represent three quarters of the Protestants and one third of the world's Christians, has not always been a simple task. Unlike other historical denominations, many of our Pentecostal brothers and sisters do not participate in the movement for Christian unity. However, in Italy, the Holy Spirit has opened a door to dialogue with Pentecostals since the 1980s thanks to the Catholic Charismatic Renewal, which shares some ways of praying with Pentecostals. The first structured and significant experiences, personally followed and encouraged by Pope John Paul II, take place precisely in Italy, between Catholic charismatic communities and some Pentecostal pastors.

In 1981, I met with Pentecostal Pastor Giovanni Traettino to begin the crucial dialogue toward unity. In 1992, Pastor Traettino was invited to speak at a Catholic Charismatic Conference in the San Nicola football stadium in Bari. On that occasion, he made a prophetic gesture, washing the feet of a representative of the Catholic Church. It was this gesture of humility that marked the beginning of a long collaboration between the Catholic charismatics and Pastor Traettino.

Another historic event followed in 1996 where, for the first time, Catholics asked the Pentecostals for forgiveness. For the ecumenists, it was a historical turning point in the dialogue between Catholics and Pentecostals in Italy.

CHARISMATIC ECUMENISM

Charismatic ecumenism has become a topic of great interest. This is partly due to the personal attention that the late Pope Francis—first as archbishop of Buenos Aires, then as Cardinal Bergoglio—reserved for this dimension of contemporary Christianity. The conferences and ecumenical meetings between the charismatics of the various denominations are multiplying extensively on a world scale.

In a sermon to the pope and the Vatican Curia, Cardinal Raniero Cantalamessa, preacher of the papal household, asserted, "We have been witnessing for some time a change that we can call epochal. All the churches of the West, or those born from them, for over a century, have been crossed by a current of grace which is the Pentecostal movement and the various charismatic renewals derived from it in the traditional churches."

Although ecumenism received more attention from Catholic Church authorities at all levels in the decades following Vatican II and particularly with popes John Paul II and Benedict XVI, Pope Francis approached this ecumenical area with a new turning point, often characterized by personal initiatives specifically addressed to the world of evangelicals and Pentecostals and apparently without any official activity on the part of the Pontifical Council for the Promotion of Unity of Christians and the usual pontifical protocols such as his famous visit to the Pentecostal Church of Caserta in 2014. He met with the evangelical Pastor Giovanni Traettino, his friend, to ask for forgiveness from the Pentecostal evangelical community for the oppression suffered in the period of fascism in Italy from 1935 to 1955.

Pope Francis said, "I ask your forgiveness for those Catholic brothers and sisters who did not understand and who were tempted by the devil and did the same thing as Joseph's brothers. I ask the Lord to give us the grace to recognize and forgive."

The pope's gesture had a singular ecumenical value because it also addressed the Pentecostal movement around the world. He wished to give public recognition to these evangelical churches for their contribution to the common mission of the gospel. He also highlighted the merit of these evangelical churches in recalling the urgency of a new openness to the work and person of the Holy Spirit and the rediscovery of adoration, a peculiarity of Pentecostal piety.

Pope Francis was particularly sensitive to the prophetic and charismatic aspects of the church. He once said, "Let yourselves be guided by the Holy Spirit, with that freedom, and please don't cage the Holy Spirit!"

DIVERSITY RECONCILED

With numerous ecumenical contacts over the years, Pope Francis built a great bridge toward Pentecostalism. Inspired by the great Reformed theologian Oscar Cullmann, he indicated as a viable path for an authentic ecumenism that of "reconciled diversity."

Speaking to the Catholic Fraternity of Charismatic Covenant Communities and Fellowships in October 2014, Pope Francis said, "The Holy Spirit makes *diversity* in the church. ... And truly this diversity is so rich, so beautiful. But then, the same Holy Spirit creates unity, and so the church is one in diversity. ... He does both: He does the diversity of charisms and then

He does the harmony of charisms. This is why the first theologians of the church, the first fathers, [in] the third or fourth century said, 'The Holy Spirit, He is harmony' because He creates this harmonious unity in diversity."

In this new method of ecumenical dialogue, Pope Francis invited Christians to overcome mistrust, to draw near, to esteem themselves, to forgive each other, to collaborate, to recognize the existence of diversity, to celebrate the differences, and to welcome the gift of unity. He said, "It is necessary to entrust the heart to the companion on the road without suspicion, without mistrust, and first of all look at what we are looking for: peace in the face of the one God."

For the future of Christian unity, I think the words that inspired Oscar Cullmann's vision, when he invited churches to experience differences in a reconciled way, can really help us. He urged the churches to love each other despite the differences and to love each other *with* the differences. Cullmann gave the analogy that all Christian churches are like different planets revolving around Christ, "the sun from which they receive light."

Pope John XXIII said, "There are many more things that unite us than those that divide us." Pope Francis affirmed, "We must learn to accept the other in his diversity. Not all differences are necessarily divisions! We have to see a church as a gift for other churches. True ecumenism is an exchange of gifts."

In fact, on several occasions, Pope Francis warned Catholics against the temptation of wanting to standardize diversity. He said, "This is the danger of uniformity. Unity is knowing how to listen, accept differences, and have the freedom to think differently, with all due respect for the other who is my brother. Don't be afraid of differences!"

We Catholics should join the example of our late Vicar of Christ toward the Pentecostals, the Waldensians, and the Hussites, asking the Holy Spirit for the ability to forgive and seek to heal wounds of the past. Thus would be fulfilled the desires that are in the heart of Christ for a rediscovered fraternity of His disciples in this third millennium.

TO THE BROTHERS AND SISTERS OF THE PENTECOSTAL CURRENT

Dear loved ones in Christ:

All who have accepted Jesus as Lord and Savior are our brothers and sisters in Christ. In this crucial hour of human history, the Lord invites us to make every effort to renounce our atavistic divisions and re-embrace as brothers and sisters in Christ, members of His own family of God. We are Catholic, Evangelical, non-denominational, Pentecostal, charismatics… Whatever our Christian denomination or background, we must have this awareness that we have not chosen one another, just as we have not chosen Christ. He has chosen us, and He has chosen us to be His, together not only to be part of this spiritual awakening, but for all of eternity. (See John 15:16.)

This contemporary Pentecost has shown us the urgency of being united in one body.

Because of the fact that we *"all were made to drink of one Spirit"* (1 Corinthians 12:13), this same Spirit urges us to witness our unity in Christ in one body: Catholics, Evangelicals, Pentecostals, and non-denominational, never again separated!

Our differences do not hinder our path toward the unity willed by Jesus. And today, we are entrusted with a responsibility and a commitment to be one *"so that the world may believe"* (John 17:21).

However imperfect our unity is, yet our differences are not irreconcilable. Not all differences necessarily represent a division. On the contrary, diversity reconciled through prayer represents a richness. Today there are so many ecumenical events that demonstrates this eloquently.

We all recognize that there is only one church of Christ—one holy, universal, and apostolic church. There is only one church because there is only one Christ and the church is His body.

Therefore, we are called by God to a fuller realization of our unity in the body of Christ, since there is *"one body and one Spirit—just as you were called to the one hope that belongs to your call—one Lord, one faith, one baptism, one God and Father of all, who is over all and through all and in all"* (Ephesians 4:4–6).

As Christians of the entire globe, we must pray and strive for our unity in Christ's love to become more and more evident as a sign to the world of God's reconciling power and for the world to believe in Him.

We must be honest: today, the body of Christ is *broken* as it presents itself to the separated world, and because of this, the awakening and evangelization of the world are undergoing a setback.

Today we Christians in the world are just over two billion out of a population of seven billion. Despite two thousand years of Christianity, about five billion men and women do not know the gospel. What will become of them? Some Christians feel powerless and are paralyzed by the tide of secularization and rampant paganism even in the continents of ancient evangelization.

Some will tell me that the fault lies with the mystery of the iniquity that rejected the light of Christ and turned to the idols of this world. Quite right! But I believe that a grave responsibility also falls on us Christians who have not loved one another according to the Lord's command: *"By this all people will know that you are my disciples, if you have love for one another"* (John 13:35).

Today, the Holy Spirit still offers us an opportunity to advance the kingdom of God on this earth. Under certain conditions. Scripture says: *"If my people who are called by my name humble themselves, and pray and seek my face and turn from their wicked ways, then I will hear from heaven and will forgive their sin and heal their land"* (2 Chronicles 7:14).

Let me suggest a few steps:

- Recognize that division among Christians is a *diabolical* sin from the enemy of our souls. There are many Christians who are not aware of this.
- Confess with sincere repentance to the Lord, telling Him: "Lord, forgive us for our divisions because when we have not honored our brothers and sisters in Your body, we have dishonored You. We broke the covenant of love that You wanted for each of us with the sacrifice of Your cross."
- Ask for forgiveness from our brothers and sisters in Christ. Ask Jesus to give us the grace to recognize that we are all sinners and to know how to forgive one another. Jesus says: *"If you are offering your gift at the altar and there remember that your brother has something against you, leave your gift there before the altar and go. First be reconciled to your brother, and then come and offer your gift"* (Matthew 5:23–24). Jesus asks for pure worship to come up from a church purified by His precious blood shed for our salvation.

Therefore, let us say to each other, " Forgive us, brother and sister, if we have offended you and have failed in the command to love one another, if we have resentments, prejudices, closures, and even mythologies toward you that did not represent reality. With all our heart, we sincerely ask you to forgive us!"

We ask the heavenly Father to purify our slanderous language that has wounded our brothers and sisters in the body of Christ and to give us a new language of men and women clothed in the love of Christ, capable of communicating peace and unity.

We ask the Holy Spirit to heal the wounds in our memory due to the divisions of our fathers over the centuries of Christianity.

We receive a new fresh anointing from the Holy Spirit to be ambassadors of reconciliation. The ministry of reconciliation is a personal initiative of God. Scripture says that God reconciles us to Himself as ambassadors of reconciliation. (See 2 Corinthians 5:18–20.) We ask the Holy Spirit for a powerful and fresh anointing to be ambassadors of reconciliation.

God never resigns Himself to the sin of man. Today He opens up new ways to live our fraternity in Christ, and we cannot escape this.

Therefore, as a Catholic, I humbly ask your forgiveness. I ask your forgiveness also on behalf of those who have shown non-Christian, even non-human attitudes of closure, division, and behavior toward you. In the name of the Lord Jesus Christ, forgive us!

God have mercy and forgive us, pour out His Spirit, and be able to manifest His glory on the face of the earth. May the Lord now renew a new Pentecost even greater than the previous ones and pour out His Spirit on all flesh before His great and glorious day comes. (See Acts 2:17, 20.)

Matteo Calisi is president of United in Christ International, headquartered in Dallas, Texas, USA, and president of the Community of Jesus in Bari, Italy. He has organized conferences on renewal, unity, and reconciliation all over the world. Connect with him at www.unitedinchrist.global.

8

LIVING IN LOVE AND UNITY AS A FAMILY

Heidi Baker
| Pentecostal Missionary |

Like many parents, I learned some of the deepest lessons about the unity God asks of us by raising children. When my husband and I moved to Maputo, Mozambique, we already had two natural born, tow-headed blondes who looked just like us. As we began to take in more and more children from the streets, we quickly realized that all of our natural and adopted children had very different personalities and ways of expressing themselves. They not only looked different from one another, they had different ways of playing, working, and praying. Through raising many sons and daughters, we learned by experience that God both accepted and cheered on their many individual personalities and also called us to live in unity as a family. We faced many hard trials together, and often it was the most difficult times that taught us the greatest lessons about unity. When we nearly ran out of money or food, when we lost property and buildings and homes, when we were threatened or flooded or faced with infectious diseases, we saw that God always blessed our choice to come together in faith and share whatever we had.

When I studied theology, I was taught many ideas about the best ways to worship and pray—whether out loud or silently in our hearts, whether in the early morning or throughout the day, whether solemnly or with exuberant celebration. But I saw that all our children had different rhythms, different ways of expressing their love to God. As the years passed, we realized more of God's heart through the way that He loved all the personalities of His children and all the genuine ways in which they worshipped Him.

One of the most moving prayers in all of Scripture is Jesus's own prayer for His disciples. I especially love the Passion translation of John 17:9–23, in which He prays that they would be one in unity and protected from evil.

My father had some Jewish ancestry, but the family line had converted to Catholicism. He had become an atheist while studying at Stanford University. My mother took me to an Episcopalian church when I was a child, but the way they worshipped had never seemed completely real to me. Mercifully, my father ultimately rediscovered a strong faith late in his life and was ordained as a lay minister in the Episcopal Church at the age of seventy-two. My mother also experienced astounding growth as we walked together through forgiveness, and she became filled with the Holy Spirit before she passed away.

I first heard about what it really meant to be born again at a Baptist church when I was sixteen years old. I was a student with the American field service on an Indian reservation in central Mississippi. A Navajo preacher came to the reservation and preached the gospel in full native American dress. He was yelling so much that I was afraid at first. He talked about all the Native American power movements he had been a part of and how he had greatly cursed white people in the past, even wishing them dead. There were only three white people present: me, another student, and the pianist. I wanted nothing more than to escape that church. Then the preacher looked over the congregation, and I felt like he was looking directly at me. He said, "But now I love all people, because Jesus has come inside my heart." What a revelation of the Father's heart for unity! What a glorious demonstration of the love of Jesus and the way that He takes away hatred and brings us into unity from the inside. That night, I was powerfully born again. Immediately after the service, an older woman from a Pentecostal Holiness church found me and told me that it was indeed wonderful to be born again, but now I needed to receive the Holy Spirit. I agreed to go to her church the next night.

To me, a teenager from Laguna Beach, California, these Holiness Pentecostals seemed like they were from the moon. The women were all wearing long dresses, with sleeves to the wrists. Their hair was all tied up in enormous buns. They didn't believe a woman should have her hair cut. The men all had short hair; they didn't believe that a man should ever have it uncut. I was greatly taken aback by all of this, but still, I felt so undone by the presence of God that I opened up my heart completely in worship. That night, my life was again forever changed as I became filled with the Holy Spirit. Jesus gave me a precious vision that has guided much of my life since, and He has never let me down.

For a while after this, though, I became deeply critical toward my mother's faith. Looking back, I see now that I allowed unjust judgments to come into my heart because I could not accept my mother's expression of Christianity as an Episcopalian. I really felt there was no possibility at all that my mother could be a true Christian. It seemed that their strict formalism lacked sincerity and life, and their rituals felt empty to me. At the same time, both my parents were shocked at my newfound Pentecostal expression of faith. They insisted that I was in a cult. They even hired a special psychologist to try to deprogram me. But as it turned out, my father was actually changing little by little from an atheist into an agnostic. After college, when I was preparing to leave America for the mission field, he finally told me, "Please pray for me because you have a direct line to God, but I can't get through to Him."

In the Pentecostal Holiness Church, they really taught me how to seek Jesus and connect to Him personally. At the same time, there were countless rules that badly affected the way that I was able to relate to other churches and denominations. I was absolutely petrified that if I broke one of these many strict rules, I would perish and go to hell. Since then, I have been a cross-cultural missionary for more than four decades. Over this time, I truly believe that I have received some revelation of God's heart of love for all His people. I have seen that there are many different ways of expressing love for God, and I know that I have no authority to minister to the body of Christ unless I have experienced genuine love for the body of Christ.

One of the first times the Lord began to correct my attitude toward His body came when I visited an Assembles of God church on the campus of Vanguard University (then called Southern California College) in California. A college admissions director met me there. She was wearing makeup and enormous hoop earrings. Even more shockingly, she had short hair. According to the rules I had been taught, these things meant she was not a Christian. But when she saw me, she smiled broadly and asked, "Hey, honey, what's your birthday?" I said, "August 29th." She replied, "No, no, no, sweetheart, I mean your spiritual birthday." I paused and said, "Well, it's March 13th, 1976." Then she told me, "Well, happy birthday! The Lord told me it was your birthday today." And it *was* my spiritual birthday. That was the moment when the Lord began to teach me real love for people from other denominations.

After arriving on the mission field, I witnessed tremendous variety in the ways that other cultures dressed and spoke and celebrated. The Lord continued to speak to me about the mistakes I sometimes made in judging His children. Year after year, He softened my heart. After a decade of ministry, I ended up going to King's College, University of London, to study for my doctorate in Systematic Theology. When it came to dealing with other Christian groups and churches, this would turn out to be one of my greatest challenges. Leaders from denominations more ancient and formal than my own were studying alongside me. There were Catholics, Greek and Russian Orthodox, Lutherans, and Reformed theologians. I think I was actually the first woman who had been admitted to that particular program in systematic theology because one of the requirements was being an ordained leader within your own denomination. I sometimes felt judged very harshly by some of the other leaders present. Many of them did not believe in the ordination of women. Many had only disparaging remarks for Pentecostals in particular. Although this was difficult, the Lord was very much working on my heart during those years of study. I began to understand that these leaders, these devout men, were really true believers in the Lord, but they expressed their genuine faith in many different ways.

I have always loved to dance and sing and clap and pray in tongues as I worship. Few of my peers at King's College could relate in any way to my manner of praising God. So I found my tribe on the streets of London, with the homeless. In many ways, I felt most comfortable with them. After I graduated, we moved to Mozambique, knowing that there were many more people in need of tangible help, and we found that most were exceptionally enthusiastic about expressing themselves energetically in church, just as we loved to do. As much as I enjoyed this, I began to realize that I still carried a lot of severe distrust for other denominations, for the rest of the body of Christ. I often made unwitting judgments against my brothers and sisters, feeling that we were superior to other denominations because of our special service to the poor. I think that at times I even thought that the miraculous signs and wonders we saw meant that we were somehow better than these others.

Another thing that influenced my change of heart was a friend who invited me to visit an Episcopalian church in New York City. It was the first time I had been in that kind of church for many years, and to my surprise, I found myself absolutely overwhelmed by the presence of God during Communion. I wept and wept, seeing that God was more than willing to touch these worshippers with the same intimate companionship that I had known among Pentecostals and charismatics. It was not a different or lesser blessing than what we knew in our worship, but the same God in the radiance of His grace and love. I knew at once that I had to repent and ask forgiveness for all the ways that I had judged the Episcopal denomination in particular.

So ... I was raised Episcopalian, born again in a Baptist church, and filled with the Holy Spirit in a Pentecostal Holiness church. Despite holding on to judgment toward the Episcopalians and many other Christians who looked like them for many years, the Lord softened my heart gradually and showed Himself to me in an Episcopal Communion service. This aspect of the church's celebration of God was a life-changing blessing, where once it had seemed like an almost cruel, ritualistic obstacle.

On another occasion, I went to a revival meeting where I was so struck by the weight of the Holy Spirit that I hit the floor and was unable to walk under my own strength for the next seven days and nights. I literally needed physical help to go anywhere or do anything. As you might imagine, this became incredibly humbling. During this time, I felt a strong impression from the Lord saying, "You can do nothing without Jesus, and you can do nothing without the body of Christ." By then, we lived in Mozambique. I felt I had learned a lot about the many different ways that God's children relate to Him, but I had never before been so dependent on others in such a direct and obvious way. During that week-long experience in God's presence, while friends and people I had never met carried me from room to room, it seemed that the Lord ripped out my remaining judgment for the church, for the body of Christ. In its place, He put a supernatural love for the whole church that I still cannot fully explain. Before that time, I had only been invited to a handful of churches to speak. One of those churches was in Fairbanks, Alaska, where my spiritual mother had encouraged me as greatly as anyone ever has. I loved her so much that I was willing to brave the unbelievably freezing Alaskan winters to go and share about what we were doing on the mission field. But after that week, I suddenly began to receive invitations from all over the world to come and preach. At first, I was very confused. Nothing obvious had changed. I had sent out no letters announcing my availability to speak. But the invitations came. God had shifted my heart in preparation to serve many more kinds of people than I had ever expected, and when the time was right, He opened all the doors He chose.

Kingdom authority comes only where you have love. I believe the Lord only trusted me with a wider ministry after He had done a kind of surgery on my heart, increasing my love for the body of Christ beyond anything I had known before. Even now, the Lord continues to stretch my understanding as He sends me to different parts of the world. I recently spoke to three separate groups of believers in three days, each one completely different. The first was a congregation of Messianic Jewish believers in Kiev, Ukraine, who worshipped in Hebrew and Russian, wore *kippahs*, and danced joyously in the service. I had a wonderful time with them, as I have always loved to dance during praise. I was next scheduled to speak to a Pentecostal church in Poland and then to a group of Catholics the following day in the same city. The Pentecostals said they too wanted to grow in their love for the whole church, but they could not quite share the same service with the Catholics. So they arranged to make the same conference hall available for that group. That was as close to unity as they could come at the time, but I took it as a good start! Worshipping with the Pentecostals, I was in the kind of setting with which I was most familiar. The Holy Spirit came and moved, and many were blessed. Then the very next day, the Catholics came and changed all the decorations in the hall. They even took away the old flower arrangements and brought new ones. A Catholic priest came with a large youth group, wearing his robes and collar, and we shared a beautiful meal together. I spoke and later we were able to sing many beautiful hymns and even some praise songs. Once again, I felt the presence of the Holy Spirit strongly, even though these worshippers looked so different from the ones I had been with for the past two days.

All three of the leaders of these Christian groups tried to persuade me that their way of worshipping was the best. In a way, it was very stressful trying to adjust to speaking in such different environments so quickly. But the truth is, despite the challenge, I can honestly testify that throughout this time, I felt tremendous joy. Inside me, there was indescribable affection for the body of Christ in all its variety. In the end, I simply felt that it was my own task to enjoy each expression of worship I experienced in those three days and to keep a grateful heart so that I could continue to enter into the presence of our heavenly Father, who has welcomed all of us through the blood of Jesus.

Several times here, I have mentioned my love for dance. I grew up studying classical ballet. As a matter of fact, dancing was one of the first things that I gave up when I joined the Holiness Pentecostal church at age sixteen. It was terribly painful, but I was told that it was a sin, and I believed it. When I was born again, I became so zealous that I would sacrifice anything for God. After a long journey in faith, the Lord did ultimately give me back the gift of dance, which I have deeply treasured ever since. During those three days with the Messianic, the Pentecostal, and the Catholic worshippers, I saw that all three of these groups also loved to dance, each in their own way. Their steps and their songs were extraordinarily different, but each time, I felt the Lord's distinct pleasure and desire to dance with every one of His children. The relationship that He has with each of them is beautiful and significant in its own right. If we ourselves love our natural and adopted children for all their unique and wildly varied personalities, how much more does our Father love the endless expressions of worship that His many children offer up to Him!

A LETTER TO THE BODY OF CHRIST

To my dear brothers and sisters,

I send my love, affection, and admiration for you. I carry you in my heart always. I pray for each one of you, that you would be possessed by the love of Christ Jesus, so that He will shine through you and release His *shalom* to this broken and shaking world. I pray that the power of the Holy Spirit would protect and ignite you. I pray that day by day, you would be empowered to stop for the one in need. I ask that your eyes would be opened with a fresh vision of the beauty of Christ's body in all its fullness.

I am thankful that the Lord has allowed my travel to slow this year because I have so treasured worship in our small family gatherings in Mozambique. Under trees, in small rooms, and in villages, we are hidden from much of the world, but not from God. I pray that as we focus our eyes on Jesus, He would undo our former lives and remake us by His grace. Let us not forsake fellowship together as believers but strengthen ourselves day and night with testimony and prayer and worship.

I pray that your heart would break as His heart breaks. Push away hatred and fear and unrighteous judgment. Be overwhelmed by His love. Father, have mercy on Your children! Have mercy on Your bride. In this time of great shaking, allow us to love through all our pain until fear melts away. Forgive me for all the times when I have not seen Your sons and daughters as You see them. Rip the judgment from my heart. Allow me to celebrate Your family with a pure spirit. Let us never go back to living in hatred again.

All around us and around my home are wars and rumors. I come to you from a war zone. I hear testimony after testimony from mothers and fathers and grandparents and children who have lost their homes, their loved ones, their families. They have seen horror, murder, violence, and torture. They suffer because of the wicked judgments of others around them who live by different doctrines. I call upon the sleeping beauty, your church, to run from all false judgment that leads only to death.

I come as a little mama with many, many children. I cry out to You with tears and sorrow. Wake up Your children. Show them that grace and love alone will win. Lead them into the unity that Jesus paid for on the cross, until we are one. Let even our enemies see by our love for one another and for every human made in God's image that we truly are brothers and sisters. I plead with the church to stop fighting, stop eating one another with bitter words and anger. I cry out for the orphans of a world turned upside down by rage and division and, yes, even religion. Walk in mercy. Share what you have been given, not only with those who are in your family of faith but also all those are hungry for spiritual and physical food. Jesus said, *"I am the bread of life"* (John 6:35). Because He died, there will always be enough bread.

Some of you have grown weak for lack of bread. You cannot live on yesterday's bread. Come to God daily. Eat and share. Open your eyes and see the starving, the suffering, and the lonely. Everyone who has the seal of adoption by God is your brother and your sister, and even your spiritual foes need to return home. Won't you love them too? How else will they know who we are? How else will they know who God is?

This week, I sat and held the four-year-old daughter of our friend Filizardo, who was crucified and set on fire by people of another faith. He has nail marks on his legs and his neck will not straighten because of the burns. His tormentors said he would suffer in the way that Jesus suffered. I pray that the body of Christ would become like the good Samaritan, the kind of neighbor who stopped for Filizardo as he burned on a cross—who rescued him, took him down, and carried him to a hospital. Let them be like the neighbor who later found Filizardo's terrified daughter, took her in, and reunited her with her father. Let them rejoice with this man and his daughter, who endured the worst of human hatred and lived to praise God. And I rejoice with those who helped us to build a new home for Filizardo and his daughter. May we be filled with compassion and joy as we build homes of healing where all of God's children can belong.

Look how we need one another! We cry out for grace—great grace, great grace, great grace.

Love in Jesus,
Heidi Baker

Heidi Baker is a Christian missionary, itinerant speaker, and CEO of Iris Global, a Christian humanitarian organization. Connect with her at www.irisglobal.org.

9

DREAMING OF ONE TABLE

Francis Chan
| Evangelical |

I fell in love with Jesus in a Baptist church. The youth pastor explained the cross in a way that was clear and alluring. Church members were eager to love me as family. One couple even took me into their home when I had nowhere else to live. As a lost teenager with deceased parents, the church quickly became my refuge. Those were wonderful and life-changing days. I thank God for that church, and I still enjoy friendship with some of those who began loving me forty years ago.

I found so much life through that church, and I embraced their theology. I questioned nothing. Why would I? It was here that I found Jesus, life, and love. To question any of their doctrine would have felt disloyal. When people with different beliefs challenged me, I could always count on my church leaders to defend our theology.

I later attended Bible college and seminary to learn how to study and teach the Bible. I was grateful for this school. A couple professors not only taught me how to study the Scriptures but seemed to genuinely care about me. Out of loyalty once again, I held to all the doctrine I learned. However, after graduating, I began to meet many Christians who held to different beliefs. As a staunch cessationist, I felt uncomfortable, literally getting knots in my stomach whenever I met someone who claimed to be Christian yet spoke in tongues or claimed to have a supernatural gift of prophecy. I viewed them as ignorant and dangerous. Then I got to know some of them.

One of the first was Pastor Jack Hayford. I held a lot of assumptions about Jack because his name often came up in my school. I also concluded that those who believed in these supernatural gifts did so because they were too lazy to study the Scriptures and relied on visions from God rather than careful study and obedience to biblical commands. As I got to know Jack, however, I realized he loved Jesus deeply and was faithful to studying the Bible. While I assumed his teaching would be shallow—not nearly to the level of scholarship of this recent seminary grad—I was shocked as he explained an Old Testament text, giving historical context and dissecting the Hebrew in a way of which I was incapable. He shattered my paradigm.

Over the years, I was able to observe Jack's character and saw an overflow of love, joy, peace, patience, and other fruit of the Spirit. Since then, I have met many charismatics who don't study the Word and are complacent toward sin, but I have also met many who are the opposite. As they have patiently explained their interpretations of Scripture, I saw that their conclusions weren't as ridiculous as I once thought. Before this, I had only learned their theology from the biased perspective of those who staunchly disagreed. I had never actually spoken to them or read their books. After doing so, I not only better understood their reasoning but I came to agree with them on some of their teachings.

Especially over the past two decades, I have rubbed shoulders with leaders of many different denominations. I have questioned some on their theology. While I disagreed with some of their conclusions, I saw that they had studied diligently. Sometimes I would begin these conversations being 99 percent sure that I was right, and I would leave being about 70 percent sure that I was right. Other times, I concluded that I was wrong. I don't feel unstable on my convictions, but I am learning that it's healthier to reexamine my understanding of Scripture rather than assume that the first theology I was taught happened to be the right one.

For example, I am currently 90 percent sure that I have been wrong about my belief that Christ is not present in the Eucharist. I'm probably about 70 percent sure that the denominations that hold the most accurate view of the Eucharist are those that marvel at the real but mysterious presence of Christ. I'm about 65 percent sure that transubstantiation as most understand it is inaccurate. I am about 95 percent sure that I was wrong about my cessationist view of the gifts. When I say things like this, I realize that some readers are eager to debate me on these issues. I understand. I was there. I once thought all charismatics were shallow and dangerous heretics. I once thought all Catholics were unsaved and lifeless idol worshipers. I never dreamed that I would actually have friends who were charismatic Catholics and that I would love them as brothers. I still have doctrinal disagreements with many charismatics and Catholics, but I have enjoyed my friendships with those who share a deep reverence for God and amazement at the cross.

Forty years after my initial conversion, I still hold to the basic foundational truths I was taught in my early days. I still spend time alone reading the Scriptures daily. I still believe that salvation is by grace alone through faith in Christ. I haven't deviated much from my Baptist roots. My biggest change is that I have come to realize that these roots are not exclusively Baptist. The gospel truths I would die for are shared by more people than I was led to believe. Because of this, I have the responsibility and privilege of uniting with the rest of those who recognize Christ as Lord and Savior.

UNITY WITHOUT COMPROMISE

Scripture makes it very clear that unity in the church is extremely important to God. Paul paints this beautiful picture of how the church is supposed to function:

> *So then you are no longer strangers and aliens, but you are fellow citizens with the saints and members of the household of God, built on the foundation of the apostles and prophets, Christ Jesus himself being the cornerstone, in whom the whole structure, being joined together, grows into a holy temple in the Lord. In him you also are being built together into a dwelling place for God by the Spirit.* (Ephesians 2:19–22)

We are all called to attach ourselves to this living temple made up of believers throughout the ages, from the apostles and prophets up until now, Jesus Himself being the cornerstone. God wants to dwell with *us*. Unity is not optional; it's commanded.

Likewise, Scripture is also very clear that the church is to be holy, as God is holy. We are to *"be separate"* from unbelievers, to keep ourselves *"unstained from the world"* (2 Corinthians 6:17; James 1:27).

So as believers, we have this twofold mandate: attach ourselves to the church and remove ourselves from the world. I think most of us would agree on those principles. The problem is, what happens when the church starts taking on worldly beliefs and behaviors? Is it possible to become stained by the church itself? How do we respond if the church begins to deviate from fundamental truths? How do we decide which issues are important enough to break fellowship over?

It's very hard to know how to be *"eager to maintain the unity of the Spirit in the bond of peace"* (Ephesians 4:3) without compromising on holiness and truth. For many years, it seems, believers have tried to navigate this by creating boundaries with various degrees of separation, reasoning, "You can call him a Christian, but it's probably best not to associate with him," or "We don't agree on these issues, but I *think* it's okay to partner on this type of event." This quickly becomes confusing, and it's hard to be consistent. Many people have asked me where to draw the lines, and honestly, I don't know.

Recently, as I was meditating on Ephesians 4:3, it dawned on me that Paul doesn't provide a strategy for how to achieve godly unity, but he does show us a type of character that we are supposed to pursue: *"With **all** humility and gentleness, with patience, bearing with one another in love"* (verse 2). So often, I just want to know what to do, but here Paul is telling us who to be: the most humble, gentle person on the earth.

In the many marital counseling sessions my wife Lisa and I have led over the years, we've never seen a humble couple divorce. It just doesn't happen! It's crazy how humility brings people together.

As I was thinking about what it means to be humble and gentle, I realized those same words are used in another passage of Scripture. In the whole Bible, there is only one place where Jesus describes His own heart: *"Come to me, all you who are weary and burdened, and I will give you rest. Take my yoke upon you and learn from me, for I am **gentle and humble in heart**, and you will find rest for your souls"* (Matthew 11:28–29 NIV).

Jesus loved perfectly, without restraint or compromise. If we want to be like Him, we need to start by shifting our focus from the boundaries to the heart. If we are diligent about forming the character of Christ in our lives, I believe we will have fewer conflicts to begin with and He will pour out the wisdom we need to walk with integrity in those that remain.

TOGETHER, WE WILL SEE HIS POWER

I love seeing power. There have been times when I experienced the power of God so tangibly that I actually felt a bit afraid. I think it's similar to the *"awe"* that all believers felt in Acts 2:43. Recently, my teenage kids described how they felt at summer camp when they saw their dear friend miraculously and completely healed of a lifelong ailment. My son said the entire group was screaming with excitement, but soon, they were on the ground trembling. The fear of God fell upon them as they realized that they were truly in the presence of a holy God. Supernatural experiences produce more than excitement. There is a fear and awe that is like nothing else in this world.

Experiencing His power is so fascinating that prolonged periods of *ordinary life* leave me frustrated. I refuse to experience life in the same way as a person who doesn't have the Holy Spirit. This is one of the reasons why unity is so critical. Biblical unity results in supernatural power. Scripture promises this, and I have experienced this. As I have loved and partnered with believers across denominational lines, I have witnessed the fulfillment of His promises in Psalm 133. Not only did I enjoy *"how good and pleasant it is when brothers dwell in unity"* (v. 1), but I witnessed, *"For there the Lord has commanded the blessing, life forevermore"* (v. 3). Miracles and salvation resulted from unified efforts at sharing the gospel with the unreached. Now that I have experienced this, I can't settle for less. I want more. Which leads me to my dream: the day when all true believers can sit at the same table.

As it stands, believers from certain denominations are not permitted to partake of the Lord's supper together. Does that statement bother you at all? Do you think it bothers God? If so, shouldn't we have faith that He can change this? I believe a day is soon coming when I will celebrate Communion with brothers and sisters who trust in the death of Christ for salvation and whose lives produce the works that accompany salvation, whether they are Protestant, Orthodox, or Roman Catholic. Even as I write that, I think to myself, "This discussion is above my paygrade." The key scholars and heads of these churches should be leading this discussion. I hope they will. The problem is that we have been waiting centuries for scholars to agree and leaders to humble themselves. Does God really want the rest of us to sit silently? Jesus's command to unity is a command for every believer, so it's our responsibility to encourage steps toward unity.

THE CHILDREN WANT TO BE TOGETHER

When I was a kid, I looked forward to seeing my friends each week at our church gatherings. We would sit by each other during service, eat lunch together, and then play football or basketball. Sundays were great. Then one week, I showed up at our gathering, and half of the people were missing. The church split. Our parents fought and decided to divide the church in two. As kids, we weren't told what the fight was about. All I knew was that I wouldn't see half of my friends again. As I got older, I discovered that the church split over some embarrassingly petty issue in light of the gospel truths that supposedly united us. In the end, the children paid the price for the sin of their parents. Some of us kids (forty years later) occasionally cross paths and talk about "the good old days" before the fight.

Today, there are millions of Christians who don't understand why our spiritual parents chose to divide. We inherited division, but that doesn't mean we have to continue in it. I'm not saying we should rebel against leadership, sneak out of our spiritual houses, and share Communion together. Nor am I saying we shouldn't. I *am* saying that something has to be done. I have yet to meet a Christian who believes that God's ultimate desire is for us to be at separate tables. It's hard for any of us to believe that His church should so closely resemble a middle school cafeteria or a prison yard, where the tables are exclusive. *"Because there is one bread, we who are many are one body, for we all partake of the one bread"* (1 Corinthians 10:17).

INCREASING OUR REVERENCE AT THE TABLE

Any time there is an appeal for unity, there will be a crowd that insists that it's impossible to unify without compromising holiness. But I think we can all agree that all believers could stand to grow in their sacredness at the Lord's Supper. Liturgy that was meant to preserve sacredness can easily become mindless ritual for some. Non-liturgical gatherings using creativity in hopes of stirring affections can lead to cheapening what was meant to be holy. The more we all grow in our reverence for the Lord's Supper, the easier I believe it will become to take together.

I have been extremely convicted about the need for greater reverence toward Communion in my own life. I grew up having a very limited understanding of Communion, and as a result, I went to the table for decades without really understanding what I was doing. It wasn't until a few years ago, when I was challenged to really study the first three hundred years of church history, especially as it pertained to the Lord's Supper, that things began to change. Since then, as I have studied the Scriptures deeply, I have only become more and more convinced of the sacredness of Communion.

COMMUNION AND THE HOLY OF HOLIES

There is something special about coming to the table, experiencing the presence of Christ in a different way. The very word *Communion* describes an intimate encounter or exchange. When we take of the bread and the cup, we commune with Christ in a way that is unique from the day-to-day relationship with Him.

I think the closest Old Testament equivalent to this is the holy of holies. God was with His people everywhere, but there was a special presence in the holy of holies. Only one person, the high priest, was ever allowed to enter, and he could only do so once a year on the Day of Atonement. When this practice was instituted, God told Moses to warn his brother Aaron that he would die if he did not follow the special ceremonial requirements of Leviticus 16. Can you imagine how seriously Aaron would have taken this warning after watching two of his sons die for their lack of reverence? (See Leviticus 10:1–2.) It is extremely dangerous to enter the presence of God casually, and the Israelites witnessed this firsthand.

What we have to understand is that the presence of Christ in Communion is no less holy than the presence of God in the holy of holies. Often, we can fall into the trap of believing that the New Testament realities are less intense than those of the Old Testament, when in fact, I believe the opposite is true. If you find yourself doubting this, I would challenge you to meditate on the book of Hebrews.

Hebrews is all about how now we have greater access to God, and with that greater accessibility comes greater intensity. Hebrews 8:5 talks about the holy of holies as *"a copy and shadow of the heavenly things."* Christ *"has obtained a ministry that is as much more excellent than the old as the covenant he mediates is better, since it is enacted on better promises"* (verse 6). Later, Hebrews 9:24 tells us, *"For Christ has entered, not into holy places made with hands, which are copies of the true things, but into heaven itself, now to appear in the presence of God on our behalf."* Thus, *"we have confidence to enter the holy places by the blood of Jesus, by the new and living way that he opened for us through the curtain, that is, through his flesh, and since we have a great high priest over the house of God, let us draw near with a true heart in full assurance of faith, with our hearts sprinkled clean from an evil conscience and our bodies washed with pure water"* (Hebrews 10:19–22).

As amazing as the Old Testament temple was, it was just *"a copy and shadow."* The curtain in heaven was the body of Christ that was torn open so we could enter into the real holy of holies. Our high priest, Jesus, has made a way for us to come before not just the ark of the covenant and the cloud on the mercy seat, but the actual throne of God. This is way more intense.

It is as dangerous to partake in the Lord's Supper in an unworthy manner as it was to enter the Old Testament holy of holies unworthily. Paul says whoever takes Communion *"in an unworthy manner will be guilty concerning the body and blood of the Lord. … For anyone who eats and drinks without discerning the body eats and drinks judgment on himself. That is why many of you are weak and ill, and some have died"* (1 Corinthians 11:27, 29–30).

There is a real possibility that you could die the next time you take Communion! This is not something to be taken lightly. Lives are at stake, and the key to our safety is *"discerning the body."* Understanding this phrase is critical. In context, Paul is speaking about the church, His body. While many believe that *"body"* might also be referring to Christ's presence in the bread, almost everyone agrees that it certainly refers to the church body. This means that our survival in Communion is directly tied to our relationships with other believers.

In the preceding verses (1 Corinthians 11:17–22), Paul tells the church at Corinth that they have made a mockery of the Lord's Supper because of their divisions and lack of concern toward members of the body of Christ. This leads him to give them warnings and commands to care for one another. If that's not enough, Paul spends the next three chapters talking about the need for unity of the body!

In the Old Testament, the high priest had to exercise extreme caution when entering the holy of holies. This included wearing proper garments, practicing proper cleansing, and making proper sacrifices to atone for himself as well as the nation. Now in the New Testament, God is warning us to exercise extreme caution as we partake of the bread and cup. This includes proper recognition of our brothers and sisters in Christ, proper relationships with them, and proper respect and care for them. Recently, in our gatherings, we have started to ask God to bring to mind any brothers and sisters in Christ whom we have offended or failed to love. We also ask the body to voice any needs they may have, so the church members can care for those needs through prayer or the sharing of their possessions. Cautiously, after these acts of repentance and love, we come reverently into His presence.

The way I understand the New Testament now is that it's not just about us having a personal relationship with Jesus Christ but also recognizing our need for one another and our utter dependence on Christ as our head. It's about coming before our Father, laying down our individual rights and coming together as one body in Christ.

Taking Communion together is a physical embodiment of these deep spiritual truths. It is a tangible act through which we profess the very core of the gospel. This is why I believe that the Eucharist needs to be central to this larger discussion about unity. Can you imagine what it would be like to see believers from all different traditions partaking in this together?

> *I do not ask for these only, but also for those who will believe in me through their word, that they may all be one, just as you, Father, are in me, and I in you, that they also may be in us, so that the world may believe that you have sent me.* (John 17:20–21)

GOD'S ETERNAL PURPOSE

As I have been studying the book of Ephesians lately, I have been embarrassed by the shallowness of my thoughts compared to the depth of God's eternal truths.

Consider Ephesians 1:4–5:

> *Even as he chose us in him before the foundation of the world, that we should be holy and blameless before him. In love he predestined us for adoption to himself as sons through Jesus Christ, according to the purpose of his will.*

The road to my union with God was paved long before I was created. He initiated His glorious purposes before I let out my first breath. He has bestowed upon me the sacred honor of being an adopted son.

So what does that have to do with Communion? Just this: If our Creator's love led Him to predestine someone as His son or daughter, are we sure that we have the right to deny them access to the bread that we break?

I'm not suggesting that it's always wrong to exclude people from participating in sacred Communion. I am saying that there should be a certain level of fear and trembling when we look a child of God in the eyes and tell them they are not welcome to the table.

Consider Ephesians 2:13–16:

> *But now in Christ Jesus you who once were far off have been brought near by the blood of Christ. For he himself is our peace, who has made us both one and has broken down in his flesh the dividing wall of hostility by abolishing the law of commandments expressed in ordinances, that he might create in himself one new man in place of the two, so making peace, and might reconcile us both to God in one body through the cross, thereby killing the hostility.*

The heavens decided, in a supreme act of love, to reconcile both Jews and Gentiles to God through Christ's excruciating death on the cross. This was to create *"one new man in place of the two."* I pray that as you read this passage, you are struck with the weightiness of this divine decision.

Any decisions we make on earth to exclude people from the Lord's Table must be made in light of these holy truths. Knowing the level of suffering endured by our Savior to make us one should motivate us toward sacrificial effort to unite His children in the presence of His body and blood.

DEAR CHURCH

I aspire to deeply love any human being who has been sealed with the Spirit of God. This has not always been the case. Even as I write this, I am asking God to bring to mind anyone I have not forgiven completely. I am also asking that He would give grace to anyone I have offended, that they would quickly forgive. The stakes are too high to live another day under the influence of our enemy.

> *Anyone whom you forgive, I also forgive. Indeed, what I have forgiven, if I have forgiven anything, has been for your sake in the presence of Christ, so that we would not be outwitted by Satan; for we are not ignorant of his designs.* (2 Corinthians 2:10–11)

Forgive me for the years I spent inadvertently dividing the body of Christ. In my zeal to defend truth, I never considered that my biblical interpretations could be errant. I neglected the command to be eager to maintain the unity of the Spirit. I casually rejected ancient church practices without thoroughly studying church history. I have been guilty of being the eye that said to the hand, *"I have no need of you"* (1 Corinthians 12:21). God has shown me the error of my ways. I am asking your forgiveness and saying to everyone who depends on the shed blood of Christ, "I need you."

We currently have a window of time. I would love to partner with you in seeking the deepest level of humility either of us have achieved. I want to kneel beside you at the cross, trembling at His holiness and marveling at His love. Though I realize there are issues that need to be addressed, please know that I have a tremendous desire to one day sit at the same table with you in the presence of our Lord and Savior.

Our Father, have mercy on us. Only by Your power can we think with accuracy regarding something as sacred as the flesh and blood of Jesus. Our pride has led us to wrong thinking and shallow love, resulting in disunity. Forgive us for overestimating our ability to reason and move us toward deeper humility. Your beloved children are far from the oneness that Christ prayed and died for. We have separated Your table and do not know how to reunite. We come to express our desire for unity and our need for divine intervention. Lord, please unite us again at Your table.

Francis Chan is an American Protestant author, teacher, and preacher. He is the founder of Crazy Love Ministries (www.crazylove.org).

10

LIVING CHRISTIAN UNITY UNDER THE SAME ROOF

Cardinal Gérald Lacroix | Catholic |
and
Bishop Bruce Myers | Anglican |

The story is told that when the Right Reverend Jacob Mountain arrived as the first Anglican bishop in Quebec City in 1793, Monseigneur Jean-Olivier Briand, Quebec's seventh Roman Catholic bishop, was waiting on the shore to welcome Bishop Mountain to his new episcopal see.

It was the auspicious beginning of more than two centuries of warm and fraternal relations between the Roman Catholic and Anglican bishops of Quebec—a relationship characterized chiefly by collegiality rather than competition, friendship rather than enmity.

This fraternity reached a new high point in 2016, when Monseigneur Briand's current successor welcomed Bishop Mountain's current successor into not only their common see city, but as a fellow resident of the Roman Catholic archbishop's own home.

This ecumenical living arrangement wasn't really planned. Bishop Bruce was moving to Quebec City to take up his charge as coadjutor bishop of the Anglican Diocese of Quebec and needed a temporary home before moving into his church's official episcopal residence.

Fortunately, Cardinal Lacroix had some spare room in his own official residence, which is situated in the heart of the oldest part of Quebec City, beside the

Roman Catholic cathedral, Notre-Dame-de-Québec Basilica, just a short walk away from the Anglican cathedral, Holy Trinity....

It was a stopgap living arrangement that we thought might last at most a few months. It ended up being a profound experience of Christian communion that continued for more than a year.

The *archevêché* is home not only to the cardinal, but also to the Roman Catholic diocese's two auxiliary bishops, a retired bishop, and a few priests. Each resident has their own individual room, but meals are shared together, *en famille* (family style).

Family is just the right word to use because our time living together helped cultivate a true sense of Christian brotherhood. Despite the different ecclesial traditions from which we come, we were daily reminded that we are held together by the waters of our common baptism, a sacramental bond even more fundamental than genetics. In this case, water is actually thicker than blood.

Life together at the *archevêché* was about much more than simply eating and sleeping under the same roof. There were also regular occasions to socialize and pray together. When not travelling, we would gather to pray the divine office and celebrate Mass according to the Roman rite, participating as fully as our respective traditions allow. These moments of common prayer were both a daily celebration of the deep and rich liturgical heritage Anglicans and Roman Catholics share, and a daily reminder of the pain of our existing divisions as churches in real but imperfect communion. It was a tangible expression of what the Anglican-Roman Catholic International Commission wrote in its 1990 report, *Church as Communion*: "Paradoxically the closer we draw together the more acutely we feel those differences which remain."

The communion we enjoyed as Anglican and Roman Catholic bishops living and praying together has continued to infuse our ministries in the mission field that we share, and in which we are coworkers with one another and with Christ.

Less than a century ago, Quebec was once one of the most religiously observant places on Earth. Today, societal attitudes toward people and communities of faith are often characterized by ignorance, disrespect, and even hostility; government policies have never been more aggressive in their attempts to limit the place of religion in the lives of Quebec's citizens. Such a climate has drawn us closer together as Christian leaders, as we recognize that our current context requires us to take to heart Pope John XXIII's insight that "what unites us is much greater than what divides us." This means being less preoccupied with what makes us distinctive as Roman Catholics or Anglicans and emphasizing instead what it means to be a disciple of Jesus Christ.

The call to be reconciled with one another as Christians is so that we might be God's agents of unity in the world God loves. In drawing into a closer and deeper communion as siblings in Christ, we have better recognized that part of our role in society is to try and draw together others who may also be divided, to try and model dialogue, and be witnesses of reconciliation by sharing our own experiences.

This spirit of charity toward one another, and this call to be symbols of unity in the world, have helped us cultivate a still wider openness to others in our midst with whom we may need to be reconciled. When our Muslim brothers and sisters in Quebec City were viciously attacked in a murderous shooting rampage at a mosque in 2017, we extended a hand of friendship, forging long-overdue links of love and support between our city's Christian and Muslim communities.

Each of our churches has a complicated and conflicted history with the Indigenous peoples of this land. For decades, Anglicans and Roman Catholics participated in the Indian residential school system, which supressed Indigenous languages, culture, and spirituality. Many Indigenous children attending these institutions suffered physical, psychological, emotional, spiritual, cultural, and sexual abuse. As our churches repent of their participation in this colonial project, we are also together trying to learn how to walk the way of reconciliation and healing with our Indigenous sisters and brothers.

In all of this—and especially as a result of our time as housemates—we have been reminded that the unity and reconciliation that we seek will not primarily be made wrought through formal agreements brokered between official institutions. Rather, the full visible unity of the church that is both God's desire and gift is most clearly revealed by disciples of Jesus Christ growing into closer and deeper communion with one another through shared experience that helps draw into sharper focus the depth of the faith we already share—through praying together, breaking bread together, and sharing the joys and challenges of our daily life and work together.

Even though each of us now lives in our respective bishops' residences—which are just a couple of blocks away from each other—the seeds of unity sown and the bonds of fraternity forged during our time as housemates have created an ecumenical friendship that informs our faith and carries into our ministries as bishops. This friendship is both personal and an outward, visible symbol of our churches' desire to grow together in unity and mission, a foretaste of the full communion that is our desire and our Lord's will.

There's another, more physical and enduring symbol of this deepening communion between us and the two churches we serve. In Quebec City's Anglican cathedral, for as long as anyone can remember, there has been a chair that sits opposite the cathedra of the Anglican bishop of Quebec. It's a chair of equal size and dignity that has customarily been reserved for the Roman Catholic archbishop of Quebec when he is formally present in the Anglican cathedral. In a ceremony in 2016, that custom was made formal, and the *Archbishop's Chair* was officially set apart as a permanent seat in Quebec City's Anglican cathedral for the Roman Catholic archbishop of Quebec.

In doing so, we recognize a few things. First, the church of Christ was present and active in Quebec before the arrival of Anglicanism. Second, in the words of Archbishop of Canterbury Justin Welby and the late Pope Francis, we are "brothers and sisters in Christ by reason of our common baptism" called to "work together to give voice to our common faith in the Lord Jesus Christ, to bring relief to the suffering, to bring peace where there is conflict, to bring dignity where it is denied and trampled upon." And third, despite our differences, our churches are in real, if imperfect, communion.

A similar gesture of hospitality is extended to the Anglican bishop when he is in Notre-Dame-de-Québec Basilica Cathedral for a liturgy, so that when we are formally present in each other's cathedrals, we face each other not as historic rivals, but as partners in the gospel, brothers in Christ, and members of the one, holy, catholic, and apostolic church.

The friendship that has developed over the years has not only enriched the two of us in Quebec City, but we are convinced that through this visible sign of a growing unity, our Roman Catholic and Anglican communities have also grown in a better awareness of who we are and what we are called to become together: a visible sign of the body of Christ in and for the world.

Christ said if we abide in His love, we will bear much fruit. (See John 15:5–9.) Walking together as shepherds and with God's holy people, may the Lord allow us to grow in unity and witness to the world. How good it is to belong and to follow Jesus Christ.

From the Rt. Rev. Bruce Myers:

DEAR CHRISTIAN SIBLINGS,

I unwittingly began my ecumenical pilgrimage from the very beginning of my life. My parents were cradle Anglicans, born and raised in Montreal. But when as newlyweds, they moved to the countryside of eastern Ontario; the closest church to the farmstead that was our family's new home was a congregation of the United Church of Canada. So that's where our family went to church, where I was baptized, went to Sunday school, and was instructed in the Christian faith. I still consider that congregation my *home church*.

It was only many years later that I recognized the ecumenical significance of my parents' decision. An Anglican congregation was a few villages away, within reasonable driving distance, but my parents readily recognized that the fundamental characteristics of church could be found in a Christian tradition other than the one in which they were raised.

My childhood ecumenical education continued unawares as I would accompany my parents to the funerals of neighbors who were also Christian but attended different churches than our own: Roman Catholics, Presbyterians, Reformed Presbyterians, and Baptists. As I would sit, stand, or kneel through these various services, I had the impression of hearing the same language spoken, but in different accents or dialects. It was then I started asking my first questions about why, if all of us are Christians, we seem to be so different—even divided.

Ironically, it wasn't until I left home to attend university that I first encountered Anglicanism. It's the tradition of the church I would eventually call home, while always honoring and valuing the United Church tradition in which I was raised.

These experiences in the early years of life planted the seeds of a lifelong ecumenical pilgrimage. When I was discerning the call to ordained ministry, my theological education occurred in the company of students and teachers from a half-dozen different Christian traditions. My two best friends from those days aren't fellow Anglicans but Presbyterians, and almost every year since graduating, we gather for a week of fellowship, prayer, and study. Further studies in ecumenical theology were a kind of full immersion experience—not only studying with other Christians from around the world and a multiplicity of church traditions, but also living, eating, socializing, and praying together. Perhaps that's one of the reasons I found sharing a roof with Cardinal Lacroix and his Roman Catholic confreres so natural!

My own Christian life as an Anglican has not only been enriched by these encounters over the years, but they have made it such that I cannot conceive of the church without the richness of this God-given diversity and feel somehow incomplete without it.

Part of what binds all of these ecumenical experiences together is that they primarily involve personal encounters between fellow Christians. It's true that the historical divisions between many of our churches are rooted in differences over doctrine or practice. That's why it's important that the work of *theological ecumenism* continue, so that the matters of faith and order that still divide us can be better understood and reconciled.

At least as important, however, is the task of *spiritual ecumenism*. This is less the work of institutional churches and councils than of individual disciples of Jesus Christ. In a way, it consists of something no more complicated than simply getting to know one another better, across the differences we bring from our different Christian traditions, to find the fundamental unity in Christ that binds us together.

The fact that you're reading this book suggests you've already got a heart for ecumenism, a desire to make more visible the unity of the church that is God's gift and God's will. That's no small thing! My invitation to you is to find some ways to give concrete expression to that heartfelt desire.

Like Jesus, pray for the unity of the church. Our prayers are part of the way God's good purposes for the world—and for the church—can be made manifest, and so we need to pray for the unity among Christians, which we seek and which God desires. Then try taking that further and pray with others who come from a Christian tradition other than your own. Discover the different accents and dialects of the language of love that different churches use to worship our one Triune God.

From praying together, you can explore the Bible together, discovering how the sacred Scriptures we all share as Christians are interpreted, prayed, or sung in ways you hadn't considered or experienced before.

You can also engage in proclaiming the good news of God in Christ together. Different churches do this in different ways too. Sometimes it's called mission, outreach, service, evangelism, evangelization, or works of mercy. Whatever the name, it's about revealing God's kingdom of peace, reconciliation, and justice here and now.

All of these things will reveal and increase what we have in common as disciples of Jesus Christ, which are much more abundant than the things that divide us. It's in abiding with each other, as sisters and brothers in Christ, in prayer, in breaking open God's Word, and in reaching out to the world God loves, that we'll truly find the unity for which Jesus prayed.

Your brother in Christ,
+Bruce

From Cardinal Gérald Cyprien Lacroix:

A LETTER TO MY OTHER CHRISTIAN BROTHERS AND SISTERS

My life experiences and my ministry have offered me many opportunities to share with brothers and sisters of many non-Catholic denominations. I was born in a French-Canadian farming town in Quebec. We were all Roman Catholics at that time. When I was eight years old, my family immigrated to Manchester, New Hampshire, in the United States. That is when I had my first encounter with non-Catholic Christians. There was an Episcopal church a few blocks from our home, and along with my younger brothers, I was invited to participate in a summer day camp. I vividly remember the warm welcome and the respect the organizers had toward our family. At the time, I did not speak English.

Although my parents sent us to Catholic schools, we frequently had contacts with other Christians in the city. I remember participating in an ecumenical Christmas choir in seventh grade. What a beautiful experience and a beautiful Christmas concert also! Someone once said that when voices learn to harmonize, hearts can learn to live in unity.

A few months before my nineteenth birthday, I returned to Quebec for a time of formation in a secular institute, in preparation for consecrated life as a layman. Those were beautiful years of many discoveries, especially the gospel.

I was touched by the story of the founder of the Pius X Secular Institute, Father Henri Roy, who grew up in Montreal and had a Protestant friend who lived nearby. He recalled that when he was invited for dinner at the Webster family's home, his friend's father would always open the Bible and read a few verses before they ate. That impressed him very much and shaped him into an apostle of the Word of God. He was very proud to share that his profound love for the Word of God was a fruit of his friendship with a Protestant family.

I have always admired how our non-Catholic brothers and sisters cherish and value God's Word. It is truly part of their everyday lives. We Catholics have grown in many ways since the Second Vatican Council, and we can now say that more and more Catholics are seriously reading the Scriptures, praying, and sharing the gospel.

I had the opportunity to serve as a missionary in Colombia, South America, for nine years. In the communities where I served, I often met with pastors and faithful of other Christian denominations. Our relationships were not always easy, but I always admired the fervor, the missionary spirit, and the apostolic zeal of these brothers and sisters. They witnessed a way of living their faith founded on a personal relationship with Jesus Christ. That is not only admirable, but it is the only way to be a disciple of Christ and to bear fruit.

I have now been a bishop for thirteen years. I have had many opportunities to meet, share, and learn from many other Christian brothers and sisters. Every year before Christmas, in our city of Quebec, I welcome into my home the pastors of the different Christian churches of the region. We share a two-course breakfast: first, we share the gospel. It is always powerful and enriching to be together with Christ in our midst, present in His Word and present in our hearts. The joy of being together, united in faith, is an experience that makes me grow. And of course, bacon and eggs follow!

I remember the first years we experienced this event; some of the pastors were shy, others were maybe wondering what the Roman Catholic archbishop was up to. But as the years pass, we enjoy the friendship that has emerged, and every year, we are happy to welcome new pastors. In the past two years, because of the pandemic, we have been deprived of this fraternal event. We miss it and are looking forward to meeting again. I truly believe that the Lord is slowly building unity among us Catholics, Anglicans, Protestants, Evangelicals, and Pentecostals. The more we meet for this pre-Christmas event and at other times during the year for diverse occasions, the more my appreciation for these brothers and sisters has grown. And for that I am thankful. Thank you for helping me open my eyes and my heart to the diversity of our Christian life.

I have learned through the journey of my life that we need to strive for unity and not uniformity. Thanks to the respect and genuine love of the other Christians I have met, my life has changed. May the Lord help me and help us all to continue to believe and work towards unity.

Gérald Cyprien Cardinal Lacroix is the Catholic Metropolitan Archbishop of Quebec and Primate of Canada. The diocesan website is www.ecdq.org. The Rt. Rev. Bruce Myers is Anglican Bishop of Quebec. The diocesan website is www.quebec.anglican.ca.

11

MAY THE LOVE OF CHRIST MOVE US TO JUSTICE, RECONCILIATION, AND UNITY

Rev. Prof. Dr. Jerry Pillay
| Uniting Presbyterian |

I took up my position as general secretary of the World Council of Churches (WCC) only in January 2023, but ecumenism has always been part of the DNA of my ministry, which has spanned more than thirty-five years as an ordained minister, general secretary, and moderator of my church, the Uniting Presbyterian Church in Southern Africa.

At a young age, I felt God's calling in my life; as a teenager, even though I was deeply rooted in the Presbyterian church, I had contacts with many churches. I was constantly invited by pastors from different churches to participate in some of their church activities. This gave me a great sense of exposure to other church traditions and encounters. I led a youth group of more than 120 young people in my church, a good number of whom came from different churches in the area. This also increased my zeal and desire to connect with other Christian churches.

Then I was selected by my denomination to attend an interdenominational youth camp in Madagascar, which further whetted my desire to be involved in ecumenical activities.

Once ordained, I had many opportunities to be involved in the ecumenical movement in South Africa and beyond. This included being president of the World Communion of Reformed Churches from 2010 to 2017, serving on the National Executive of the South African Council of Churches, serving as a trustee on the Board of the Council for World Mission, a member of the Central Committee of the WCC, and in many other ecumenical organizations. All of these different experiences and opportunities further deepened my passion for Christian unity and involvement.

VISIBLE UNITY IN A FRAGMENTED WORLD

The world today is in crisis. There is an abundance of pain, suffering, turmoil, and conflict. Violence, fear, terrorism, political unrest, natural disasters, unemployment, poverty, gender discrimination, famine, pandemics, religious tensions, religious fundamentalism, wars, factions, forced migration, political dictatorship, and abuse of women and children surround us daily. And the list goes on.

I constantly ask myself, "How do we as Christians, how does the church, and how does the WCC respond to these challenges?"

Visible Christian unity is absolutely necessary to witness to such a broken and suffering world. A divided church is a weak and feeble witness to an already fragmented world. My vision for Christian unity is based on John 17:21 (NIV): *"That all of them may be one, Father ... so that the world may believe that you have sent me."*

SPIRITUALITY AND SUFFERING

Coming from South Africa, I know from personal experience how the WCC played a vital role in dismantling apartheid, in standing with Christians and others in solidarity. Today, our country has been liberated from such oppression.

Living through apartheid for many years, one of the things we learned is how suffering and spirituality are intertwined. We were inspired by figures like Mahatma Gandhi, Desmond Tutu, and Nelson Mandela. One of the things that kept us sane in the midst of the insanity of apartheid was our sense of spirituality.

As the general secretary and then moderator of a church that is predominantly Black, I was often in the townships in South Africa. I would be deeply inspired and yet also troubled by the fact that I would see people on the streets laughing and praying and rejoicing and dancing in the midst of the apartheid experience.

I thought, "How in the world can you do this in the midst of suffering?" Then I realized that is spirituality that keeps people going in the midst of their sufferings.

In the South African context, spirituality has always been part and parcel of our way of life. The majority of people who have lived through that experience will say that spirituality and faith are fundamental to life and have brought us through our struggles. This spirituality is indeed very deep.

This aspect of spirituality is crucial, and this is one of the things that I am encouraging and emphasizing in my position at the WCC. This has been a wonderful strength in the WCC, where spirituality and devotion have taken center stage in terms of the work we do and the decisions we make.

What I wish to emphasize is the need to follow God's command and God's will in terms of proclaiming Christ to the world. This is the most important task that we do together as Christians.

The cross and the resurrection speak of life, hope, and victory in the midst of despair, defeat, and death. More significantly, the cross speaks of suffering, love, grace, forgiveness, and restoration. It reminds us that Jesus came not to condemn the world but to save it.

As we serve God, we need to constantly stop and ask: Are we in tune with God's will and plan for us? Are we remaining faithful in proclaiming Christ in Word and deeds? Are we fulfilling the Great Commission as expressed in Matthew 28:19? Are we caring for the poor, hungry, thirsty, stranger, naked, sick, and imprisoned as expressed by Jesus in Matthew 25:45 (NIV): *"Truly I tell you, whatever you did not do for one of the least of these, you did not do for me."*

Jesus makes it abundantly clear where He stands. He stands with the poor, oppressed, and captives. (See Luke 4:18.) The gospel makes it clear where the church should stand if we choose to stand where God stands.

And of course, we declare the lordship of Jesus Christ together in our common witness and our common faith with all our sense of diversity, the different experiences that we have, and different backgrounds from which we come.

HEALING AND TRANSFORMING THE WORLD

The Great Commission is a call not only to save souls but to transform the world and the lives of people who live in it as we care for the environment and the earth. Making disciples requires this!

So my vision is of a united, flourishing, sustainable, and contextually relevant Christian fellowship that is praying, worshipping, witnessing, and working together to impact and transform the world with God's love, justice, peace, reconciliation, and unity, participating in God's reign on earth and the fullness of life for all creation.

We need to strengthen the fellowship and visible unity of churches; engage God's mission together to save, heal, transform, reconcile, and unite humankind and all creation; and work toward unity and justice in the world, holding both together. We cannot have unity without justice.

So I see our task as Christians not only to work toward visible unity but to uphold and champion the call for justice and peace in the world.

We need to stand where God stands, standing with the oppressed and the poor, seeing ourselves as part of one humanity, and seeking to find ways together to address the challenges that we all face in the world. We need to reflect God's justice—including economic, gender, and ecological justice—in the world. Unity and justice need to go together like two wings on a bird. You need both to soar and make a difference.

Christian churches are often disunited and disagree about doctrine, polity, political affiliations, and ethical issues. It is important that we do not forsake our unity in Christ while we are divided on these issues. I believe we need to continue to strengthen and facilitate safe spaces where churches can meet, dialogue, and find one another on potentially divisive issues, safe spaces where the unity of Christ and the Holy Spirit are at work. What troubles me much is that many churches that tend to have increased conflicts seem to think the only solution is to break away and form another church. Unfortunately, while we get stuck on the divisive issues, the importance of unity and Christ's prayer that we "*may be one*" gets completely sidelined.

At the same time, we need to create not only safe spaces but *equal spaces* for marginalized and neglected voices to be heard, respected, and appreciated. It requires from all of us a willingness to engage a kenotic, self-emptying experience as, following Christ, we take seriously the needs of the *other*. This will help us to keep the vision of unity in the forefront so that we work toward it at all times.

ONE, HOLY, CATHOLIC, AND APOSTOLIC CHURCH

The Nicene Creed reminds us that we are "one, holy, catholic and apostolic Church."

To speak of the church being *one* reminds us that God has called us to unity, and unity is a gift from God. Unfortunately, churches continue to fragment. The church is divided by theological, doctrinal, and ethical views; sadly, it's divided by political, economic, social, and ethnic issues as well, among other things. A divided church can offer nothing but a weak and fragile witness to a broken world.

To speak of the church being *holy* reminds us that we are set apart, distinct, and different from the world. As John Calvin put it, we are the "theater of God's glory." But are we? We are called to live in the world, to participate and share in it, because this is God's world in the first place. But we are reminded that sin, evil, and selfishness are quite prevalent. Therefore, inasmuch as we are *in* the world, we should not be *of* the world by living, doing, wanting, and behaving as it does. Instead, we should live as followers and disciples of Christ. We are called to live out our holiness as salt and light in the world. How will the world know the difference if we as believers do not live an *alternate lifestyle* as taught by Jesus? We need to live a life that propagates justice, righteousness, peace, unity, and love.

To speak of the church being *catholic* speaks of its universal nature. It encompasses the whole of this planet. Therefore, it is concerned about what goes on in other parts of the world, and it stands in solidarity with those who suffer from all kinds of evil systems and oppressions. The church is reminded that as the one body of Christ, it suffers when others suffer and rejoices when others rejoice. (See 1 Corinthians 12:26.) We are called to be church in partnership with other churches. The church is called to be the sacramental presence of God and a servant serving with the sacrificial love of Jesus Christ, proclaiming hope to a fallen world.

To speak of the church as *apostolic* tells us that it is a *called out and sent out community*. We are called by our triune God, blessed by His presence, and sent out to call and bless others in His name. We come so that we may, "*Go therefore and make disciples*" (Matthew 28:19). The church does not exist just for believers; it exists for the world. The apostolic dimension reminds us that we are a missionary church, the people of God constantly on the march for God, and we will not stop until God's reign and return in Christ has come fully.

DEAR SISTERS AND BROTHERS IN CHRIST,

In a world that is riddled with conflict, war, factions, political instability, injustices, restlessness, suffering, strife, and pain, we need to pause and take a deep ecumenical breath to breathe afresh God's life and hope into the world. In the face of injustices, war, conflicts, and the danger to life and the earth, we need to reclaim our prophetic witness. Let us take strength from the message of the 11th Assembly of the World Council of Churches, held in Germany in 2022, around the theme, "Christ's love moves the world to reconciliation and unity":

> As reconciliation brings us closer to God and each other, it opens the way toward a unity founded in God's love. As Christians we are called to dwell in Christ's love and to be one (John 17). Such unity, which is a gift from God, and which arises from reconciliation and is grounded in his love, enables us to address the world's urgent problems.

Article III of the Constitution of the WCC states its vision and mission as follows:

> The primary purpose of the fellowship of churches in the World Council of Churches is to call one another to visible unity in one faith and in one Eucharistic fellowship, expressed in worship and common life in Christ, through witness and service to the world, and to advance towards that unity in order that the world may believe.

I would like to say that in my life thus far, I have seen many miracles happen in the area of Christian unity. I have personally facilitated mediation processes bringing different groups of people together. In my own church, eight groups of people were disrupting the unity of the church. I was given the task of bringing them together into four church fellowships. Many thought this was an impossible task given cultural, personality, and economic differences, as well as other factors. However, by God's grace, even though it took over fifteen years, the uniting of these organizations was completed in 2019 and is still going strong. This was and is a great witness to the world.

In my former roles as pastor of a congregation, moderator of the Uniting Presbyterian Church in Southern Africa, and president of the World Communion of Reformed Churches, I have witnessed the gracious hand of

God in so many churches and groups as they found reconciliation and unity. Thus, we must never give up on praying and working toward Christian unity.

I know that while many people continue to yearn, pray, and work for visible Christian unity, some have become disenchanted and despondent on the journey, believing that such is a farfetched dream far from reality. Personally, I believe that we must never stop praying and walking and working together to reach that vision and goal. We need to affirm and deepen the desire for Christian unity, knowing that this is what Jesus prayed for in John 17:21. Unity is a gift already given to us to appropriate in Christ; unity is not uniformity. This broken and suffering world is in need of Christians working together for reconciliation, justice, and peace. Our inability to live up to the calling of visible Christian unity should not diminish or blur the ultimate vision. Let us continue to pray and work together so that the world may believe!

For seventy-five years, the vision of the WCC has been expressed as a commitment to *stay together, pray together, move together,* and *act together* as a fellowship of churches seeking visible unity and common witness. In September 2022, the WCC's 11th Assembly invited the churches to continue their journey together as a pilgrimage of justice, reconciliation and unity. WCC's adopted Unity Statement reads in part:

> We affirm the vision of the WCC for the visible unity of all Christians, and we invite other Christians to share this vision with us. We also invite all people of faith and goodwill to trust, with us, that a different world, a world respectful of the living earth, a world in which everyone has daily bread and life in abundance, a decolonized world, a more loving, harmonious, just, and peaceful world, is possible. In a world weighed down with so much pain, anguish, and fear, we believe that the love we have seen in Christ brings the liberating possibilities of joy, justice for all, and peace with the earth. Moved by the Holy Spirit, compelled by a vision of unity, we journey on together, resolved to practise Christ's love, following his steps as his disciples, and carrying a torch for love in the world, trusting in the promise that Christ's love moves the world to reconciliation and unity.

I believe in the Christian message of justice, reconciliation, unity, and peace. I believe that as Christians, Christ has called us to follow His example. The prayer Jesus offered for the unity of believers is a prayer we need to constantly be reminded of as we seek to be Christ`s followers in the world. May we trust and lean on the work of the Holy Spirit to continue to lead us to justice, reconciliation, and unity.

It is in this spirit that I offer the following prayer:

Loving, uniting, and reconciling God, remind us that even though unity is a gift from You, it does not come without effort and sacrifice. In our common witness to Jesus Christ as Lord and Savior of the world, help us to emphasize that which unites us rather than the things that divide. May the love of Christ move us all to justice, reconciliation, and unity. We offer this prayer in the name of the triune God: Father, Son, and Holy Spirit.

The Rev. Prof. Dr. Jerry Pillay is General Secretary of the World Council of Churches in Geneva and Dean of Theology and Religion at the University of Pretoria in South Africa. He may be reached through the WCC at www.oikoumene.org.

12

LOVE KEEPS US IN UNITY

Archbishop Foley Beach
| Anglican |

Grace to you and peace from God our Father and our Lord Jesus Christ! What a privilege it is to be a part of the kingdom of God on earth today with so many expressions of the biblical faith!

We live in an unprecedented time for the church of Jesus Christ to share the gospel and reach those in need with God's saving and healing power. With technology and transportation advances and with progress in language adaptations, the gospel message and God's *agape* community can shine forth literally all over the world.

However, we have a huge obstacle: the divided church. Not so much that we are divided, but how we treat other parts of the body of Christ from whom we are divided. When unbelievers hear us putting others down, condemning them for their tradition of the faith, or discounting their understanding of the faith, walls and hurdles are created that hold them back from following Jesus. I invite you to join me in repenting of these sinful and unhelpful comments and actions toward faithful sisters and brothers around the world. Let us work together for the unity of the body of Christ as Jesus asks us to do in John 17 so that our witness for Him draws others to Him.

FROM BROKENNESS TO BEAUTY

My understanding of the importance of the body of Christ began when I was a young child. All my life, I have experienced the varied expressions of Christianity to be meaningful and personal. As someone from a broken home whose mother was active in the drug culture, I moved from place to place as a child. At every new location, friends and neighbors included me in their church activities. In first through third grade, we lived in Sandy Springs, Georgia, and I was taken to a very small Baptist church. In the first part of fourth grade, I attended the local Presbyterian church near Grayton Beach, Florida. For the last part of fourth and fifth grade, I attended and sang in the children's choir in an Episcopal church in downtown Atlanta. After my mother was arrested for selling drugs on my twelfth birthday, my father took my sisters and me to the local Baptist church in Sandy Springs, Georgia. In sixth grade, I attended a small Methodist church in Cherokee County, Georgia. Additionally, my aunt, uncle, and cousins were active Roman Catholics, and they included me in many church activities. All these expressions of the body of Christ ministered to me in my times of need and guided me toward following Jesus as my Savior and my Lord.

Attending my father's Baptist church, I had a personal encounter with Jesus Christ and began a personal journey with Him. This included interacting with not only friends from other Baptist churches, but friends from other expressions of the body of Christ. In high school, we attended each other's churches—Roman Catholic, Baptist, Church of God, Methodist, Presbyterian, and Episcopal—and I began to value different perspectives of following Jesus from others who knew Him as their Savior and Lord.

I AM A CHRISTIAN FIRST

The nondenominational ministry of Young Life impacted me greatly at this time, and I realized that not one church was perfect or had all the answers, even though we all thought we did. Each denomination looked at and practiced the Christian faith in their own way and had important theological insights and contributions to the body of Christ on earth. I began to describe myself by saying, "I am a Christian first, and I just happen to be a Baptist." Then it was, "I am a Christian first; I just happen to be Episcopal." Now it is, "I am a Christian first; I just happen to be an Anglican." I began to view my relationship with other Christians from a perspective of what we had in common rather than our differences in theology and practice. Our differences were (and are) important, but I quickly realized what we had in common dominated our relationships instead of our differences, and what we had in common overshadowed the few differences we had.

UNPHASED ACCEPTANCE

One significant event in my early years was when I was hired to be the youth minister at the Episcopal Cathedral of St. Philip in Atlanta, Georgia. I was currently a Baptist and a Young Life leader at that time. In my hiring interview, the dean of the cathedral, David Collins, asked me if I had any questions for him. I asked, "Does it bother you that I am a Baptist and not Episcopal?" His response was, "We are looking for God's person for this job, and that person may not be an Episcopalian." I was amazed and inspired by his response. That kind of openness to other Christian expressions was not very common back then in my small world, but it perfectly expressed my sentiment.

Serving as the youth minister at the Cathedral of St. Philip, we regularly had youth pastor gatherings with the other large churches in metropolitan Atlanta. I found that even though we were Episcopal, Methodist, Baptist, Roman Catholic, Pentecostal, Presbyterian, Church of God, and nondenominational, our love for teenagers and our desire to help them follow Jesus overrode all our theological differences.

Later, as the rector of St. Alban's Episcopal Church in Monroe, Georgia, I was active in the county's ministerial association. In a town where the churches *never* did anything together or cooperated in ministry activities, we were able to work with one another to bring churches together to create "Faith in Serving Humanity" (FISH), a ministry to help those in need in our community. All of us—Episcopal, Roman Catholic, Baptist, Presbyterian, Methodist, Christian, and Church of God—committed to work with each other to serve our community. Thirty years later, FISH is thriving with over fifty churches working together to serve and do gospel ministry throughout the community.

ONE IN THE HOLY SPIRIT

There is one other important factor from this era of my life that contributed to my ecumenical outlook. While serving in the Episcopal Church, the charismatic renewal movement touched our congregations in a strong way. Soon we found ourselves worshipping with Holy Spirit-filled believers from across all denominations. It didn't matter what church we went to, followers of Jesus filled with the Holy Spirit were worshipping, fellowshipping, and studying the Bible together. The richness in our diversity became quite apparent, yet we all grew in our understanding and application of the Bible in our lives and ministries. When I look back, I find myself grateful for the ministries of David Collins (Episcopal), Charles Stanley (Baptist), Cardinal Leon Suenens (Roman Catholic), Paul Walker (Church of God), Charles Marsh (Baptist), Tom Atkins (United Methodist), Frank Harrington (Presbyterian), Ron Ervin (Baptist), and Michael Youssef (Anglican).

As a bishop and later the archbishop of the Anglican Church in North America, I find myself interacting with denominational leaders from all over the world. Most are attempting to follow Jesus in their own tradition, their historical understanding of the Bible, and in the culture in which they find themselves. For the most part, I have found these leaders to be godly and desiring to honor the Lord. With these faithful servants, unity is possible. Where unity is not possible is when people have departed from the clear teaching of the Bible in theology and morality. When leaders in the body of Christ teach that what the Bible calls sin is not sin and model Christian behavior that is more in line with the fruits of the flesh (Galatians 5:19–21) than the fruit of the Holy Spirit (Galatians 5:22–23), it creates disunity in the church. It is very discouraging to see this occur because it always leads to more division in the body of Christ.

IN ALL THINGS CHARITY

The theologian Rupertus Meldenius (1582–1651) wrote a pamphlet on Christian unity in which he said, "In essentials unity, in nonessentials liberty, in all things charity." I think his words still hold true today and can serve as a model for us in the twenty-first century.

In Essentials Unity. There will not be unity if we can't agree on the essentials of the faith—that is, what has always been believed about the faith since the days of the New Testament. During the first few centuries of the church, official councils were held to discuss and affirm the essential doctrines of the faith, such as the doctrine of God, the authority of Scripture, the Person of Jesus Christ, the work of Jesus Christ, the deity of the Holy Spirit, salvation, and marriage. Today, we use the creeds to summarize these biblical doctrines. These theological doctrines are the essentials.

In Nonessentials Liberty. It is often the nonessential issues that get in the way of unity more that the essentials. What color to paint the front door. What kind of music, classical, contemporary, or gospel? Whether to stand or kneel for the prayers. Meldenius is suggesting that in these nonessentials, we grant each other freedom and liberty to follow our conscience. By granting others the grace to practice their version of the essentials, it gives unity a big boost forward.

In All Things Charity. Regardless of other Christians' or churches' perspectives, the gospel commands us to love them. We are to love our brothers and sisters, and we are to love our enemies and those who persecute us. This is different from breaking fellowship with them as many are prone to do today. *In all things charity.*

LOVE IS THE GLUE OF UNITY

When we are in agreement on the essentials of the faith, we are able to have unity. I have personally found this to be true again and again. However, we are living in a time when *cancel culture* is manifesting itself in many church environments. When someone doesn't agree with the pastor or another member, they are written off with no contact, no conversation, no engagement. If we are to have unity in the church, we must intentionally seek to overcome this mentality and practice it in our lives and churches. Jesus calls us to a different standard—love, *agape* love, unconditional love, God's love toward those we disagree with. We are to love our sisters and brothers (see John 15:12), and Jesus even tells us, *"Love your enemies"* (Luke 6:27). Love is the glue of unity; it *"binds everything together in perfect harmony"* (Colossians 3:14). Love doesn't create unity—this comes from agreement in the essentials—but love keeps unity and deepens unity. Unity comes from being bound to something higher than ourselves: the love of Jesus Christ and the truth from the Word of God. Love keeps us in this unity.

In this time in which there is so much hate, so much division, so much violence, and so much misunderstanding, brothers and sisters in Jesus, let us love one another in the power of the Holy Spirit. Let us build one another up in the faith, in our lives, and in our ministries. Let us not condemn, cancel, or act cruelly toward others. Jesus calls us to reflect Him and His glory, and this is best manifested in the act of love. Let us go out of our way to know, support, encourage, and pray for other followers of Jesus.

DEAR SISTERS AND BROTHERS IN CHRIST JESUS,

I have been following the One who is to be followed for the past fifty-three years, or at least I have been attempting to follow Him. Jesus asked us to love one another, and though I have often failed, it truly brings heaven to earth. Selfless, caring, patient love opens the door for the outpouring of the Holy Spirit, the Spirit of unity.

This love of God toward other followers of Jesus sounds a loud message to our hurting, lonely, and conflicted friends. Love, in the biblical *agape* sense of 1 Corinthians 13, is an incredible witness for the power of the gospel. Loving someone who is different from you, who believes or practices their faith differently, is a remarkable demonstration of the fruit of the Holy Spirit in one's life. While we may not have organizational unity in the church of Jesus Christ, we can practice our faith by loving our neighbor as ourselves and imparting to them the love of Jesus Christ.

I have found my most difficult challenges in loving others are with those who also call themselves followers of Jesus. When mistreated, hurt, or betrayed (in the name of Jesus), love and forgiveness can seem impossible. Yet love—God's love—*"covers a multitude of sins"* (1 Peter 4:8). Through the power of the Holy Spirit, we can love anyway! And when we do, God does His thing.

Lord Jesus Christ, You stretched out Your arms of love on the hard wood of the cross that everyone might come within Your saving embrace: So clothe us in Your Spirit, that we reaching forth our hands in love, may bring those who do not know You to the knowledge and love of You, for the honor of Your Name, Amen. —*2019 Book of Common Prayer*

In Christ Jesus,

Foley Beach

The Most Rev. Dr. Foley Beach is the archbishop and primate emeritus of the Anglican Church in North America and now bishop of the Anglican Diocese of the South. You may connect with him by visiting anglicanchurch.net.

13

BECOMING LEAVEN OF PEACE

Brother Alois Loeser of Taizé
| Taizé Community |

There have been times in history when, in the name of the truth of the gospel, Christians have separated. Today, in the name of the truth of the gospel, it is vital to do everything possible to come together.

Christians could do much to promote reconciliation in the world; they could become a leaven of peace in the human family. However, such a commitment is only credible if they themselves seek their visible unity. When we remain separated, what we say is hardly audible. We can only fully transmit the message of peace and communion announced by Christ if we are together.

Let us dare to go toward visible unity; this is the gospel call that our Taizé Community would like to carry. It is part of the heritage we have received from Brother Roger, the one who initiated the life of our community when he came in 1940 from his native Switzerland to the small village of Taizé, located in Burgundy, France.

A PERSONAL DISCOVERY

To share a few personal thoughts on Christian unity, I recall my first visit to Taizé in 1970. Personally, it was the image of the church as a *parable of communion* that struck me at that time. I was very young, and I was impressed by the prayer, the silence, and the communion that was perceived in the brothers' way of life. As a Catholic, it was in Taizé that I discovered more deeply the catholicity of the church.

It was also in these years of my youth that I became more deeply aware of the radical nature of the vocation to follow Christ. One day, I was walking along a road near my parents' old village in the Czech Republic; the Germans who had lived there with Czech people for generations had to leave after the Second World War. I sensed that the borders that separated our countries in Europe and generated so much suffering would not always exist. And I suddenly had the very clear feeling that, as Christians, we were in a position to prepare another future, a future of peace and reconciliation.

It also became clear to me that, by its very existence, the Taizé Community was already creating the first concrete expressions of this, and I was somehow being offered the chance to participate in it. I said to myself, "Reconciliation is possible. It may take time—it took a lot for my parents to be reconciled with the Czech people—but it is not unattainable. For me, this reconciliation was linked to my involvement with the Taizé Community. Thus, my personal history and that of my family intersected with the vocation there. This gave me great joy, great hope.

Back in Taizé, I was ready to hear the call of Christ to make a total commitment of my person. Community life became a call for me: to share the gospel with others and not just live it on an individual level. I was won over by Brother Roger and the other brothers, by the spirit of reconciliation that animated them day after day. I was struck by their desire to find new ways to communicate the gospel to young people.

I also realized little by little that this *parable of communion* had to be lived out very concretely, and that this search for unity was not a theory, but a daily process.

After joining the community, I have always lived in Taizé. Brother Roger wanted us to deepen our formation, so he asked brothers who were more qualified in theology and biblical exegesis to teach us. I discovered the Bible and the church fathers. Even though my parents were devout Catholics, we never read the Bible; we didn't consider it necessary. My father had only one book, containing the Sunday Bible readings, and he always kept it with him. He didn't need anything else.

The study of Scripture became the heart of our pastoral work with young people. When I arrived in Taizé, the community was already organizing youth meetings every week, but in the mid-1970s, Brother Roger made a significant change. He asked us brothers to put the reading of the Word of God at the center of these meetings. Since then, and still today, the young people we welcome listen to a biblical introduction given by one of us every day for a week.

Brother Roger had realized that, after a complex period in the late 1960s and early 1970s, it was first and foremost necessary to help young people go to the sources of faith. He certainly must have drawn on his own experience, his own history. His Protestant origins inclined him to return constantly to the biblical sources.

From Brother Roger, I learned this passion for communion, for the search for unity in a great diversity. Still today, from the outside, it's hard to imagine how different we are as brothers: we come from more than thirty countries, from all continents, and we belong to different Christian denominations.

On the day of his tragic death in August 2005, Brother Roger called one of our brothers in the late afternoon and asked him to write down the words that had come to his mind: "To the extent that our community creates in the human family possibilities to widen..." Then he stopped, fatigue preventing him from finishing his sentence.

Pronounced by Brother Roger on the very day of his death, these words have obviously taken on a particular value for me. And I still wonder: what did he mean by "widen"? More and more, I think he meant doing everything to make more perceptible the love that God has for all human beings without exception.

Indeed, all his life, he wanted for our community to reveal this mystery of universality. At the beginning of our community, writing the Rule of Taizé, Brother Roger addressed this call to every brother: "Make the unity of the body of Christ your passionate concern."

So up until today, my brothers and I would like to take up this challenge and advance along the path where God constantly widens our steps. (See Psalm 18:36.)

THE PRACTICE OF UNITY AT TAIZÉ

The passion for unity, the passion for communion, is a starting point that stimulates us to a continual widening at the level of our common life, a very simple daily life, and at the level of Christian reconciliation, which for us is strongly connected with our pastoral work with youth.

The specific parable that we, the brothers of Taizé, would like to offer through our lives is that of communion. Communion, reconciliation, trust—these are keywords for us. We would like to show that a community can be a laboratory of fraternity.

Fraternity is one of the deepest human aspirations. But seeking to live as brothers and sisters is a huge challenge in everyday life. And here lies a first call to widen the space of our hearts. If the resistances to fraternity cannot be overcome in the concrete reality of a community, how can this occur on a larger scale?

In a community, one does not choose one's brothers or sisters. The community is a place to work to overcome our resistances. Each member is invited to reflect: what more is asked of me now? It is not necessarily a matter of doing more. What we are called to do is to *love more*. To choose to love, over and over again.

Life in community stimulates an ever-deeper communion based on mutual love. That is a priority. Without it, although a community might perform impressive works, the sign of God would remain veiled.

Each of the brothers is a living stone in the microcosm of church that the community is. Otherness not only has to be accepted but requires us to discover ways of dealing with it. A great joy for us is that the common prayer always brings us together again. When tensions arise, the common prayer is the gift that allows us to find the path of forgiveness and peace of heart so essential for us who wish to be a parable of communion.

By the sign of our common life, we would like to contribute to the search for communion among other Christians. By bringing together Protestant and Catholic brothers, as well as an Orthodox monk from time to time, our community seeks to anticipate the unity still to come.

This everyday ecumenical life has become very natural to us. Certainly, it sometimes involves limitations and renunciations, but there is no reconciliation without renunciation. We are placed on a narrow ridge: to live by the conviction that Christ already unites us, and then to journey in communion with the different churches that are still separated. This is what enables us to stimulate a gospel life in so many young people, whatever their church tradition.

ANTICIPATING THE RECONCILIATION OF CHRISTIANS

When we gather three times a day in the church of reconciliation, the prayer of our community brings together young Catholics, Protestants, and Orthodox. Some of them have a strong sense of belonging; they are often accompanied by their priests or pastors. But other young people come to Taizé who have no religious identity. Brought by their friends, they are searching and sometimes are very receptive to the gospel.

So this diversity among the young adults who come to Taizé is huge. Many are seekers rather than believers. And yet, in the simple common prayer three times a day—which consists of singing, listening to the Word of God, waiting in silence, and interceding for those in difficulty—we discover that we are all guests of Christ, welcomed into the house of God, whoever we are.

A new challenge thus appears: what to propose to those who have no religious affiliation but who love Christ? We feel a tension here. On the one hand, we want to allow them to discover the gospel and we are happy to see trust in God come to birth in them, even a rudimentary trust because they are not always clear about the content of the faith. We are also aware that we are called to awaken them to the meaning of the church, the communion between all the baptized.

What we seek earnestly is to help young people experience communion. Not everyone can immediately call this experience of communion by name; they speak rather about friendship, respect, mutual aid. They are surprised to find themselves going beyond cultural and denominational barriers, and they look for the reason why. And some find in Christ the source of a unity without borders.

For one week, they agree to put themselves under the same roof and turn to Christ. Praying together, reading the Bible together, in the simplicity of a shared life, they anticipate unity. They live it in advance. If this is possible at Taizé, why could it not be possible elsewhere?

We have always refused to organize a youth movement around Taizé. To continue on the way they have deepened in Taizé, we refer them back to the churches they came from. To help them on their journey, there is a *pilgrimage of trust* made up of meetings, large or small, held on different continents.

At every stage of this continuous pilgrimage, we closely collaborate with church leaders from all denominations, and the young participants are received in the local communities willing to receive them.

One of the specific features of these meetings is the hospitality offered by families. Young people from different countries do not only gather together among themselves, but each morning, they pray and then have exchanges with the people of the parish where they are staying. By offering hospitality, older people build trust between the generations.

It's astonishing to see how the young participants and those who open their homes to host them for a few days feel profoundly united without reducing their faith to a lowest common denominator or leveling their values. A harmony is established between people who belong to different faiths, cultures, and generations.

It is as if the hospitality practiced in the monasteries was being extended to thousands of families. When people open their doors to young people whom they do not know, whose language they may not speak, at a time when people are often afraid of foreigners, this highlights the vocation of the church to be a place of communion.

STEPS TOWARD VISIBLE UNITY

If this experience of communion is possible in specific gatherings, which concrete steps could be taken on other occasions to express more visibly the unity of all those who love Christ?

Could our Christian churches and ecumenical institutions make a visible communion, perhaps imperfect but real, among all those who love Christ? Could we not find the courage to turn to Christ together without waiting for all the theological formulations to be fully harmonized?

More than fifty years ago, the Catholic theologian Karl Rahner observed a "new pluralism." Today, our church synods and ecumenical conversations often highlight positions that seem—and sometimes are—incompatible, at least conceptually. Rahner reflected on "a unity that can never be secured by concepts alone" and proposed what he called a "practice of unity."

Our ecumenical conversations attempt to move from a unified profession of faith to unity. Rahner wondered whether taking things in reverse might not be a real theological possibility: that the people of God gathered in common prayer might move toward a unified confession of faith.

One of the documents of the *Groupe des Dombes,* a group of Protestant and Catholic theologians in France, provided a solid basis for this view by calling for priority to be accorded to baptismal identity over denominational identity. The document explains that, to define Christian identity today, churches have put denominational identity first. People define themselves as Catholics, Protestants, or Orthodox. The Dombes theologians suggest that all Christians should define themselves first of all as baptized persons. The document therefore calls on churches to enter into a "dynamic process of conversion."

One day, Jesus used this beautiful expression: *"In my Father's house there are many dwelling places"* (John 14:2 NAB). We should gradually manage to make this reality visible: various dwellings under one roof, diverse expressions of the same faith.

Whenever I have the opportunity, I ask, "Has not the time come for the separate churches to dare to come together without further delay? And how could we live *under one roof* or *widen the space of our tent?"* The answer is to do together everything that can be done together and no longer doing anything without taking the others into account.

To make this happen, in my opinion, the only way is to develop among us an attitude of mutual welcome, of reciprocal hospitality. And such a reciprocal hospitality asks for an effort of translation, for beliefs can be like foreign languages to each other. Translation requires us to be patient so that we can translate into our own language what the other is saying. A true attitude of hospitality leads us to the point of accepting the others in their otherness.

When the faith of the other remains inaccessible, let us at least be attentive to its authenticity. Recognition also means gratitude; there should be a festive element in the wondrous discovery of the other!

Finally, such reciprocal hospitality requires a spirit of humility and conversion:

- *Humility* because no theological concept can express the truth of the gospel in its entirety. That truth is not owned by anyone; it is always beyond all its expressions.
- *Conversion* because we must recognize that we have not always acted according to the will of Christ.

To increase this sense of mutual hospitality within our Christian communities, I would like to list four concrete suggestions:

1. In the local community, we can gather under one roof, neighbors and families, in so-called *base communities*, to pray together, help each other, and get to know each other better.
2. Between parishes of different denominations, there already often exist collaborations in the study of the Bible, in social and pastoral work, in catechesis. These could be intensified.
3. Let us come together more often in the presence of God, listening to His Word in silence and praise. Could it be possible, in many cities, for the cathedral or the main church to become a common house of prayer for all the Christians of that place?

4. Would it be possible to conduct theological dialogue while emphasizing the framework of common prayer and with an awareness that we are already together? When living and praying together, we tackle theological questions differently. Perhaps one might say the same of ethical reflection.

One more word to finish this part of my reflection: it is true that churches and ecclesial communities sometimes demonstrate different paths to achieving this communion. However, the more deeply each one belongs to Christ, the more they are enabled to see the others correctly, seeing them as sisters and brothers. We should even go further: recognizing the others as sisters and brothers is the sign that one truly belongs to Christ.

There are many people who serve as inspirations for today's ecumenism. Among them is the Rev. Dr. Larry Miller, who for many years served as general secretary of the Mennonite World Conference. At Taizé, we got to know him more personally as secretary of the Global Christian Forum from 2012 to 2018.

Larry's ecumenical commitment goes back to his time as a student in the late 1960s, when he took part in anti-war and anti-racism protests alongside Christian believers from several churches. Many years later, in the context of the global forum, he played a key role in creating bridges of dialogue between leaders and believers from all Christian confessions.

When I met him last year at Taizé, I asked him how we could hope to advance on the way of Christian unity. He replied, "It is not good to start by saying, 'This is who we are and this is why we are right.' Rather, it is to recognize our weaknesses and ask other churches to help us receive what we lack. This is receptive ecumenism, which allows us to welcome what comes from others."

Isn't this pastor's vision right? We all carry the treasure of Christ in clay vessels and it perhaps shines out more clearly when we humbly acknowledge what we lack. This vision of a receptive ecumenism seems very relevant to me.

When we approach the search for unity with this attitude, we can be led to this joyful discovery: the remaining differences do not divide us but can even be an enrichment. The gifts of our respective traditions can be shared with each other in a spirit of mutual respect.

MY DEAR CHRISTIAN SISTERS AND BROTHERS IN THE MIDDLE EAST,

At Taizé, we often pray for your countries and for the Christian churches of your beloved region. In the last years, we have had several youth meetings there: in the Holy Land, in Syria, and in Lebanon. Each of these meetings was also a concrete reminder of the importance of coming together, of praying for peace.

During our last pilgrimage in the Holy Land, with three hundred young adults from many countries, it was extremely moving to pray in the land where Jesus lived, where He was crucified, and from where He rose again. Let me take just one example: in Bethlehem, we could feel so close to the place where the One we follow was born, the One who gives meaning to our lives, the One who awakens hope.

But how can we speak of hope and joy when we know of the wars and violence in the world, when we think in particular of the unbearable suffering of women, men, and children? All this weighs heavily on us all, but most of all on those who are directly exposed to the consequences of war and violence.

I have a very strong memory in my heart from my visit to Syria during Christmas 2015. The extent of the destruction I saw in Homs was unimaginable. A few families returned to settle and try to live again in those ruins, then without water or electricity. In the center of Homs, in front of the destroyed Greek Catholic cathedral, the parishioners had celebrated a Christmas party for the children. The young people had prepared gifts and the children were singing. I had rarely experienced a Christmas party where the message of the gospel was so intensely lived. Christ is also born there, in the heart of such a situation.

In spring 2022, we supported a meeting of eight hundred young Christians from Syria in this city of Homs, together with the local church communities. When I looked at the photos and short films of the preparation of the meeting, one thing struck me: the joy and energy that emanated from the faces of the youth. I thought, "What vitality! What potential to dare to invent the future."

In your region, Christians are witnesses to a long tradition of faith. The multi-secular history of the church continues to be written today. In the past, Christian divisions have often been a heavy burden; today, we are discovering with you all the ways of living together, precisely in the name of our faith.

To seek this unity means first of all to let Christ have the first place—He is the one who brings us together. Christ already unites us; it is up to us to do all we can to reveal this unity, already accomplished mysteriously in the heart of God.

Another point I would like to mention in this letter is your incredible sense of hospitality. We had a powerful experience of this in Egypt during a pilgrimage to the Coptic Orthodox Church and a year later in Lebanon, in spring 2018, when for the first time, we had an international meeting with almost two thousand young people from all over the world.

By practicing such hospitality, you remember the treasure mentioned in the holy Scripture: *"Do not neglect to show hospitality to strangers, for thereby some have entertained angels unawares"* (Hebrews 13:2). And you also try to live, very concretely, this hospitality with those who come from another religious background, which is not always easy.

This is part of an important reflection that the Middle East Council of Churches (MECC) has launched in their document, "We Choose Abundant Life," published in September 2021. It shows a way how, in faithfulness to your traditions, you can open new ways of communion in the Middle East. I hope that this document will bear fruit.

Thank you, dear brothers and sisters, for making the gospel shine out in your countries. You can be sure we accompany you with our prayers at Taizé. Let me conclude this letter with this prayer:

Lord Jesus Christ, universal Brother, it is through Your life, death, and resurrection that we discover the unconditional love of God. Today, some of Your disciples in the Middle East and in other places in the world are suffering martyrdom and persecution. May Your presence open our eyes and enable us to look at the realities of our lives in a new way, with hope and trust, a way that transforms us. We entrust to You the peoples of the Middle East. May the Christians in that region be creators of peace and reconciliation.

Your brother, in Christ our Lord.

Brother Alois Loeser is prior emeritus of the Taizé Community in France. He led the community from 2005 to 2023, succeeding the community's founder, Brother Roger. To connect with Brother Alois, visit www.taize.fr/en.

14

UNITY FOR WITNESS AND PURPOSE

Darlene Zschech
| Pentecostal |

I love the word *unity*. I treasure it. I love the scenes that the Bible paints for us around unity. I love the thought of the *"precious oil"* spoken of in Psalm 133:2, and the idea that it is only by the purpose and power of the Spirit of God that we can live in the wonder and blessing that true union of hearts and minds brings to our lives. The beautiful thing about oil is that it's hard for other things to stick to you that shouldn't when you are covered in His oil of anointing.

> *A new commandment I give to you, that you love one another: just as I have loved you, you also are to love one another. By this all people will know that you are my disciples, if you have love for one another.*
> (John 13:34–35)

When I think of the call to unity, this passage of Scripture in the book of John has always held my heart to account and tied my dreams to a picture of what God has made possible for us and how *He* sees the power of unity, but wow! at times I have fallen way short of my part of the picture.

Growing up in a performance culture from a young age and being part of a family who loved to watch me and my siblings perform, the people pleaser in me was alive and well, right into my early twenties and long after I had become a committed Christian. I think I mistook unity for simply "going along with the loudest voice"—kind of making myself small to blindly please others rather than speaking up when needed and being mature enough to bend my selfish ways to a higher way if it meant a godly outcome for all.

When Jesus models ultimate servanthood and humility in John 13 by washing His disciples' feet, He was able to showcase an incredible way of living. Not from a position of pleasing people or false humility, but from a position of knowing who He was as the Son of God and from His beautiful heart of endless *love*.

The word unity is easy to say, easy to sing, wonderful to proclaim and dream for ... and yet to walk it out, to see unity outworked at a deep level in our relational and kingdom frameworks, we can often find ourselves in a sea of frustration and unmet expectation.

Over many years, I have had the profound privilege of watching the lives of many prominent Christians from *behind the curtain*. And the ones who I have ultimate respect for are not the ones who were most fabulous on a platform, but the ones who modelled unity, love, and making sure people were seen and appreciated in all the spaces that nobody sees. Unity is one of the great byproducts of living with love for one another, enabled by the Holy Spirit.

As a writer of songs of worship, and one who *loves* to write with others, there is no way you can enter into a writing session without understanding the blessing of unity combined with a sure sense of knowing who you are in Christ. To bring something of worth that is flexible and pliable to fit hand in glove to someone else's creative and worshipful thoughts and expressions requires a commitment to humility and a godly confidence that doesn't feel threatened while honoring another above yourself. This is all a part of growing up *into* Christ.

So why is unity so important? As the days we live in get darker, I sense that unity across the body of Christ will become so paramount to how we advance the kingdom of God that there is really no room for us running to isolate from one another or war against each other. Again, John 13:35 says everyone will recognize us by our love for one another.

We constantly see an emphasis on oneness throughout the Word of God. Not sameness, but oneness, which in the end always comes back to a heart issue. And the Word of God teaches us that those who are onlookers on God's church will see and *know* that we are disciples of Jesus by our love one for another. *Witness and purpose*.

When you understand the higher witness, the godly purpose of yielding your own way for the sake of the kingdom, somehow the childlike tantrum that wants to rear its ugly head finds itself bowing in honor of godly pursuit.

This is not simply *staying quiet*, but stepping into a deeper understanding of assignment, trust, legacy, and miracles.

In all of our doing the work of the ministry and works of service—and you know what the word *work* means right? It means work—we equip others so that Christ's body may be strong, unified, and grow in maturity.

Work isn't very glamorous. It comes without titles and privileges. But Jesus asks us to tend to the work, and it's here we find that not only do we need to be infused with the power of the Holy Spirit to see the power of God doing what only He can do in our midst, but also so that we can work in harmony doing the work of the ministry.

GOD'S GLORIOUS ARRAY

It's hard for me to explain my passion for the worship of God. It stems from many life-changing encounters where the power and presence of Jesus has wonderfully interrupted my natural life, leaving me changed, challenged, and desperate for everyone to experience His great love. Music finally made sense to me after receiving Christ. And every day, I'm aware of His song and its ability to express the inexpressible from the core of our being. I think this is also why I've never really made it my battle to haggle around the issues of diversity within the body of Christ that has traditionally only brought division. You might be surprised, learning where I have been during some of these life-changing God encounters. You can challenge my theology, but you cannot take away or diminish the permanence and wonder of my personal experience. I love God's church. Her diversity is her beauty—ancient songs and styles woven together with modern melodies and musings all straining to give voice to praise that will never be exhausted. If we were all the same and expressed our worship the same, what a sad reflection of our Creator we would be. His vast array of colors painted across the sky, every single moment of every day, should give us a hint as to His surpassing beauty, ongoing fun, and endlessly creative nature.

CHEERING EACH OTHER ON, SIDE BY SIDE

One of my favorite stories of unity in God's Word is found in Nehemiah 3. Nehemiah is a cupbearer to the king of Persia, Artaxerxes. After much prayer, Nehemiah asks the king if he can go and rebuild the walls of Jerusalem, which are in ruins. The king gives Nehemiah all that he needs to start the process of fixing the problem. Oh, such favor here! The miracle of favor when you are tending to things that matter to God is quite unexplainable.

Nehemiah *"told the Jews, the priests, the nobles, the officials, and the rest who were to do the work"* (Nehemiah 2:16) that the hand of God was upon him for the project. *"And they said, 'Let us rise up and build.' So they strengthened their hands for the good work"* (verse 18).

Then Nehemiah 3 lists everyone who works to rebuild the walls of Jerusalem—Eliashib, the high priest; the men of Jericho; Zaccur, son of Imri; the sons of Hassenaah; Meremoth, son of Uriah; Meshullam, son of Berechiah; Zadok, son of Baana; the Tekoites; Joiada, son of Paseah; Meshullam, son of Besodeiah ... The list goes on and on.

When we read the third chapter of Nehemiah, we are reminded that no gifts are unimportant, that God knits us together. There are ways that *you* will build up the people of God that I cannot do and vice versa.

Can you visualize the number of people who stood shoulder to shoulder and worked together to see the wall complete, to bring security to so many? It's a remarkable account of ordinary people who built and labored together to do something for God and one another.

"Eliashib the high priest rose up with his brothers the priests, and they built the Sheep Gate" (Nehemiah 3:1). A high priest would not normally do this work, but can I say with a heart of love that *nobody* is above doing the work. His example is so awesome, and the people saw him doing something holy and with a oneness, for a purpose greater than himself.

And throughout the chapter, we read, *"next to them"* and *"next to him."* They were all together, cheering each other on. There is such a power in coming together and doing God's work. Part of our common calling is we are all ministers, partnering with God in building His kingdom on the earth.

Hebrews 12:1–2 tells us:

> *Therefore, since we are surrounded by so great a cloud of witnesses, let us also lay aside every weight, and sin which clings so closely, and let us run with endurance the race that is set before us, looking to Jesus, the founder and perfecter of our faith, who for the joy that was set before him endured the cross, despising the shame, and is seated at the right hand of the throne of God.*

This is the picture of unity from an eternal perspective. The heroes of the faith cheering us on while we keep our eyes on Jesus and allow the Holy Spirit to continue to equip us with every fruit of the spirit that enables us to walk together in holy rhythm.

The "Prince of Preachers," Charles Spurgeon, said, "Unless I can leave off loving Jesus Christ, I cannot cease loving those who love Him." Such a poignant quote from one the masters!

JESUS, THE AUTHOR AND PERFECTER

Unity takes humility; unity takes people willing to let go of their own way for the benefit of the greater good. Unity takes a willingness to prefer others. This does not mean allowing ourselves to be stepped on to hide truth, but it does mean that because God has called us to love others, we operate in the gifts of the spirit to bring self-control to our responses and reactions.

I don't know how you respond when there is a lack of oneness within your family, or team, or wherever you find yourself. I tend to be a peacemaker, so that when there is a lack of unity in any environment close to me, I find myself going to either extreme—charging in to help fix things, or pulling away to avoid the messiness that seems to get messier before peace is at the table.

But I have learned that through open and honest, respectful communication, and a prayerful approach to the conversation, a solution can often be found.

Fully loving can sometimes leave you at risk of being hurt, but I want to live like this. Jesus says to come to Him like a little child, uncomplicated, trusting, open armed, accepting and believing the wonder that surrounds you. And before you jump to be critical next time at a style or sound that is different from yours, take a breath, be slow to speak, and ask the Holy Spirit to keep working on your capacity to love even the things you don't understand.

Every time our diversity or preferences bring fractures or cause others to take their eyes from Jesus and onto a meaningless display of immaturity, we need to rethink our practices, lift up our eyes, and look to Jesus, the Author and Perfecter of our faith. Ask Him for grace and understanding and a genuine love for others who display their worship expression in a different way than our own.

As Augustine said, "Our lives should be lived as a hallelujah from head to toe." Living our lives in response to the great love of God, in all its diversity, should be our 24/7 thank you!

TO MY DEAR SISTERS AND BROTHERS...

Across the earth the ones reading this today, the ones who are aware of their *for such a time as this* moment in history:

With all my heart, I pray today that each one of us would be Spirit led as we put any thoughts to words, public or private, as we daily navigate this tremendously critical time on the earth. Let *love* be the guide.

I pray that our lives would be used by God to build and encourage the body of Christ rather than quickly criticize the things we don't fully understand. Over my lifetime, I have learned that I can love my brother or sister even without agreeing with them. This is the whole point of Christian unity and is the mark of maturity.

I pray that we would obey the Bible as it asks us to go to a brother or sister face to face when we are out of alignment if it is in our power to do so, to listen, forgive, and walk in healing and wholeness. I pray that we would increase our commitment to pray for our enemies, to bless those who persecute us, to watch God do what only He can do as our commitment to Christ strengthens and matures us in ways we may not fully understand right now.

This is the life of faith. Even when we don't see it, even when we don't understand it, the Holy Spirit continues to reveal Jesus to our hearts every step of the way if we welcome it.

No one is immune to these challenges, and no one is too far from the grace of God to walk in the unity that I believe the Lord is requiring of us. I have had to learn these same lessons as I walk out my own journey, and I must say that when I yield my way to God's way, the result is so miraculous, it's hard to put into mere words. Grace is robust. It is not flowery or sugary, but strong and made possible by an empty tomb.

I pray you find the grace to bring the peace of Jesus Christ into the chaotic places of your world, and that we find God's love for others to flow from our lives in ways we never imagined.

With so much love,

Darlene Zschech

Darlene Zschech is an award-winning Australian singer-songwriter, pastor, and author. Connect with her at www.darlenezschech.com.

15

BABEL HAS FALLEN … AND PENTECOST IS RISING!

Bo Sanchez
| Catholic Charismatic |

If my chapter title reminds you of movie titles, that was deliberate. I like watching movies.

A few years ago, a couple of action movies came out with the words "has fallen" in their titles. First was *Olympus Has Fallen.* Next came *London Has Fallen.*

But another story came out much earlier than that.

A few thousand years earlier.

The title? *Babel Has Fallen.*

Sadly, this drama is still going on.

The story of how Babel fell is found in Genesis. But you still find the exact storyline being played out even among God's people to this very day.

Nevertheless, by God's endless mercy, He caused an anti-Babel event to happen too: Pentecost.

Babel and Pentecost are opposites on the spiritual spectrum.

BACKGROUND ON BABEL AND PENTECOST

The story of Babel is told in Genesis 11:1–9. "*The whole earth had one language*" (verse 1), and the people, descendants of Noah, were moving eastward, finding a plain in Shinar. Historians say Shinar was one of the cities in Babylon, the capital of Babylonia in southern Mesopotamia, some 60 miles south of what we know now as Baghdad, Iraq.

As they settled in Shinar, Noah's descendants had this great idea to build a tower. Perhaps they had learned their lesson after the great flood, and they wanted to build a tower so high no flood could reach it. That's just my conjecture.

The Bible says they had another motive. They said, *"Come, let us build ourselves a city and a tower with its top in the heavens, and let us make a name for ourselves, lest we be dispersed over the face of the whole earth"* (Genesis 11:4).

But their plans did not escape our omnipotent God's attention. When the Lord saw what was happening, He said, *"Behold, they are one people, and they have all one language, and this is only the beginning of what they will do. And nothing that they propose to do will now be impossible for them. Come, let us go down and there confuse their language, so that they may not understand one another's speech"* (Genesis 11:6–7).

So now our word for "confusing language" is *babel* or *babble*.

It was a whole different story during Pentecost. After Jesus ascended to heaven, the apostles were staying together in a room in Jerusalem. And there, one day, the Holy Spirit appeared to them in the form of *"tongues of fire that … came to rest on each of them"* (Acts 2:3). This happened at the time the Israelites were celebrating their spring festival called *Shavuot*, fifty days after Jesus's resurrection. And thus, we have this festival we now know as Pentecost, from the Greek *pentecoste* meaning fiftieth day.

BABEL IS ABOUT DIVISION; PENTECOST IS ABOUT UNITY

After the Tower of Babel, people spoke different languages and could not understand one another. But at Pentecost, everyone was able to discern what was being said no matter whether they knew the language or not.

Babel is about building a tower of pride.

Pentecost is about building a church of humility.

Here's a spiritual truth some may have missed: *Unity is born from humility, not uniformity.* We may come from different religious traditions, speaking different religious languages. But because of the Spirit, unity is possible.

BABEL PEOPLE VS. PENTECOST PEOPLE

There are two kinds of people in this world: *Babel people* and *Pentecost people.*

The mistake of Babel people? They started believing in their own Instagram posts. That's dangerous. Because on Instagram, you post only the good side of life. You rarely post your failures. You rarely post your most embarrassing mistakes.

Babel people are proud. And they think they're the center, the source, the boss. In their arrogance, they want to become gods.

Pentecost people are humble. They know their weaknesses. They know they're not the center, the source. They acknowledge God.

When there's disunity, you're going to smell the stench of pride.

But Pentecost people are different in two aspects.

FIRST, PENTECOST PEOPLE WORSHIP GOD

Worship is the biggest difference between Babel and Pentecost.

In Babel, people worship themselves. At Pentecost, people worshipped God.

In Babel, their fulcrum, their reference point, and their source of power is themselves. At Pentecost, it's God.

In Babel, they do everything *"so that we may make a name for ourselves"* (Genesis 11:4 NIV). But at Pentecost, they are *"telling in our own tongues the mighty works of God"* (Acts 2:11).

Here's what I notice: *When there's war, there's self-worship.* Babel people say, "Hey, I'm important. How dare you bypass me? How dare you fail to recognize my importance?"

And the conflict begins.

But Pentecost people say, "It's okay if you bypass me because in my world, I'm not god—God is God. And I don't need you to tell me I'm important. God thinks I'm important. And that's enough for me."

May I go deeper with this?

ARE YOU BUILDING A TOWER OR BUILDING A CHURCH?

What unites people?

It's not the belief of Jesus. As you know, many who believe in Jesus are fighting each other. There are now 41,000 Christian denominations in the world. Some churches fight over their principles, while others fight over their properties. Some fight over their theology, while others fight over their money. Some fight over big things, but others fight over petty things.

What unites people? It's not believing in Jesus but acting like Jesus. (Chew on that for a while.)

Like Jesus, we need to die to ourselves.

Every kind of unity is very expensive. Unity comes at a very high cost. *Unity comes from death.* Someone has to die.

Will you be that someone?

Will you die to your pride? Your self-righteousness? Your judgmental attitude? Your bias? Your hatred, being so quarrelsome and adversarial? Seeking vengeance rather than forgiveness?

Babel builds a tower of pride. Pentecost builds a church of humility.

Churches, not towers, are God's main strategy for blessing the world.

You are the church.

SECOND, PENTECOST PEOPLE KNEW WHEN TO WAIT

In Babel, people didn't wait. They took matters into their own hands. They said to one another, "*Come, let us make bricks*" (Genesis 11:3) and "*Come, let us build ourselves a city*" (verse 4).

But on the day of Pentecost, they didn't say to one another, "Come." They said to the Holy Spirit, "Come." For nine straight days, they waited for God to make His move.

Imagine Mary and the apostles praying in the upper room, waiting for something to happen. They didn't even know what that *something* was. Jesus just told them to wait.

The first day, nothing happened. The second day, nothing happened. The third day, nothing happened. The fourth, the fifth, the sixth, seventh, and eighth days, still nothing happened.

Imagine if on the eighth day, one guy—Mr. Impatient—stood up and said, "Well, I've waited long enough. I'm going fishing."

And off he walked into the sunset. But the next day—BOOM!—the Holy Spirit fell upon the entire gang ... minus Mr. Impatient. He gave up one day too early.

I urge you: Wait on the Lord. Unity will happen to His church. And only the Holy Spirit—and our humility to receive the Spirit—can make it happen.

But let me backtrack a little. Let me tell you my story...

MY SPIRITUAL JOURNEY STARTED WITH SOME WEIRD STUFF

How did I meet Jesus?

When I was a kid, my dad would put his arm around my shoulder and say, "You're my *favorite* son."

"Gee, Dad, thanks," I'd say, feeling wonderful. Until I realized he didn't have much choice. I was his only son.

But I'm the youngest with five older sisters.

Dad used to say in jest, "I almost named you Atlas. Because when the doctor said I had a boy, I said, 'At last!'"

Mom and Dad were very Catholic. Together with my evil sisters, er..., I mean my elder sisters, we went to Mass, wore a scapular, and prayed the Rosary together every night. My sisters and I learned religion in a Catholic school.

So I knew about Jesus. Sort of.

But something radical happened when I was twelve years old.

It was another Friday night, and my mother invited me to this little Catholic prayer meeting she attended with my dad and sisters. For six months, they had been attending something weird on Friday nights. They'd come home with stories about how people prayed in tongues, got healed, and received miracles. Really strange stuff.

Even young as I was, I knew something real was happening to them. First, I noticed my sisters were behaving kind of crazy. They were kinder to their cute and lovable brother. Second, my entire family was excited about God. That had never happened before. They kept talking about Jesus like He was a real person.

But one day, they wanted to pull me into their weird realm. It was okay just watching them from a distance go through this transformation, but when my mom wanted me to join them, I told her, "Sorry, Mom, I'm too young to give my life to God. Besides, isn't this thing only for old people and women?"

My thinking was, "Gee, I haven't yet puffed my first cigarette, tasted my first bottle of beer, or had a girlfriend. Perhaps when I get older, I'll attend that prayer meeting."

Like when I'm seventy-five years old.

MY FIRST PRAYER MEETING

My father, however, was a stubborn man. He said, "If Bo doesn't want to go to the prayer meeting, we'll bring the prayer meeting to Bo."

I didn't know what he meant by that.

One night, after we prayed the Rosary, Dad stood up and said, "We're going to have a prayer meeting right now."

"Jeepers, Dad. It's *Starsky and Hutch* on TV!" (Yes, that's how old I am.)

"Sit!" my father commanded, and so I did. He then asked all of us to close our eyes and hold hands. No way! For a twelve-year-old boy, holding hands with your sisters is a nightmare! And so, clowning around, I closed only one eye, curious about what my father would do next.

I was expecting another barrage of formula prayers, like *Our Father* and *Hail Mary*, but Dad simply *talked* … to God. Talking from his heart, his face looked so at peace. And I realized he actually believed God was listening to him.

Was God really there in front of him? Didn't the Almighty have more important chores to do than be in our living room?

I didn't want to admit it, but praying with Dad made me feel warm and fuzzy inside.

But lest my family discover that I was being *touched*, I tried instead to look infuriated by it all.

That was when the most unpredictable thing happened. My dad saw my stony face, stood up, and firmly placed his hand on top of my head. He then said, "In Jesus's name, devil, get out!"

What did he say? The devil was in me?

And, to my horror, everyone in the family stretched their arms toward me and, in unison, attacked me with, "Amen!"

Actually, I guess Dad didn't know exactly what he was doing. He just wanted me to get closer to God, and he was determined to try anything, including imitating TV evangelists' exorcisms.

With all the authority he could muster, Dad bravely shouted, "In Jesus's name, devil, get out! In Jesus's name, devil, get out!"

But because he really was new to this whole thing, he started uttering something else: "In Jesus's name, devil, get out! Jesus, Jesus, Jesus! Get out! Get out! Get out!"

At once, my mother's eyes popped out. She glared at Dad, elbowed him hard, and exclaimed, "Your prayer is all wrong! You're asking Jesus to go out!"

Whoa, Dad had just committed heresy!

So, his face turning white—as in drained of blood—Dad panicked and promptly told everyone, "Quick! Let's pray again, let's pray again!

"Jesus," he implored out loud, "come back!"

PERSONAL ENCOUNTER

That happened many, many years ago. For the next six years, my father still felt dull pain in his lower left rib cage, thanks to Mom's timely jab.

My life has never been the same since that day.

I read this fun quote written by the prolific Mr. Anonymous, and I said to myself, gosh, this realization is what changed my life: "If God had a refrigerator, your picture would be on it."

God loved me. How could I not love Him back?

Thus, in my teens, Jesus became very real for me.

I came to know Jesus as the God who loved me perfectly and completely. The God who knew me through and through, including all my weaknesses, and still accepted me, treasured me, and celebrated me. The God who was involved in my daily struggles, no matter how tiny or trivial they were.

I realize that all the Catholic stuff I did as a kid was a beautiful foundation. And the moment I got to know Jesus, I began to understand my Catholic faith. Little by little, I discovered its depths. And so, for the past forty-some years, my mission and passion have been to invite everyone to encounter this Person named Jesus.

In that time, God has given me the privilege and joy of meeting the most amazing pastors from evangelical, nondenominational, and born-again churches, who saw me as a brother.

No, we didn't form organizations or ministries together. We were busy enough with our own churches and ministries; the last thing we needed was more work.

Here's what we did: *We became friends.*

We listened to each other.

We laughed and ate together.

We shared wisdom.

We gave gifts.

And we prayed together.

In these simple friendships, we tried to recreate Pentecost.

WHAT DOES PENTECOST LIFE LOOK LIKE?

When you hear the word *Pentecost*, you automatically think of miracles, signs, wonders, and praying in tongues.

But here's what happened right after Pentecost: "*They devoted themselves to the apostles' teaching and to fellowship, to the breaking of bread and to prayer. . . . All the believers were together and had everything in common. They sold property and possessions to give to anyone who had need*" (Acts 2:42, 44–45 NIV).

This was our first local church. It all started in Jerusalem and Luke described them as a loving family. They didn't just pray together, or listen to teaching, or break bread together. *They loved each other in very concrete ways.*

This, I believe, is the essence of Pentecost.

The pope's retreat master, Cardinal P. Raniero Cantalamessa, a coauthor of this book, has said, "The evident sign that one possesses the Spirit is not to speak in tongues and do miracles, but to love unity."

This is how Pentecost will happen—by all of us loving each other in concrete ways.

A PERSONAL LETTER TO MY "PROTESTANT" FRIENDS

Before I go on, let me point out here that I put quotation marks around the word *Protestant* because it's a word some no longer consider politically correct or a kind word to refer to our brothers and sisters in faith. But let me use it anyway because that's the backstory of where we're coming from.

Dearest "Protestant" friends,

I have three messages in this short letter.

Forgive us. Thank you. I love you!

PART 1: FORGIVE US

You are my brother.

You are my sister.

We belong to one Father.

We're part of one family.

For the many times a Catholic did not recognize this as a Jesus follower, forgive us.

For the many times a Catholic maligned you, or belittled you, or insulted you, or ridiculed you for your faith, we ask for forgiveness.

PART 2: THANK YOU

You inspired me to love Jesus more.

You reminded me that the center of life is a personal relationship with Jesus.

You stirred up within me a deep love for the Scriptures.

You made me enjoy more spontaneous and expressive worship.

You taught me how God smiles when I dance and jump and sing like a little child in a prayer meeting.

You pulled me into loving small groups where fellow Jesus followers *do life* together, sharing deeply, becoming vulnerable and accountable, and journeying toward Jesus.

You helped me depend more on the power of the Holy Spirit.

You emphasized how miracles still happen to this day.

You modeled for me the burning passion needed to bring more people closer to Jesus.

You reminded me that the church is not just:

- A behavior modification movement, teaching people good moral character, even though we do end up being transformed.
- A social action movement, helping the poor and all those living in the periphery of society, even if this is 100 percent central and essential to our faith.
- About performing obligatory rituals that will gain us a ticket to heaven, even if there are beautiful sacred rituals that are channels of grace.

Instead, you reminded me that the church is a spiritual family gathered around a Person named Jesus. And you told me that if I don't get this, I'll get the ribbon, the wrapper, the box ... but not the gift.

I'm a better Catholic because of you. Because I love Jesus more.

PART 3: I LOVE YOU!

Today, I express my commitment to all my brothers and sisters in various churches.

Let's do life together.

Let's leave Babel behind.

Let's live Pentecost today.

In Jesus,
Bo Sanchez

Bo Sanchez is a best-selling author and international speaker based in the Philippines. He has founded many organizations to help others. Connect with him at bosanchez.ph.

16

7 LESSONS I'VE LEARNED ABOUT CHURCH UNITY

Dr. J. Norberto Saracco
| Argentine Pentecostal |

On April 9, I celebrated fifty-five years of being ordained as pastor in a Pentecostal church in Argentina. I have had the privilege of pastoring on the outskirts of the city of Buenos Aires, then in Costa Rica, and finally in the city of Buenos Aires, where I still serve as a pastor. Throughout my ministerial pilgrimage, I have been amazed by the move of the Spirit that transformed my mind and heart, led me to love His church intensely, and sowed in me a passion for the unity of the body of Christ. I look back and recognize that I am the fruit of a miracle of grace.

In these brief reflections, I want to share what I learned along the way about the unity of the church. These are not academic lessons but experiences that the Lord of the church has taught me over the years. Some things I see with total clarity, others with some shadows, but what I know for sure is that the church *is one* and this church is the one for which the Lord will come.

FIRST LESSON: IGNORANCE DIVIDES

The year was 1964. I was sixteen years old and had just finished hearing about the Second Vatican Council. The youth leader of my church invited me to listen to Pastor Míguez Bonino, who had been one of the Protestant observers at the council. Our church was a Pentecostal church, and my entire religious world was limited to that small community of faith. In truth, I could not conceive that outside our walls, there were really Christians who were truly saved. Saying it sounds like a lie or exaggeration, but I'm being truthful.

I agreed to meet my leader at the door of the Faculty of Theology. Some churches of historic Protestantism were part of this institution. For a few minutes, I refused to go in. I doubted that this was a place that pleased God. My "moral" problem was not with the issue of Catholicism or the council. Both things were totally alien to me and did not cause me problems. It was clear to me that the Catholic Church and its institutions were a perversion of the true faith and were doomed to hell. My doubts were with the Methodist and Lutheran churches that I didn't know and therefore I feared that I would be in rebellion with God just by entering their facilities. At last, I entered and attended the conference. I did not understand or remember what was being talked about, and for many months, I retained the fear that I had betrayed my faith and my God. My vision was so shortsighted that to me, the whole church was the one to which I belonged. Today I look back on that distant youthful experience and think about the power of ignorance. Ignorance about the other fills us with prejudices, erects barriers, builds walls. Ignorance leads us to see our differences as obstacles rather than as riches of God's manifold grace.

Thirty years ago, together with four other pastors from different denominations, we decided to form the Council of Pastors of Buenos Aires; we did so under the premise of establishing bonds of friendship that would allow us to get to know each other. The temptation was to create a kind of alliance of city churches. But we preferred to build another path not based on institutions but on the people who form them. This did not mean losing our denominational identity but building new relationships based on the knowledge of others as they were and not as we had been told they were. Today, thirty years later, the Council of Pastors works under the premise that in the city, there is only one church. It has no authorities but is based on the recognition of the grace that God has given to each one. We see the differences and particularities of the more than four hundred churches in the city as richness. *Christianity Today* magazine called this "Something Better Than a Revival."

SECOND LESSON: THE SPIRIT'S MOVEMENT BREAKS DOWN BARRIERS

In 1972, I traveled to Costa Rica to study at the seminary. I was ordained pastor three years earlier in a small church on the outskirts of Buenos Aires. My father-in-law, a man of prayer, a layman, had come into contact with missionaries influenced by the Latter Rain movement. This opened him up to a deeper experience with the Holy Spirit and worship. Those were days of spiritual searching. A few months after my arrival in the Central American country, a Brazilian classmate invited me to a charismatic meeting in a Catholic chapel. I went out of curiosity. My concept of the Catholic Church hadn't changed, but I wanted to see with my own eyes what was going on.

I was amazed when I entered the place and saw that everyone was praising God full of the Spirit, just as I had experienced in recent times. I can't deny the feeling of confusion I had. I couldn't put together a move of the Spirit of God and the Catholic Church. It wasn't long until I had to accept that it was the Spirit of God pouring out on that Catholic community. I had a thousand questions and doubts, but I could no longer deny that they were my brothers. We have seen this ecumenism of the Spirit all over the world. It is the same experience that the early Jewish Christians had when they had to accept gentiles into their communities. (See Acts 10:43–45.) It requires of us nothing more than accepting God's sovereignty and embracing what He embraces. This in no way ignores differences or detracts from theological dialogue and discussion but relegates them to second place. Unity is not given by our agreements but by who we are in Christ. The challenge is to live up to who we are and work through our differences in the light of this truth.

THIRD LESSON: THE ECUMENICAL POWER OF WORSHIP

I'm aware that I'm not talking about something original. Most of us who have overcome the barriers that divide us have done so, initially, through worship. As we well know, worship is not singing religious hymns. It is a spiritual experience that involves our whole being, spirit, soul, and body. The Spirit unites our tongues, human or angelic, and our divided hearts in a single expression of praise to the Lord. The reasons for the division, the walls that history has built, and the theological arguments that have underpinned our separation take second place. It is not that they have not been or are not important but in the perspective of a spiritual movement, they acquire a relative value. This is what we call the ecumenism of the Spirit. Just as speaking in tongues allows us to worship beyond what our words can say, the manifestation of the Holy Spirit makes us live in unity beyond what we can humanly build. Every time I have participated in worship with brothers and sisters from other traditions, the certainty of unity is renewed in me.

FOURTH LESSON: WITH THE SPIRIT, BUT NOT ONLY WITH THE SPIRIT

There is no doubt that a powerful movement of the Spirit has a special force that leads us to unity. When we are able to see the move of God in the other, we inevitably come to the conclusion that if God is working in him or her, they are my brother and sister, beyond what we can understand or explain. However, if we remain only at this level, our unity is superficial. If we are not able to work on our differences, to know them, value them, and accept them, our unity will not go beyond the emotional and affective. This is how we value, for example, the Catholic-Pentecostal dialogue that has developed over the last fifty years. It has not been a sterile job. The majority of Pentecostal and Catholic pastors, priests, leaders, and bishops may be unaware of the existence of this space for dialogue and encounter, but ignorance does not negate the value of the effort. I firmly believe that in order for unity to have roots and continuity over time, it must take into account our differences and work on them in a framework of seriousness and respect.

Certainly, we will reach irreducible points, nonnegotiable affirmations for one or the other, or irreconcilable differences, but it will be in the recognition of these obstacles that unity will be strengthened. It is a pity that there are no such instances of theological dialogues at the level of the members of our communities in the different contexts. I'm talking about dialogue between Catholics and Pentecostals/Evangelicals, at least in Latin America, which is what I know. In the 1970s, we had made some progress with spiritual ecumenism, but then it weakened because, among other things, it did not have the roots of serious, deep, and loving reflection.

I have learned that there are at least two paradigms that make up our understanding of unity: the paradigm of Babel and the paradigm of Pentecost. From my participation in these spaces, I prefer the latter. Babel is unity under a single thought, with no divergences or different opinions. Babel puts all of its energy in one direction, with a single conviction. There is no place for others. Pentecost is unity in the midst of diversity. At Pentecost, different languages are spoken and everyone understands without renouncing their language and culture. The wonder of Pentecost is that it breaks down barriers, not to make us all the same but so that despite our differences, we appreciate and value each other in our uniqueness. Pentecost is God's irruption into the midst of His people to remind us that His church is the space in which the different, even the antagonistic, unites. In first-century society, there were Jews and gentiles, Romans and slaves, prostitutes and holy women, poor and rich, but in the church, the Spirit made them one. The paradigm of Pentecost impels us to overcome the differences that separate us, not by ignoring them, but by bringing them under the influence of the Spirit.

FIFTH LESSON: RELATIONSHIP FIRST

In 1998, the Latin American Council of Churches (CLAI) and the Latin American Episcopal Conference (CELAM) convened a meeting of Catholics and Pentecostals in the city of Quito, Ecuador. It was the first meeting of its kind in Latin America. The idea was not to discuss theological or doctrinal issues but to create a space for mutual knowledge within a framework of respect. It was decided that building relationships was the first step toward unity. On the plane ride home to Buenos Aires, three pastors and two priests who had met in Quito had time to talk. At the end of the trip, we agreed to see each other and continue our dialogue. A bishop joined the next meeting. For more than three years, we met every two months at the home of one of the participants, on the condition that the host should cook lunch. What was special about these meetings was hearing the life stories of some of the participants. For instance, the bishop had been an active opponent of the presence of Pentecostals in his diocese, going so far as to denounce them to the authorities and trying to prevent their meetings. On the Pentecostal side was a *patriarch* who belonged to the founding families of Argentine Pentecostalism.

As we progressed in our relationships, prejudices began to crumble, and we were able to include deeper and more challenging topics in our dialogues. As time went by, the personal relationships moved to the faith communities they represented and was the basis for an important rapprochement that took place between Pentecostals and Catholics years later. We learned from this experience that when we can develop a deep personal relationship, theological issues and divergences can be addressed in a more fruitful and constructive way. We discovered truths, emphases, and riches that our presuppositions had hidden from us. Moving forward in a relationship makes prejudices disappear; we can open spiritually and mentally to each other. The relationship enriches and creates solid bonds of unity.

SIXTH LESSON: THE POWER OF COMMON TESTIMONY

Matteo Calisi, a lay Catholic world leader in the charismatic movement, visited Argentina in 2003. A little more than a year prior, the country had suffered the biggest economic crisis in its history; despair and frustration abounded in the population. Matteo met with Jorge Himitian, a leader of the evangelical charismatic movement in Argentina. The Catholic brothers in charge of Matteo's agenda organized a lunch with Pastor Himitian and other pastor friends. From this meeting of Matteo, some charismatic Catholics, and some pastors, a relationship began that went beyond a simple friendship and led to a common witness. They decided to organize events in which there would be a visible participation of Catholics and Evangelicals. The first event at the headquarters of the Catholic University in 2004 drew a thousand participants. This was followed by events in an evangelical church in 2005 with 1,800 participants and in a stadium (Luna Park) with 7,500 attendees.

The common witness strengthened the relationship and served as an inspiration and encouragement for a hopeless and anguished society. From this initiative, CRECES (Renewed Communion of Catholics and Evangelicals in the Holy Spirit) was born. The former archbishop of Buenos Aires, the late Pope Francis, actively participated in CRECES and was inspired by this path of unity. These events led to a more concrete unity that was expressed in the joint distribution of the Bible, testimonies of common evangelization, a united presence in the city of Buenos Aires, and intimate meetings of prayer and intercession. From deep spirituality, we moved on to influence society with gestures of unity that became visible and challenging for our faith communities. CRECES has served as an inspiration for other unity movements around the world. Those of us who have been part of this have learned the power of common witness when the relationship becomes mission.

SEVENTH LESSON: UNITY IS A JOURNEY AND A LEARNING PROCESS

The unity of the church depends on us, on our will. This is why Jesus did not pray that the church would be one, but that *we* would be one. (See John 17:21.) The unity of the church is not only between Roman Catholics, Orthodox, and Evangelicals. Today there are more than forty thousand Christian denominations or groups. In every generation and in every context, we face the challenge of being one in Christ Jesus. Unity is not something that is given instantly by the goodwill of some. It's a long and winding process that requires will and perseverance. Understanding this will avoid the frustration of expecting immediate results; at the same time, it will make us aware that we are all responsible for making the essential unity of the church visible.

I think it's important to point out here that those of us in a leadership role must bring the vision of unity to our faith communities. One of the most significant experiences we had at CRECES was getting our communities involved. For example, in September, the month of the Bible, we go out to offer God's Word. We set up booths in the streets or markets, and Catholics and Evangelicals together offer their versions of the Bible. This simple gesture is a powerful testimony to the community.

I fear that many ecumenical efforts remain at the level of the ecclesiastical hierarchies. However, we would be surprised to see how easily people are willing to live the truth of our unity. At least this has been my experience every time we proposed a joint action. The process of unity also involves learning from each other. The willingness to learn is more than listening or receiving information. It implies that we are willing to modify our beliefs and perceptions when we discover value in the other's argument. This may be the most difficult instance, but it is necessary and will prove to be of great value.

The path of unity is a permanent and never-ending process. It is not a document that we sign that remains static over time. It is true that we can reach, and have reached, significant agreements regarding the unity of the church, but they must be transformed into actions, gestures, and experiences. Jesus's prayer that we may be one appeals to us in every generation, and every generation must face the challenges that come with it. Situations constantly arise that push us to division. Whether it's because of what we say or do, there's always a latent temptation to walk alone without the burden of other people's convictions. The history of the church shows us in many ways how many times we have succumbed to this temptation. However, we are encouraged to look back and see how far we have come on the path of unity. In the face of the real enemies—such as anti-life ideologies, the systematic destruction of the family, the hedonistic conception of life where enjoyment is the supreme good, and the contempt for childhood and old age, among others—we need more than ever to fight this cultural and spiritual battle together. The unity of the church today is not just a divine demand but a moral imperative.

In my pilgrimage for unity, I have learned some lessons, perhaps not all there are, but I thank God for having enlightened me to leave my *little kingdom* and love His whole church, in its weaknesses and holiness, in its diversity and plurality, in its poverty and majesty.

To the Lord of the church be honor and praise forever! Amen.

A LOVE LETTER TO THE PENTECOSTAL CHURCH

My heart is grateful to God for giving me the privilege of being born into a Pentecostal family. Years passed, I was able to earn a doctorate, minister in many countries, serve God in organizations of worldwide reach, and pastor a contemporary church in the mega city of Buenos Aires. However, it was in the bosom of that small Pentecostal church that I learned and received what was most important to my life and ministry. There I learned to live always open to the work of the Spirit, to believe God, to love His Word, and to hope against hope. I learned to pray when I saw the worn knees of my grandfather's pants. I learned the passion for evangelism by preaching on a street corner and the transforming power of the gospel by changing entire families.

Thank you for teaching us that the Spirit blows where He wants and how He wants. Beloved Pentecostal brethren, my debt of gratitude to you is infinite. You have been the great gateway to the work of the Holy Spirit that transformed twentieth-century Christianity and its influence continues to this day.

Because I love you, I remind you that you are a movement, not a denomination. Your faithfulness is not to the past but to what God has ahead. Do not allow structures to stifle the fresh movement of the Spirit. Your tradition should inspire you but never become a longed-for past to which you want to return.

I encourage you to watch with joy as God fulfills His promise to send His Spirit upon all flesh, not just all Pentecostal flesh. Your greatest contribution at this time is to be an example of openness to the surprises of the Spirit who surely moves in very different ways than He did in your tradition.

Thank you for what you have been and are. Thank you for what you taught us. Thank you for what you have sown in faith in millions of people who honor God today and tens of thousands who serve Him today.

With appreciation... and hugs

Dr. J. Norberto Saracco

Dr. J. Norberto Saracco is the pastor of Good News Church in Buenos Aires, Argentina. He is the founder and rector emeritus of the Instituto Teológico FIET (International Faculty of Theological Studies). Connect with him at fiet.com.ar.

17

JOINING GOD IN HIS WORK

General Brian Peddle
| The Salvation Army |

The playwright Henrik Ibsen said, "A thousand words leave not the same deep impression as does a single deed," which inspired the phrase "a picture is worth a thousand words." The best picture of the church is when it presents itself as a *serving* church. When I am able to travel internationally, I am often able to see His church with its sleeves rolled up, tending the sick, feeding the hungry, and sheltering the poor and vulnerable. I rejoice in such images because they provide ample evidence that God is at work.

The Salvation Army is at work in 133 countries across the world. We are engaged in a work that is God-given and larger than we are capable of achieving by ourselves. We, The Salvation Army, and all churches need to partner with God in the *missio Dei*, recognising God's gracious invitation to join in His mission, His work. God could save the world and rectify all the presenting and endemic issues by Himself at a single stroke, yet He chooses to invite the church and believers to partner with Him, to learn from Him, to journey with Him. Hmmm ... I think God may be trying to show and teach us something here.

We are brothers and sisters in Christ, sinners saved by the grace of God as revealed in Jesus Christ, seeking to live each day as disciples through the power of the Holy Spirit. Our respective churches are engaged in various ministries, but we share core basic beliefs, and we are concerned about the most marginalised, downtrodden, and exploited within society. Whenever I meet with other Christian leaders, we do not meet as rivals engaged in some competitive war for the largest slice of the Christian pie. We meet as God's fellow workers, as fellow disciples of Christ, called by God to lead a global church seeking to speak into and address global issues. Our shared convictions and concerns mean conversation is easy, and the grace of God is abundant in our sharing.

During my term in 2018–2023, I took a positive and proactive approach to our ecumenical relations. Not only did this mean fully supporting our secretary for international ecumenical relations but also being an active participant in conversations with leaders of other denominations. While at the Vatican for a private audience with the late Pope Francis, I was able to meet with members of the Pontifical Council for the Promotion of Christian Unity. From 2007 to 2012, the Roman Catholic Church and The Salvation Army were engaged in dialogue covering a range of issues. In my 2019 meeting at the Vatican, we decided to set up another series of informal talks between our respective churches on shared areas of interest and concern. While the COVID pandemic presented some challenges and pushed back schedules, it has not completely halted ecumenical progress. I have also been conversing with the leaders of the Lutheran World Federation, exploring opportunities for joint working and gathering information regarding existing projects and working partnerships. Similarly, we are engaging with the World Methodist Council for a joint webinar. The Salvation Army grew out of Methodism, and we still align ourselves with Wesleyan Holiness, so we have much in common. Early in my tenure, I was privileged to be present at a celebration held in our international headquarters for the late Gregorious Theocharous, the Greek Orthodox archbishop of Thyateira and Great Britain. While this was our first time meeting each other, the grace and peace of Christ emanated from the archbishop, and he commented that we were both brothers in Christ and what we had in common was greater than that which differentiated us.

In June 2019, I had the privilege of visiting Palu, Indonesia, shortly after the devastating earthquake. The Salvation Army was involved in rescue operations, disaster relief, and providing medical and pastoral support. It's one thing to see a news report or watch a video online, but it is sobering when you witness the aftermath of a disaster firsthand. On the Sunday morning of our visit, we held a thanksgiving service attended by 17,000 people. At the beginning of the event, a group of Muslim boys brought some local cultural music as a means of greeting and celebration. At the conclusion of the event, I was able to meet some community leaders. The field in which we were holding the thanksgiving service for this significant crowd was close to a mosque, and leaders had worked together so that the mosque's prayers were delayed until the thanksgiving service had concluded. While this particular example of unity may be multi-faith, it demonstrates the reality that opportunities exist to work together for the common good, particularly in times of crisis and disaster. Such opportunities provide a means to share the gospel in word and deed.

In Ilford, London, the unique and exciting Project Malachi started with a young boy donating his money from the tooth fairy. Malachi's mother volunteered at The Salvation Army's night shelter, so when Malachi received £5 from the tooth fairy, he donated it with a note saying to use it to help homeless people. His donation kickstarted a campaign to build a hostel in a community where ten homeless had died. The Salvation Army partnered with the Roman Catholic Church and City Gates, an independent church, in addition to the local mosque, the Sikh community, and Citizens UK. The collaborative working reflected the constituent parts of the community. Each church and organization worked to their strengths to build a pop-up hostel to address the homeless issue. While not purely ecumenical in its focus on unity, Project Malachi is an exemplar of unity across faiths and throughout a community. Such is the success of this particular project of unity that other organizations and councils are examining it as a prototype to follow.

The Salvation Army has been involved with the World Council of Churches for a number of years now, and we have observer status. It is vitally important that we engage with our sisters and brothers in Christ on local, regional, national, and international levels. When we work together to address global issues, our collective voice is wiser, more diverse, more representative, and more powerful. The church universal can speak with clarity and impact when it speaks from a place of unity.

I have always had a deep appreciation for the gathered church, and I enjoy being a part of worship with others. In my neighborhood, there are a number of churches, with multiple denominations, steeples, storefronts, church halls, and quiet places. On my journey to worship, my curiosity often takes me inside, and despite the style, standing or sitting, liturgical or free, I catch an image of His church. Equally inspiring is the benediction, the opening of doors, and the sending of His church into the world. So much of faith presents as the invisible. To many, God is invisible. I find myself praying, "Let the invisible God be seen in me … in us." As much as we enjoy gathering, we must understand we are also integral to the sending.

The purpose of our gathering is to worship God and be equipped to go out into the world. Jesus was clear in His instruction to the eleven disciples gathered at the time of His ascension to heaven: *"Go therefore and make disciples of all nations"* (Matthew 28:19). The sent church has a united mission of making disciples. In Luke 10, Jesus sends out seventy-two people on a mission. Our God is a sending God, so His church should be a sent church. Jesus taught in the Sermon on the Mount in Matthew 5:13–16 that we should be salt and light, not kept in the salt cellar or covered up, but spread liberally to bring out the God flavors and shining brightly to illuminate the God colors. How rich the taste is when God's church in all its diversity lives to share and point people to Jesus in united mission. How glorious the spectrum when God's church reveals His glory through a unified approach. Individual churches and denominations should work to their strengths but that does not necessitate isolated working. Instead, we should join in a complementary, strong, and unified mission.

What could that look like in reality? Churches could unite to feed the hungry, house the homeless, welcome the refugee, shelter survivors of violence, campaign on social issues, put on Alpha courses, provide a holiday Bible club, or engage in youth work. The possibilities are only as limited as our blinkered outlook.

Contextualization is critical when considering unity. Often our impatience takes over, and we desire concrete evidence of unity that displays monumental leaps of progress. Sometimes unity comes through incremental steps taken over a long time, yet these infinitesimal steps still represent significant progress and forward momentum. In certain contexts, a mere change of heart so that unity is desired is worthy of celebration, even before any outward evidence can be witnessed.

For example, Ireland is well known for its political and religious polarization that famously resulted in over three decades known as the Troubles. A few years ago, the European Union funded the Irish Churches Peace Project. The very need for this project is indicative of the disunity that existed. One may be tempted to believe that the project did not achieve much, but that would not be accurate. The very fact that Roman Catholic and Protestant clergy were in the same room conversing with each other is almost miraculous, especially when you consider that clergy from both sides were not always able to tell their congregants about their participation. At the conclusion of the project, are there still theological differences between the Roman Catholic and Protestant churches? Yes. Are there still significant differences that would preclude joint worship from taking place? Yes. But despite such differences, clergy have met who would not have done so otherwise, stories have been shared, listening has taken place, understanding has developed, and small yet significant steps have been taken toward unity. One activity that took place as part of the project was a group of clergy visiting Belfast to meet with a Roman Catholic priest and a Protestant minister in their respective churches to hear of their experiences and attempts at unity before going on a tour of the city's peace walls. This is where contextualization is critical because some clergy and congregants may be working for peace and unity in a city that still has high walls and gates that prevent them from connecting with each other.

Perhaps, then, some key components and foundational elements of unity include sharing stories, listening and seeking to understand the other. If we are mature believers and committed disciples, then there is no room for stereotypes and prejudices. We should reach out to our brothers and sisters in Christ, even when they may take a slightly different theological stance, and do so respectfully, to engage and listen, to provide opportunities for stories to be shared and questions to be asked. What would be the impact if we focused our energies on understanding and personal growth as opposed to asserting our perceived dogmatic accuracy?

Consider with me for a moment the essential presence of the Holy Spirit. In Acts 1:8, Jesus promised we would receive power to be His witnesses in every location when the Holy Spirit came. The early church was *"all together in one place"* (Acts 2:1), waiting for the Holy Spirit, and when the Paraclete came, *"all who believed were together and had all things in common"* (Acts 2:44). I would dare to suggest that there is a direct correlation between unity and the powerful presence of the Holy Spirit. I would contend that unity is a precursor to a move of the Holy Spirit. Many of us long to see a mighty move of God in our day, but I wonder whether we could hasten such a visitation if we proactively and intentionally chose to strive for unity with our brothers and sisters in Christ. Despite the dynamism of the early church, the vast majority of the past two thousand years have been marked by disagreement, discord, schism and, to be brutally honest, a lack of Christlikeness. We know that these things break the heart of God, so how much more will unity bless the name and heart of the One God who is Father of us all.

We have choices open to us. We can proactively make these choices or passively default to unhelpful attitudes and behaviors. Let me briefly outline some of the choices currently available:

- **The choice to learn from each other:** to listen to the story and perspective of another, to ask questions, to set aside prejudice, to forego the need to be right, to eschew the belief that we already know everything.
- **The choice to focus on unity:** to intentionally direct energy and resources to those things that bring cohesion and unity as opposed to the ineffective prioritization of our differences while the world and its people suffer and hurt.
- **The choice to work for shared outcomes:** to decide the bigger picture of unity in the body and holistic salvation for the world is worthy of collaboration as opposed to working solely on our individualistic agendas and empire building.
- **The choice to respect and celebrate difference:** to see our sisters and brothers in Christ as different, then respect their distinctiveness, their faith journey, their mission and place within the body of Christ, and to celebrate the diversity that is the kingdom of God and the universal church.
- **The choice to highlight unity:** to focus on and speak of *us* and *we* and lay down any predisposition to focus on and speak of *me*.
- **The choice to put the kingdom first:** as Jesus taught in Matthew 6:33, we are to *"seek first the kingdom of God."* When we prioritize the kingdom, when we love God with all our heart, soul, and might (Deuteronomy 6:5), when we love our neighbor as ourselves (Mark 12:31), and when we love each other as Christ has loved us (John 13:34), then the world will take notice. We will be so consumed by the positive outcome of loving, honoring relationships that are the hallmark of the kingdom that disunity, discord, factions, and schisms will be an anathema.

Carol Cymbala penned some powerful words that we would do well to make our prayer and live to make a reality. She prayed:

Make us one, Lord, make us one;

Holy Spirit, make us one.

Let your love flow so the world will know

We are one in you.

TO MY DEAR SISTERS AND BROTHERS IN CHRIST,

Psalm 133 makes a declarative statement, provides a profound comparison, and confirms a promise. There is a lot contained within the three verses of this psalm of David. Here is a word to the church universal that all believers would do well to heed. The Word of God declares it *is "good and pleasant"* when the people of God live together *"in unity."* How often we long for things to be good and pleasant within the body of Christ, but that can only be achieved through unity. Let's not simply seek beneficial outcomes without committing to the hard work of intentionally seeking and embracing unity. Such unity brings the anointing and blessing of God, an oil of anointing that brings the healing of God, that softens a hard, wiry beard, that helps the beard be shaped and refined. Do we eagerly seek the blessing of God? Then we need to learn to live in unity with each other. Discord within the body is unhealthy, breaks the heart of God, and prevents us from experiencing His blessing and anointing.

As if to emphasise the importance of unity, Jesus makes a specific prayer in John 17:21 that all who believe in Him would be *"one"* just as God the Father and God the Son are One. Unity does not equate to uniformity, thus robbing us of individual and denominational uniqueness. God the Father is a distinct Person from God the Son. They are both God, and together exist in Triune unity, community, and relationship with God the Holy Spirit.

Our world is so used to disunity and fragmentation because we see it everywhere. How can the church be salt and light if we are as broken, fragmented, argumentative, and hateful as the world? There is power in unity. Unity provides a means by which the church can provide a countercultural example of the value-based kingdom of God, demonstrating the glorious, wonderful, and abundant life of the kingdom. In an era when the Pharisees and Sadducees did not agree, when Jew and gentile were hostile to each other, when the populace loathed the subjugating Roman Empire, Jesus prays a prayer that should captivate our attention and stir our curiosity. What would it mean for believers to experience unity? What impact would that unity have in our world? How could such unity lead to more impactful mission, greater discipleship, and more effective evangelism?

Denominational distinctiveness should be an obedience to a calling from God and specific missional context. Such distinction and difference do not negate unity but rather enhance and reenforce it. How much more apparent could the expression of unity be when the world sees that we are one even when we are different! The apostle Paul reminds us in Ephesians 4:3–6 of the one Lord and one faith that unite us. Rather than argue over theological minutiae, let us wake up to the dynamism of ecclesial unity that unleashes the blessing and anointing of God. How are we going to answer God on the day of judgment when He asks us why we were engaging in internal politics while multitudes were dying without knowing Christ and experiencing salvation?

My brothers and sisters in Christ, we are family. Families disagree and go through challenging times, but strong families retain the familial bonds, united by love and a shared identity. As the various denominations that form the body of Christ, we will not always agree and there will be points of tension. We live as salt and light in the way we respectfully dialogue, listen, learn, walk, and serve together. As Jesus said in John 13:35, *"By this all people will know that you are my disciples, if you have love for one another."* I encourage you to love each other, even when it is challenging and there is disagreement, and keep loving each other when such love may not be returned and is costly. The way of love is the way of God. Will you join me in loving our brothers and sisters in Christ? Together let's commit to this. Together let's rely on the empowering and equipping of the Holy Spirit to help us. Together let's demonstrate and share the love of God to a broken, hurting world that desperately needs the healing only love can bring.

General Brian Peddle (Ret.) is the former leader of the International Salvation Army. Connect with him at Brian.peddle@salvationarmy.org.

18

THAT THE WORLD MAY BELIEVE

Leif Hetland

| Nondenominational |

By this all people will know that you are my disciples,
if you have love for one another.
—John 13:35

The night before Jesus went to the cross, His last hours with His disciples turned into a prayer meeting. (See John 17.) Jesus lifted His eyes to heaven and prayed for His followers, and near the end of this beautiful prayer, He revealed two great objectives: *"That the world may* ***believe*** *that you have sent me"* (verse 21); and *"that the world may* ***know*** *that you sent me and* ***loved*** *them even as you loved me"* (verse 23). The whole redemptive plan depended on people looking at Jesus's followers and being able to see how much Papa God loves them.

This is a prayer that has not yet been answered.

When God created the world, He started with a family, and He plans to end with a family. In the perfect family in the beginning, the Father loved the Son and the Spirit, the Son loved the Spirit and the Father, and the Spirit loved the Father and the Son. The three persons of the Trinity honored each other. They weren't competing with each other. No one was asking why He couldn't be like another. They have always lived in perfect love, and they have always honored each other because honor is what love looks like.

God loved all of His creatures with perfect love too. The one who first rebelled did not love himself the way the perfect family loved him, and it led to the fall. Lucifer did not recognize who he was. He was not content with just being loved by God and loving God in return. So he left the family and went his own way. He became a homeless orphan and took one-third of the angels to be homeless orphans with him. Their primary mission has been to create division by questioning God's love, and we see the results today: a worldwide orphanage with nearly 8 billion orphans in it.

The Father has always wanted to grow His family. He began by creating human beings in His image—actually *"in our image, after our likeness"* (Genesis 1:26)—so we could look like the family in heaven. He wanted a visible manifestation on earth of His family's perfect love. But the fall of humanity led to shame, blame, and division, not perfect love.

The Father wants His family back.

Jesus took that shame, blame, and division on Himself. For the first time in all eternity, He was separated from perfect love so we could be brought back into it. He promised, *"I will not leave you as orphans"* (John 14:18) and became an orphan so we could be adopted back into the family as sons and daughters. On the cross, He cried out, *"My God, my God, why have you forsaken me?"* (Matthew 27:46)—not "My Father" but "My God."

- He became sin so we could become righteousness. (See 2 Corinthians 5:21.)
- He took our shame so we could share in His glory. (See John 17:22.)
- He took on our bondage so we could share in His freedom. (See Philippians 2:7; Luke 4:18.)
- And He became divided from the Father so we could become united in Him.

Earlier in the evening when Jesus prayed that beautiful prayer for love and unity, He demonstrated what it looked like. He had given His disciples a *"new commandment"*—not a new suggestion—to love each other in the same way He had loved them. (See John 13:34.) How had He loved them? He washed their feet—even the feet of the one who was about to betray Him and the one who was about to deny Him. He changed the golden rule of loving others the way we want to be loved to the diamond rule of the heavenly family—loving others as He loved. That kind of love is ultimately how the world would see who we are and therefore who He is. (See verse 35.)

A PICTURE OF UNCOMMON LOVE

Jesus's prayer, "*That the love with which you have loved me may be in them, and I in them*" (John 17:26) is a verse I had been meditating on for several years. God recently gave me a picture of what it really meant. I was in the Middle East visiting the headquarters of a prominent imam I had known for a long time. He always showed honor in such a beautiful way, but he apologized for not having a feast for me this time. His son had fallen and broken his neck and was on a ventilator in the hospital. He was paralyzed and almost lifeless.

I asked if I could pray for this man's son, and even though other imams were around, I had enough favor with him that he nodded his approval. So I prayed in the name of Jesus that his son would be healed. After we had some tea, I asked if we could go to the hospital. Again, he was gracious enough to allow me to do so—although I had to leave the rest of my team outside, and it was a little intimidating to be surrounded by two men with machine guns and a group of Muslim leaders at the hospital. But as I saw this young man lying there hooked up to a ventilator, I felt the Father's compassion for him. I was sure he was going to be healed. "Jesus," I thought, "if You heal him, leaders from all over the Arab world will hear about it, and You will be glorified." So I prayed again, declaring healing every way I knew how. And nothing happened.

The next day, I was in my hotel in a city about eight hours away, feeling very disappointed. I did not understand why God would miss such a good opportunity to show who He is. I was also missing my own son, Leif Emmanuel, because I had been away from home for a long time. As I was thinking about him, I could sense the Holy Spirit say, "Leif, why do you love with a hook? Why do you have to have an agenda?"

That hit me hard. And then I heard Him whisper, "Would you take your only son, Leif Emmanuel, and have him trade places with this imam's son so your son would be a vegetable for the rest of his life and this man's son would be healed and set free?"

At first, I rebuked such a thought. But it came back a second time, a third, and a fourth. I started to weep. "Father, I don't know how to love this way." A few moments later, waves and waves of love came over me. I just sat there overwhelmed, and I could feel myself being washed by this love.

About twenty minutes later, I talked to my coordinator, Marqus. He had gotten a phone call from my friend the imam, who was asking, "Where is Dr. Leif?"

"He's here right now," Marqus told him.

"No, no, I just saw him at my headquarters. He said he was going to the hospital. And I just called the hospital, and they said my son was well enough to be taken off the ventilator."

I was eight hours away, and I don't know how this man saw what he saw, but I broke down thinking about what God had done.

The Holy Spirit whispered again, "What you just experienced is like a small glass of water compared to what I am preparing to pour out." And He took me to that verse I had been meditating on: *"I made known to them your name, and I will continue to make it known, that the love with which you have loved me may be in them, and I in them."*

I thought I had gotten John 17:26, but that day, it got me. I realized how much the Father must have loved in order to give His only begotten Son, and also how much Jesus must have loved to leave the perfection of heaven and come to earth with a very clear purpose for us to be one, just as He and the Father and the Spirit are one.

The Father is going to create a wave of this kind of love around the world so people can see it in us—for each other and for the world. This is who we are, where we get our identity, where we become worshippers in spirit and in truth—Christ in us, the hope of glory, visible to the world. And this is how the world will know, just as Jesus said. His prayer in John 17 will be answered; in the book of Revelation, His people are there—a vast family representing every tribe, tongue, and nation, worshipping Him in unity.

The question for each of us is, "Will I be a part of the answer to Jesus's prayer?"

LIVING AS ONE IN A DIVIDED WORLD

In the spiritual realm, our unity is already a fact. We *are* one. But Christians have not always lived in the unity we are called to experience. The enemy has sown division not just in the world but also in the church.

I learned about division early in life. I was born in Norway to Christian parents, but my father was from an evangelical background and my mother was Pentecostal. In my hometown, we had three different soccer teams, and everyone was *for* one and *against* the others, an us-against-them mentality. Later, I learned as an evangelical that I could not get confirmed with all of my friends who were part of the state church. I was different, and our town divided over differences in many ways.

I went to a boarding school in 1983 and was introduced to Tamil refugees who had been persecuted by Sinhalese in Sri Lanka. In 1984, I found myself in a city in Northern Ireland that I would call Derry among my Catholic friends but Londonderry among my Protestant friends. My first experience with the Holy Spirit happened when a Catholic priest prayed for me in Waterford, Ireland, and I stayed with other priests in the rectory for six months. I later visited a very racially divided community in Selma, Alabama. I've been a youth pastor in a Presbyterian denomination that split off from another Presbyterian denomination. At Bible college, I experienced division between conservative Southern Baptists and more liberal Southern Baptists. I was in South Africa in 1994, the year apartheid officially ended, and I was friends with Serbs and Kosovar Albanians in the late 1990s, when tensions between them were at a peak. I have spent much of my ministry in places where Sunni and Shi'a Muslims are bitter adversaries and both are strongly opposed to Christians. Like most people, I have seen division throughout my life.

But after my baptism of love in 2000, I went from living in fear as an orphan to experiencing the Father's perfect love as a beloved son. And I realized then that part of my assignment was to be a minister of reconciliation—one of the answers to Jesus's prayer. On my journey of learning to love well, I realized that love is the language that blind eyes can see and deaf ears can hear. I have seen it bridge divisions between Christians and non-Christians—and recognized the power it can have between people who share faith in Jesus. When the world sees that kind of love among God's people, it pays attention.

I recently had an experience with an imam who had stirred up chaos and persecution against me and our ministry's spiritual family in the Middle East. I faced death on several occasions because he had falsely accused me of burning a Quran and blaspheming Prophet Muhammad. Because of him, we once had to cancel an event in which we had invested many resources and spent much time planning. He told me later that when we had once shaken hands, he went away and washed his hands because he had touched an infidel and been made unclean. I could easily have developed animosity toward this man. I was not feeling much love for my enemies.

One day, the Holy Spirit said, "Leif, why are you prejudiced against someone who is prejudiced?" I knew I was about to learn something in the school of Jesus. I needed to allow Jesus to wash my feet so I could be willing to wash this imam's feet.

I was soon given an opportunity to demonstrate uncommon love. I was in a meeting with many Muslim leaders in this country, many of whom were friends I had known for years, and I was one of the honorees. I was being commended by the grand imam who had authority over every leader there. As I looked around the room, I noticed the imam who had spread all of those false accusations that nearly got me killed. I could have seen this as a great opportunity to put him in his place and clear my reputation. But perfect love does not respond that way. When our unworthy feet have been washed by Jesus, we learn to see situations like that as an opportunity to serve and to bless.

The perfect love from the perfect family in heaven transforms us. It becomes part of us and then flows out from us. So when I had a face-to-face encounter with this man in a room full of Muslim leaders, we embraced without a word about anything that had happened in the past. Instead of shaking my hand and then quickly going away to wash his, we hugged. Love broke down the wall of division. He now considers me his brother.

WHAT TIME IS IT?

If love can break down walls of division in a context like that, it can unite people from different parts of the body of Christ. And when the world sees that unity among His followers, it starts to see the nature of God and the power of the gospel.

Someone recently asked me what was going on with all the conflict and tension in the world. I gave two answers: (1) the Father is answering the prayer of His Son, Jesus, that we may be one; and (2) the restoration of His family is the next major revival on earth. Thinking I misunderstood, this person described all the issues going on in the world today. I explained that I am aware of what the enemy is doing; he is a thief who "*comes only to steal and kill and destroy,*" but Jesus came to give abundant life (John 10:10). So if we are seeing the enemy repeatedly attacking the world in a particular way—in this case, attacking families and polarizing God's people—we can know that God is working in that area to bring abundant life. He is unifying the body of Christ and restoring His family.

The time for uncommon love and unity is now. I believe that the immune system of the body of Christ is going to be so healthy that the world will see how amazing God is and how loved they are. The goodness and kindness of God, demonstrated through His people, will lead to mass repentance. God does not want billions of orphans; He wants billions of sons and daughters. So even though we are seeing a lot of shaking, Christians and churches are being transformed—no longer operating as orphans and orphanages but becoming healthy kingdom families in which we find unity in our diversity.

I have been asking Papa God for years, "What do you most love about Catholics? About Baptists? About Anglicans, Methodists, Pentecostals...?" And when I think of each of these families and the value they are given at the larger family table, I become overwhelmed. I feel the same way when I ask that question about an individual. But when I ask the Father how He sees that person, I get a different picture. I begin to honor what God honors. This has been one of the most valuable lessons I have learned.

I founded Global Mission Awareness in 1999. We are a family of families who are on a mission to grow the kingdom family larger, deeper, and stronger. We have sons and daughters of glory becoming the answer to Jesus's final prayer in twenty-two countries. The highlights of my year are our family gatherings all over the world—in the U.S., Cuba, Pakistan, Malaysia, the Philippines, and other places where God is reaching people and unifying His body. At these gatherings, Charismatics, Pentecostals, Baptists, Methodists, Lutherans, Anglicans, Catholics, and others are all finding a place at the larger family table. They are finding their identity not in doctrines or denominations but in being sons and daughters of the Father and deeply loving Him and each other.

They are living from their inheritance in the kingdom rather than living for it.

They are celebrating one another rather than tolerating one another.

They complete each other rather than compete with each other.

They each bring a "special sauce" to the family table.

It's not a perfect fellowship, but it's beautiful.

My wife and I have been married for more than three decades—a Norwegian Viking and a Cherokee Indian have become one. Jennifer and I come from different countries, grew up in different denominations, and have different backgrounds and traditions. Our four children and their spouses represent different interests, political views, and races. We're a colorful family in many ways. But when we gather as a family, no one would be able to identify our doctrinal differences or tell the Republicans from the Democrats. We may disagree, but we love each other, cover each other, and protect each other. If one of us is attacked, all of us are attacked. We are one.

This is what is taking place at a greater level in the body of Christ. Our ministry works with other ministries and many other "family" gatherings. Divisions in many parts of the body of Christ are being healed. The challenges Christians face have made many realize that we must face them together. Jesus's prayer is being answered—and will continue to be answered until that scene around the throne in Revelation is complete. And every one of us has the opportunity to be part of that answer before it is finally fulfilled in the fullness of His kingdom.

A LOVE LETTER TO THE SOUTHERN BAPTIST CHURCH

My journey with you began in 1985, when I first stayed in the home of a Southern Baptist family. I still remember your southern hospitality, the way you opened up your home, your faithfulness to the Word of God, and your impact in my life.

A few years after that first experience, I was leading a Christian theater group called Covenant Players at Edgewood Baptist Church in Columbus, Georgia. When we performed one night in 1988, I met a beautiful young Southern Baptist, Jennifer Hildebrand. A year later, we got married in the very conservative church where her father was a Southern Baptist pastor. I am very grateful for my time in that church. They taught me about the importance of God's Word. I learned to find security in my salvation, and I learned spiritual disciplines.

During that time, I met Stephen Olford, a powerful preacher who had prayed for Billy Graham when he had an encounter with the Holy Spirit. Dr. Olford said, "Young man, you have a calling to preach." I had been trying to decide whether I should go into ministry or be a lawyer, but I followed that calling to preach, went to a Baptist college and seminary, was ordained, and spent seven years in Baptist ministry. Though that time ended in a painful separation from the church where I served, my love and honor are still there. I am so grateful for everything I received from Southern Baptists, for the friends who influenced me, and for the Word of God that shaped me. And every time I drive by a Southern Baptist church, I release a blessing.

I also want to honor my Southern Baptist family for the way you steward missions—your dedication to world evangelism and discipleship. The mission virus I have today is very much connected to the fire of missions burning in the hearts of so many faithful Southern Baptists. I still remember the two major missions offerings each year, where people make sacrifices so that the least, the last, and the lost would receive the good news. It is still a part of my life and the culture of our Kingdom Family Movement to love the world that God loves so much.

All of our family of families on a mission, and the one million names added to the Lamb's book of life through our family, have been impacted by the gift you gave me. I celebrate the Southern Baptist family of families as a gift to the rest of the body of Christ, and my years as a part of your community continue to shape me.

My prayer is that you will continue to grow Great Commission churches with great commandment hearts. I am praying for uncommon unity within the Southern Baptist Convention—for there to be a fresh baptism of love so every one of your members will be known for the way they love one another. My prayer is that you would continue to seek first God's kingdom and His righteousness so that all of these other things will be added to you.

—Dr. Leif Hetland

Dr. Leif Hetland is president of Global Mission Awareness, based in Atlanta, Georgia, USA. Connect with him at leifhetland.com.

19

WALKING TOGETHER TO BECOME ONE

Archbishop Christopher Prowse
| Catholic |

The fervent prayer of Jesus at the Last Supper is yet to be fulfilled. Jesus prayed: "*That they may all be one, just as you, Father, are in me, and I in you*" (John 17:21). When I pray this profound petition of Jesus, I think of the continuing divisions among Christians in the world. Christian unity is a priority still aching to be realized today. Yet there are many positive signs that the Holy Spirit is with us on this long journey toward unity.

THE SCANDAL OF DISUNITY AND THE POWER OF THE HOLY SPIRIT TO UNITE US

The fact that we have become so familiar with the divisions among the Christian churches is surely part of the problem. Sometimes we need others to place a mirror in front of us all and remind us of the scandal of disunity.

I recall some years ago, ministering in a local parish, when a young Chinese student began attending inquiry sessions for those interested in the Catholic Church. She asked quite innocently at one of these sessions, "If Jesus is the one God, why are there so many different Christian churches?" We needed someone from a very non-Christian cultural background to remind us of this scandal. Our cultural setting had blinded us to this obstacle to true evangelization.

My own personal pilgrimage toward Christian unity began when I was a small boy. Our next-door neighbors were Presbyterian. All my family and friends up until then were Catholics. Indeed, it never occurred to me at this stage of my life that others were not Catholic. Was not everyone in the world

Catholic? Yet when one of our neighbors' children was to be married, our family was invited. My mother seemed reluctant to accept the kind invitation. I could not understand why.

I recall her having a serious phone conversation with someone about the matter. She had phoned the cathedral to ask for advice; she was told, "You can attend but stay at the back of the church and do not actively participate." Therefore, we all went. It was the first time I had entered a non-Catholic church. It seemed so different; the liturgy and hymns were strange to me. We all lived so happily in the one neighborhood. Why were our expressions of Christian belief so diverse? Even a young boy can unreflectively sense the historic burden of Christian disunity.

A major personal step in my ecumenical pilgrimage happened soon after I joined the seminary. Up until this time, my life's contacts had been almost entirely Catholic—Catholic family, Catholic school, Catholic parish, Catholic friends, and now Catholic seminary.

Yet something wonderful happened in my first long Christmas break from the seminary. We were all encouraged to find some employment over the three-month period, so I sold alcohol at the nearby hotel drive-in. And in the midst of this abundance of alcoholic spirits, I personally experienced a fresh outpouring of the Holy Spirit!

One of my coworkers was a married man who had lapsed in his attendance at his Pentecostal church. We often shared lunch together. He seemed intrigued once he realized I was a Catholic training to be a priest. He had little to do with Catholics in his life, and I had even less to do with Pentecostals. Yet we both enjoyed talking about religious topics. I noted that he talked much about the role of the Holy Spirit. Until then, my own experience of the Holy Spirit was more academic. In comparison to him, my personal experience was remote. I seemed to have forgotten about the Third Person of the Holy Trinity.

Such remoteness was about to change.

After a time, he confided in me that our conversations had raised his desire to return to his church. He was tentative about doing this. As a sign of support, he asked me to accompany him on his first return after many years. I answered affirmatively. However, I had never entered a Pentecostal church and did not know what to expect. Nonetheless, I was keen to support him on his first day back.

The hot Sunday afternoon arrived. We gathered outside his church and entered together. First, it did not look like a church to me; it seemed more like a concert hall. The place was full of young people, and I was used to a more senior demographic. The songs were vibrant and emotional, with music provided by a loud band rather than an organ. The people seemed to be very excited, with hands clapping and extended. Bodies were swaying, and people were yelling out in unrecognizable tones.

I was quite shocked. It was all new to me. I thought I was going to church, not a pop concert! My coworker could see I was frightened, so he tried to reassure me. He too was anxious in returning after so many years of absence. Yet a few people seemed to recognize him, and we were both ushered up to the front. My strong preference was to remain discretely at the back. However, this was not an option.

A long sermon was delivered. It really startled me when I heard the preacher make some comments that were anti-Catholic, especially toward the pope. I wanted out but needed to endure the entire service. Later on, we were both invited to a small group of about twelve people. This was more refined and less confronting. Indeed, the atmosphere was prayerful, and the people truly loving. We shared a common meal together and then group prayer started. I felt at peace at last.

As we were both new to the group, we were invited to introduce ourselves. My coworker spoke of his homecoming to the congregation. They offered him such a nonjudgmental welcome back. I started to feel anxious again. What was I to say? I simply stated the facts that I was a committed Catholic who was present to support my friend on his return to his church. They thanked me for this. I expected to be the object of some type of proselytism but this did not happen.

Rather, toward the end of the evening, they asked me if I wished to be prayed over. No one in my life to that date had asked me such a question. From observing others, I could see that this was simply a matter of going into the center of the little circle. Then people would place their hands on my shoulder and ask God's blessing. It all seemed rather harmless. I accepted their gentle invitation.

Then the pastor asked me an extraordinary question: "Have you accepted Jesus Christ into your heart as your personal Lord and Savior?" No one had ever asked me this. To formulate an answer seemed impossible. I heard myself saying, "Of course, I am a Catholic!" He smiled and then started leading the others in prayer for me.

I cannot remember what was said, but I do remember feeling very much at peace. I was humbled that strangers were taking the time to pray earnestly for me. The evening concluded joyously. I never returned to this Pentecostal church.

SPIRITUAL ECUMENISM

When I returned to the seminary in 1973, my prayer times seemed different. A hidden treasure awaited me. The thirst for prayer had heightened. The Scriptures seemed as if they were written for me personally, especially the Acts of the Apostles. The reception of the sacraments, especially the Eucharist, were a real delight. In addition, I seemed to have a new language to praise Jesus like never before. I really felt the love of Jesus personally for me as Lord and Savior. My theological studies became more of an adventure than a burden. Without explicitly being able to define it at the time, I had received the baptism of the Holy Spirit.

Another surprise of the Holy Spirit awaited me. I tentatively shared my experience with some of my friends. Would they consider that I had apostatized from the Catholic Church? On the contrary, they told me about the charismatic renewal in the church, something I had never heard of before. They took me to a few of these prayer gatherings, which were similar to those in the Pentecostal church but far more sedate and disciplined—a true Catholic version! Nonetheless, an ecumenical dimension was truly present.

So a few of us started a little prayer meeting in the seminary. We met every Sunday evening in the seminary chapel. This continued for several years, and I always looked forward to it. The seminary staff were intrigued by our weekly prayer gatherings. At first, they were suspicious at what was happening. Although they seemed to just tolerate our presence, they never dissuaded us from gathering. Ecumenical dialogue was encouraged but this was something more than simply academic sharing. It was a conversion experience deeper into the life of Jesus. In my case, it was initiated by a Pentecostal pastor rather than guided by a Catholic spiritual director! The spiritual power of the Holy Spirit and the personal sharing of Jesus alive in the Scriptures attracted many to join this prayer meeting over those years. This group did attract several from various Christian churches as well. Indeed, it was a time when our yearning for inner conversion and renewal was communal rather than individual. It was a kind of prayer for Christian unity from a "heart speaking to heart" posture, using the motto of Saint John Henry Newman (1801–1890). At times, it seemed we were in the cenacle of the apostles. We awaited together a type of new Pentecost.

Sometimes, I reflect that I may not have continued in the seminary unless this renewal of my baptism and confirmation had affirmed me in the vocation of becoming a Catholic priest. It was a kerygmatic grace of the Holy Spirit for me. It was also a grace that this encounter experience happened after a few years of Catholic theological education. It enabled me to be confident in my Catholic faith and not to be too attracted to the allure of Pentecostalism. Some years ago, I came across the following surrender prayer of the late Pope Francis:

"Lord, I have let myself be deceived. In a thousand ways I have shunned Your love. Yet here I am once more, to renew more covenant with You. I need You. Save me once again, Lord. Take me once more into Your redeeming embrace."

This verbalized closely for me my prayer in these years. May you too be blessed by it.

Yet another expression of spiritual ecumenism occurred simultaneously. The seminary, located close to a major secular university, invited seminarians to participate in studies there while still residents in the seminary. So for three years, in addition to my seminary studies, I took classes at the university and also joined the Evangelical Union, an ecumenical students' group. We gathered for prayer, talks, and practical charity. It was a great blessing for me. I still keep in contact with some of the new friends I made in this group; they became friends for life.

The leadership of this student group at that time were mainly Baptists, who truly impressed me as committed Christians. They taught me how to be fluent and comfortable with spontaneous prayer to Jesus. There were other Catholics in this rather large ecumenical group. None of us were concerned about carrying the historical burden of Christian disunity. Australian egalitarianism and the new but ancient culture of Australia would not permit this. Our eyes were focused on Jesus. It was a spiritual ecumenism of friendship.

The ancient practice of praying with the Scriptures, especially the Gospels and Psalms, continued on here in this young ecumenical demographic. Prayers of intercession for global, Australian, and personal realities featured prominently in our sessions together. The teaching inputs from speakers representing various Christian denominations varied in quality. I was so grateful to have already learned much from my Catholic theological studies, which helped me to objectively assess what I heard.

Of course, being the only Catholic seminarian in this group was a cause of considerable interest from the other members. After establishing friendly relationships, they were very keen to ask all sorts of questions about the Catholic Church. There was much to discuss! Over the years, I invited quite a few people to join the seminary community for meals and events. Many accepted the invitation, albeit after initial trepidation. I was amazed how much ignorance or bias there was against the Catholic Church. However, a meal together with the seminary community was, unwittingly, a great ecumenical gesture to dispel myths and bring about unity through friendships. When I left the seminary, I was delighted that a few from the Evangelical Union joined us on the day of my ordination to the priesthood. Together, we had been on quite an ecumenical journey in our youthful years.

ECUMENISM OF LOVE AND TRUTH

My ecumenical life pilgrimage continued after my ordination to the priesthood. Now I was immersed in parish life. Every day was filled with a huge variety of pastoral experiences. Many of these provided occasions for ecumenical unity. For example, I was called to assist in the preparations of many marriages between a Catholic and a person from another Christian denomination. Here the challenge was to begin with our common baptism and explore the implications for their lives together. What do your parents think about this marriage with a person of another denomination? How will you continue to live out your particular church life when your spouse does not share this commonality? If children arrive, into what denomination will they be baptized? I found the couples were generally more concerned with immediate, practical issues, such as the wedding ceremony. The couples would acknowledge that such questions were significant, but they seemed in the future and remote to the present. Altogether, it was quite a pastoral challenge.

The initiation of people into communion with the Catholic Church was always another ecumenical challenge. Becoming a Catholic involves a period of inquiry and rites of liturgical passage based on our ancient practices. On the one hand, proposing and not imposing the Catholic faith on others is a delicate task. Catholics are not proselytizers. On the other hand, there are a surprising number of people who are genuinely attracted to our theological teachings, who wish to become one in the faith of their spouse and children or are searching for deeper meaning and purpose in life. The Holy Spirit "*blows where it wishes*" (John 3:8)! Having stated this, one of the housekeepers in a presbytery I resided in for some years was a strong defender of all things Catholics but remained a staunch Anglican!

In parishes in general, there was the general intention to join in the ecumenical tasks of joint Week for Christian Unity prayer vigils, study weeks during high liturgical seasons, and joining together to protest legislation antithetical to our shared Christian mores. However, the response from parish to parish was rather piecemeal. It seemed largely dependent on the friendship between the relevant parish priest and the local pastors. The Anglican based Alpha courses, however, have generally been well received as a joint ecumenical outreach over the years. Its simple format of informal meal, inspirational input, and question and answer session seem to offer a persuasive expression of evangelization.

For several years, I had the privilege of participating in a formal theological, ecumenical dialogue on holiness that involved Australian Anglicans and Roman Catholics. The discussions were conducted in a formal and systematic manner. Scriptural, theological, historical, and pastoral dimensions were carefully considered. The *language* of this ecumenism of truth was synodal. We walked together with great respect for commonalities and divergences in our respective traditions. Intentional listening and locating the gift of the Holy Spirit in our common search for truth is time-consuming and hard work. At mealtimes, we relaxed with each other and talked through issues informally. Our liturgical shared times and ritual silences were essential but could be painful. The pain of disunity was expressed in our inability to share holy Communion all together. Even this indicated that the synodal journey toward unity requires much patience and repentance. The hope was always there that we were not wasting time but waiting for the impulse of the grace of unity that only the Holy Spirit can bring in the fullness of time. Eventually, a joint statement on holiness was published. This was a point of arrival and yet a point of departure in our ecumenism of seeking the fullness of truth, found only in Jesus.

A sense that Catholics and Lutherans had reached a point of historic agreement after centuries of discord came about in 1998 with the publication of the *Joint Declaration on the Doctrine of Justification*. I was involved in several anniversary celebrations around Australia in the subsequent years. What a landmark moment of the Holy Spirit it was to now have "a consensus in basic truths of the doctrine of justification." Although divergences remain, great encouragement was given to Catholics and the Lutheran World Federation to continue on this unity road to truth regarding justification. The fact that an Australian Catholic, Cardinal Edward Idris Cassidy (1924–2021), then president of the Pontifical Council for Promoting Christian Unity, was among those responsible for the declaration gave us Australians extra joy. The cardinal sometimes joked that this signing was one thing he could confidently cite on his behalf on judgment day. To add to our joy was the subsequent signing of this declaration by the World Methodist Council in 2006 and the World Communion of Reformed Churches in 2017.

ECUMENISM OF LIFE

I was ordained a bishop in 2003. As a result, I was offered several wonderful opportunities to advance Christian unity in a variety of international gatherings. First, there was my appointment to the Pontifical Council for Interreligious Dialogue. Sometimes I was called upon to represent all Christians at interfaith forums. This was new for me. What a grace! It was ecumenism walking with interfaith dialogue. Once I served on a panel with representatives from Judaism, Islam, and Buddhism—just the four of us in front of a large crowd. It was not a formal philosophical symposium, simply a forum whereby the importance of religious belief could be showcased in a world of unbelief. We shared stories about faith and living life fully. I suppose this was an ecumenism of life.

I recall the beautiful story shared by the Jewish representative, who quoted from an ancient text. In the story, a Jewish teacher asks his students how they can tell when the night is over and the dawn has arrived. One student suggests it is when you can look out and a person can be distinguished from a dog. Another suggests it is when you can look out and distinguish the difference between a house and a tree. However, this Jewish theologian told the crowd and the rest of us on the panel that one can tell when dawn has arrived when one can look into the eyes of another and say, "You are my brother; you are my sister." Upon receiving such universal wisdom, a certain silence came over us. We had all been fed internally.

I also served on the International Anglican-Roman Catholic Commission for Unity and Mission (IARCCUM). The idea is that pairs of bishops from many countries—one Anglican and one Catholic—would meet with others from around the world and then plan for joint regional expressions of practical charity and outreach. There was an unforgettable international gathering of such pairs. We met for one week in Canterbury, England, and then one week in Rome, Italy. The then-archbishop of Canterbury, Justin Welby, was our host in England. After one meal with us, he spoke spontaneously to us for some time. It was such an incredible speech about Christian unity and its importance. When we were in Rome, Pope Francis led an ecumenical vigil with Archbishop Welby for us. How humbling it was to be commissioned to return to our own countries to live out practically an ecumenism of life close to the poor.

In one of the small groups of the conference, I observed that, on the one hand, in the big cities of Australia, ecumenism seemed to specialize in the gathering of small groups for prayer or study. I observed that there was a satisfactory knowledge of church ecumenical documents. Friendships were rather formal and interactions between gatherings somewhat rare. On the other hand, since becoming a bishop of a largely rural archdiocese, I observed that in remote rural townships, ecumenical friendships were plenty, but knowledge of church documents was rare. Practical Australians seemed to know everyone in the town, and they came together frequently. Most especially, they worked as one in times of calamity—bushfires, floods, and droughts. In these life-or-death situations, ecumenism was so strong. Churches, halls, and homes were all common property in the times of emergencies.

I shared with the group one of most touching expressions of this ecumenism of life that I had witnessed as a bishop. I went to visit a very remote, rural parish. The parish priest was elderly, arthritic, and somewhat in a panic with my visit. When I arrived and entered his home, the local Anglican parish priest was on his knees helping the seated Catholic priest to put on his socks and shoes in preparation for my visit. To me, this was the one of the best examples of lived ecumenism I had witnessed.

The verse from the high priestly prayer of the Lord Jesus to His Father, "*That they may all be one*" (John 17:21) takes on many expressions. Some expressions are doctrinal, some liturgical, and some practical. Surely, from the point of view of the ecumenism of life, this humble gesture of good will by the Anglican priest to his brother Catholic priest is a symbol that at some level, the Lord's Last Supper plea has been answered.

MY DEAR PENTECOSTAL BROTHERS AND SISTERS...

I thank the Lord Jesus for this opportunity to thank you all so much for awakening the kerygmatic dimension of Christianity into my heart. When one of your leaders asked me at an impressionable moment in my life, "Have you accepted Jesus Christ into your heart as your personal Lord and Savior?" I really did not understand what you were asking. Now I do. Indeed, it is a question, albeit rephrased somewhat, that I frequently ask others. You have been used by the Holy Spirit to awaken the deafness in my spiritual life. It is a gift; please God in His mercy that I will carry into eternity.

Please forgive me for the times I have wrongly judged you or dismissed your joyful exuberance in the Lord as superficial. After carefully praying over the Acts of the Apostles many times over the years, I believe such joy and praise are true signs of the presence of the Holy Spirit. My own narrowness was a sign of something other than the Holy Spirit. Thank you for your forgiveness.

Since my ordination to the priesthood forty-five years ago, I have seen much coming together of the Pentecostal and Catholic churches around the world. The charismatic renewal movements throughout the centuries are seen as times of visitations of the Holy Spirit inviting us all to conversion and unity in our Christian lives. Pentecost lives on! It is not simply a noun but a vibrant verb in our shared Christian life. Jesus is leading us always to the Father through the Holy Spirit. We seem to be in the middle of a new outflowing of the Spirit, blowing where God wishes.

In 2017, I participated with thousands of people from around the world at an international gathering in Rome to celebrate fifty years of Catholic Charismatic Renewal. I found it incredible, given our past fractured relationships, to observe Catholic and Pentecostal leaders coming together in this prayer gathering at the Circus Maximus. Just a few years ago, I was invited to an Australian biblical college that trains future Pentecostal pastors to give an address on the history of the sacrament of reconciliation, also known as confession, in the Catholic tradition. That was a true sign of the Holy Spirit. More recently, I accepted an invitation to give the homily/talk at a Pentecostal church in my archdiocese.

All of this proves the truth of Colossians 3:11: "*Christ is all, and in all.*"

Archbishop Christopher Prowse

Christopher Prowse is the Catholic archbishop of Canberra and Goulburn, Australia. Connect with Archbishop Prowse at cgcatholic.org.au.

20

THE GOSPEL OF JESUS CHRIST UNITES US

Prof. Timothy George
| Southern Baptist |

I was born in Chattanooga, Tennessee, on January 9, 1950. My father was an alcoholic; my mother had polio. Neither was able to care for me or my sister, Lynda, who was two years younger. She was brought up in a Baptist children's home whereas I was left to be reared by two of my great-aunts on my father's side, Aunt Mary and Aunt Hattie, wonderful women who loved me and nurtured me during my earliest years, through at least the first grade.

Aunt Mary was a Baptist. She took me to the Boulevard Baptist Church in Chattanooga. There I received my early Christian religious training. My paternal grandmother also had a great influence on me, though she lived a little distance from Chattanooga. I would spend the summer months with her and visiting her country church, Mount Pisgah Baptist Church, near Ringgold, Georgia. My early days were very rural. Even though we were in inner city Chattanooga, the people in that church had all grown up in the country, and they still smelled like the country, they worshipped like the country, and so it was a little bit of the urban-rural mix.

Growing up in the American South, I was nurtured in a community of faith that was part of the one, holy, catholic, and apostolic church, but had no idea that this was so. I never heard those words used to describe the church. We were separatist, biblicist, and baptistic. We were also dogmatic, but in a very bad sense of that word—quarrelsome, self-assertive, and guilty of the two major diseases that afflict the church today: amnesia and myopia. I remember hearing a number of very bad jokes about "ecumaniacs" and the need to avoid them at all costs. That was the background I brought to the study of theology as a young student. It began very early for me, even though I came from a family that was, in every sense of the word, on the margins of respectable society.

Growing up as a Baptist in the American South (though not yet a Southern Baptist), I was an evangelical without being aware of it. As a teen-age youth evangelist, I greatly admired Billy Graham and also had personal contact with figures such as Stuart Briscoe, Major Ian Thomas, and Robert G. Lee, a Baptist icon known for his pulpit oratory who had also been present at the inaugural meeting of the National Association of Evangelicals in 1942. But it was Francis Schaeffer, more than anyone else, who really introduced me to the broader evangelical family outside my own Baptist briar patch. As a student in college, I devoured Schaeffer's early books on apologetics. He showed me how the Christian faith could engage with art, music, competing worldviews, and diverse religious thought.

We lived in a Chattanooga neighborhood that was already racially integrated in the 1950s. It was integrated not because we were social liberals trying to make a political statement, but simply because we could not afford to live anywhere else. There was a small Unitarian church in my neighborhood, and I recall stopping by there one day to challenge the minister as to why he did not baptize in the name of the Father, the Son, and the Holy Spirit, as we did in my church and the Bible says one should. I recall being surprised to discover that not only did he not baptize in the name of the Holy Trinity, he did not baptize at all. This was a strange kind of church! There was also a Roman Catholic church in my town, and I remember calling the priest one day to ask why the Roman Catholics held such unbiblical teachings about purgatory, Mary, and the Mass.

For some reason, those kinds of questions were percolating in my mind at that very early age. But it was really through my great uncle, Willie Nash, who lived next door to me in that same little community, that I first learned to become a theologian. Uncle Willy was a convert to Mormonism. His life's mission was to convert me to becoming a Mormon. I, of course, wanted him to become a Baptist. We both failed in our projects but in the process, I became a theologian. He brought the missionaries from his church to give me religious instruction. Uncle Willy and I talked about all kinds of things—golden plates, marriage in the Mormon temple, the celestial underwear, baptism for the dead, and where the Baptist church came from. We discussed those issues at great length. I scoured the Bible for deeper answers and also read the Book of Mormon.

I was called to preach in 1961. I began to preach because I came out of a tradition that said if God called you, you do what He asks you to do. I started to preach in youth meetings and youth revivals. I became a youth evangelist and preached widely throughout the Southeastern United States, Tennessee, North Georgia, North Carolina, and Alabama. As I was serving as a youth evangelist, one of my mentors, a wonderful pastor named Sam Sharp, said to me, "Timothy, you need to really invest your life with Southern Baptists." He sold me on being a Southern Baptist. Several years later, I was ordained at Brainerd Baptist Church in Chattanooga, a mainstream, Bible-believing, conservative Southern Baptist Church.

My real entre into *ecumenicaldom* began during the seven years I spent at Harvard Divinity School. I did not go there to break away from my past or sever the ties I had to southern evangelicalism. I went there to learn, to grow, and to be open to what God was doing in my life. I learned a lot there about the wider body of Christ outside the South and outside the Baptist family. Several of my Harvard professors introduced me to the wider Christian world: John E. Booty, an Anglican church historian; Krister Stendahl, our dean and sometime bishop of Stockholm, who introduced me to Lutheran liturgy; Heiko Oberman and David Steinmetz, both of whom were visiting professors at Harvard in my day; and, above all, my major professor, George Huntston Williams.

Williams is best remembered for his magnum opus, *The Radical Reformation*, but that great book represented only one small sliver of his church historical expertise. A medievalist with a deep knowledge of the patristic tradition, East and West, he wrote about Celtic monasticism, New England puritanism, majority world Pentecostalism, and much more. A fourth-generation Unitarian who nonetheless steadfastly affirmed the doctrine of the holy Trinity, Williams had been an observer at all four sessions of the Second Vatican Council. There, he met and developed a fast friendship with a young Catholic bishop of Krakow, Karol Woytwa, and in 1982 published one of the first books in English about the new pope, *The Mind of John Paul II*. From Williams, Oberman, and others, I came to appreciate what Jaroslav Pelikan once called "the tragic necessity of the Reformation." Both aspects are important for ecumenism—the necessity of reform and the tragedy of scandalous division—as we continue to groan for the fulfillment of Jesus's prayer that His disciples would be one, as He and the Father are One, *"so that the world may believe"* (John 17:21).

It was in New England that I really became aware of Christian traditions outside my own little bailiwick. As much as I came to deeply love and appreciate my own Baptist and Reformed Baptist roots, I also came to recognize that God had been active with Free Methodists, Nazarenes, Lutherans, and Anglicans. In the early 1990s, I became involved with Evangelicals and Catholics Together (ECT) as a result of this awareness of the wider body of Christ as well as my own immersion in Reformation theology. The Reformers never intended to start a new church. They wanted to reform the one, holy, catholic church. There were Catholics, even if they could not remain *Roman* Catholic.

Elsewhere, I have proposed a "hierarchy of ecclesial realities." What do I mean by this? While I recognize myself as a Protestant, an Evangelical, and a Baptist, none of those labels defines my spiritual and ecclesial identity at the most basic level. Being an evangelical Protestant, a Baptist, indeed a Southern Baptist are all important markers of my place within the community of faith, but there is a more primary confession I must make: I am a trinitarian Christian who by the grace of God belongs to the whole company of the redeemed through the ages, those who are "very members incorporate in the mystical body of Christ" as noted in the *Book of Common Prayer.*

PROTESTANT

Tragic necessity of the Reformation. It is not hard to find champions of the one side of this antinomy or the other. The tragic side of the Reformation is obvious to those who care deeply about the unity of the church and also feel keenly the dire evangelistic impact of a fractured Christian community and its muted, broken witness. But the necessity of the Reformation is also evident to those who hear in the teaching of Martin Luther, Huldrych Zwingli, John Calvin, and Thomas Cranmer the good news of God's grace, unfettered grace in the doctrine of justification by faith alone—and who rejoice in the recovery of Bible-based proclamation at the heart of the church's worship.

So if we cannot quite say with the great Philip Schaff that the Protestant Reformation was the greatest event in history of the church since the day of Pentecost, can we nonetheless give thanks for the springs of spiritual and ecclesial renewal unearthed in the great upheaval of the sixteenth century? In some ecumenical initiatives, it is tempting to bypass the Reformation altogether, to get back to the early church to reclaim the common patrimony of all Christians in the fathers and mothers of the church of the first centuries. However, this approach ignores the fact that the Reformation was itself an age of great patristic ressourcement. In that new age of printing, we get the first critical editions of the Bible as well as the first critical editions of the church fathers. But overlooking the Reformation in ecumenical discussions is a luxury we Christians in the West cannot afford. It reflects the same reductionist impulse of those biblicistic Christians who transmute the principle of *sola scriptura* (by Scripture alone) into *nuda scriptura* (bare Scripture) and read the Bible as though the councils of Nicaea, Ephesus, or Chalcedon never happened—no creed but the Bible.

EVANGELICAL

While the patristic and Reformational roots of evangelicalism are more often assumed than explicitly acknowledged, the spiritual awakenings of the eighteenth and nineteenth centuries produced many of the forms and modalities of evangelicalism that we still recognize today. The awakenings were international, interdenominational, transatlantic movements of ecclesial and spiritual renewal embracing pietism in Germany, Methodism in Great Britain, and revivalism in the American colonies. A new kind of interdenominational cooperation arose based on a distinctively evangelical version of mere Christianity. Without ever denying the doctrinal fundaments of the wider catholic and Reformational heritage, evangelicals put primary emphasis on the preaching of the gospel and the call to personal conversion.

BAPTIST

So why am I a Baptist? I am a Baptist because it was through the witness of a small Baptist church that I first heard the gospel of Jesus Christ. Many of the things I still believe in I first learned in that modest Baptist community of faith: that Jesus loves me and died on the cross for my sins; that the Bible is the totally true and trustworthy Word of God; that all human beings are made in the image of God and are infinitely precious in His sight. Through the loving nurture I received from that small Baptist congregation, I confessed my personal faith in Jesus as Savior and Lord of my life. I was then baptized by immersion in the name of the Father, the Son, and the Holy Spirit. When I was called to preach the gospel, it was in a Baptist church that I was set apart and ordained as a minister of the divine Word.

It is important to say that all of this came to me as a gift from beyond myself. It is not as though I had studied carefully and weighed objectively every religious possibility before committing myself to the Baptist cause. My experience was rather of a person who finds himself standing, wading, and eventually swimming in a flowing mountain stream. The Baptist formation I received as a young Christian was a gift, unbidden and undeserved, for which I can claim no credit. Later as I studied the Bible more deeply and became aware of many other church traditions, doctrines, and denominations, my Baptist convictions grew stronger. I gradually came to understand the meaning of what I believed: *Fides quaerens intellectum* (Faith seeking understanding), a quest that continues still. What I first intuitively grasped or only dimly glimpsed I came to own with greater clarity and confidence. I came to see that being a Baptist was for me the most faithful way of being an Evangelical, a Protestant, and a Christian.

Being a Baptist is a blessing but also sometimes a burden. From time to time, I have considered the possibility of becoming something else. I once prepared a talk called "The Confessions of a Catholic-Friendly, Pentecostal-Admiring, Reformed Baptist with a Hankering After Lutheranism and a Strong Affinity for the *Book of Common Prayer*." Each of these ecclesial traditions, among others, has enriched my life and calling to serve the body of Christ. Each brings distinctive treasures to our common labors *pro Christo et ecclesia* (for Christ and the church). Being a Baptist gives me all the freedom I need to appropriate as fully as I can the gifts they offer without abandoning the Baptist principles and ways that I cherish.

There is a strand in Baptist life that celebrates fences while neglecting foundations. Now I am all in favor of Baptist distinctives such as believers' baptism, congregational church governance, separation of church and state, and so on, but I would like to see a stronger emphasis on the basics—the Bible, the Trinity, and salvation by grace. It is possible to believe strongly in the separation of church and state while denying biblical miracles such as virgin birth of Jesus, and even putting a question mark around the bodily resurrection of Jesus. Fences have their place, but without a solid foundation, the fences will not long endure.

I believe in an ecumenism of conviction, not an ecumenism of accommodation. We do not advance the cause of Christian unity by abandoning our biblical understanding of the church. But how do we hold these together? First, we recognize the centrality of Jesus Christ. The closer we come to Jesus Christ, the closer we come to one another as brothers and sisters in Him. Second, we study the Bible together. The Bible belongs to the whole people of

God, not just to one denomination or church tradition. We can clarify differences and find a deeper unity by going deeper into the Scriptures. Third, we pray. Jesus prayed to His heavenly Father that His disciples would be one so that the world might believe. We can join our prayer to the prayer of Jesus and in so doing become a part of its fulfillment.

MY DEAR BROTHERS AND SISTERS IN CHRIST,

The way to true unity is always focused on the gospel of Jesus Christ. This is where we begin. This is where we take our stand. This we cannot negotiate. This we cannot compromise. It is a gospel that leads to and produces and brings a unity in Christ. Now, this must be accompanied by love—the type of love stressed in 1 Corinthians 13. It's not just human love; it's the love that comes from Christ. It is only by Christ, the undivided Christ, that I have come to know Jesus, that I have come to have eternal life, that I have come to share a fellowship with brothers and sisters.

Wouldn't it be wonderful if instead of only talking about the church of the undivided Christ, we could talk about the Christ of the undivided church? We're not there yet, but in the meantime, we can remember what Paul is saying to the Corinthians and is saying to us, "The way to unity is the way of the gospel. It is the way of love. It is the way of grace, an amazing grace." We do not get there by compromising our purity, our integrity, our diversity. We get there through our appreciation of the grace of unity made possible by the One who purchased our redemption with His own blood on the cross.

To close, I wish to humbly bless each of you in Christ to receive a renewed yearning in your heart for the same oneness Jesus prayed for so earnestly before His death. May God's light dawn afresh and lead you to experience the colorful richness of your unmet fellow believers along the glorious path of unity as we prepare the bride to be presented without spot, without wrinkle, on that great day.

—Dr. Timothy George

Timothy George is the founding dean of Beeson Divinity School at Samford University, where he is a distinguished professor of divinity. Connect with him at www.samford.edu/beeson-divinity.

21

CHURCH: DENOMINATIONAL BRAND OR JESUS MOVEMENT?

Bishop Todd Hunter
| Anglican |

Some people take church branding very seriously. Not my long-time friend and colleague, Barry Crane, who recognizes that church unity—and the effective mission that flows from it—cannot be achieved by making denominational loyalty a first-order issue. Barry is appropriately committed to his tribe, *Converge*, formerly known as the Baptist General Conference, but his eye is always on the prize of the will of God that transcends all things.

Barry is a long-time resident of the Seattle area and pastor of North Sound Church in Edmonds, Washington. Barry and North Sound see the core of ministry through the lens of Jesus's announcement of the final inbreaking of God's kingdom, not brands of churches. Barry loves and respects denominations but sees them as penultimate. For Barry, the ultimate thing is God and His kingdom and the followers of Jesus who are formed by and comprise the people of the kingdom. The mission of North Sound is to "extend the kingdom of God by making mature disciples of Jesus Christ in the context of a life-transforming community."

Contrariwise, denominationalism has to do with labeling, naming, and classifying. The impulse underneath denominationalism is to categorize people not by what they hold in common with others, but by distinctives. This then gives us the ability to insist on difference. Denominations separate from others over theological disputes, practices of worship, personality driven fights, ethnic divisions, language barriers, economic classes, and more.

Labeling others gives us a sense of power or control. It facilitates the protection of a brand.

Within our habit of noting difference and particularity, we do well to keep in mind the whole. For instance, all coins and bills are *currency*. In the same manner, *church* is fundamental, more whole and unifying than denominational branding. Church can never be reduced to denominational branding that creates religious consumer choices.

The church, created by the rule and reign of God, is huge and whole and fitted for God's global, cosmic purposes.

UNITY IN ACTION

Who could be against church unity? Jesus prayed for unity. (See John 17:21.) It's often just a notional value, but Barry and North Sound are different. At significant cost to themselves, they do good for other church groups. I know because I am an Anglican bishop who was a recipient of their generosity—an openhandedness that flows from them practicing their kingdom-based mission statement.

To have unity in action, one must have clear priorities. For instance, one must practice a key principle: *In necessariis unitas, in dubiis libertas, in omnibus caritas* (commonly translated as *in necessary things unity; in uncertain things freedom; in everything compassion*). Secondly, we must see that the rule and reign of God precedes and predates everything—light, space, time ... and the church. The historical and present action of God creates the church. This means that as unspeakably important the body of Christ is, it is formed within and for the eternal purposes of God.

But our thinking must be careful here. The church is not simply utilitarian. It's not analogous to a lawn mower in God's tool shed. The church is people connected organically to the living Jesus, people who have been called, gathered, and sent in specific ways. When Jesus *called* disciples, He also *sent* them to preach and do the deeds of the kingdom. (See Matthew 10:1; 5–8.) Jesus said, *"As the Father has sent me, even so I am sending you"* (John 20:21).

A BAPTIST CHURCH PLANTS AN ANGLICAN PARISH

In 2010, Pastor Barry was thinking about how to best interact with his city, his mission field. Barry knew one way to do mission was to plant churches. He also knew that most church planting was geographical in nature. A denomination realizes that it does not have a church in a certain city or neighborhood and decides to start a branch there.

But Barry took a decidedly different tack. He did not ask, "Where do we need another Baptist church?" Instead he pondered who in the community was not being reached by existing churches. His research revealed an unreached group of about 17,000 people within a three-mile radius of North Sound who preferred a liturgical form of worship. Most of these people were unserved. Although it has been a challenging half-century for all churches in America, it has been especially so for mainline liturgical congregations. From 1965 to 2005, they have lost anywhere from 15 percent to 46 percent of their adherents.

Barry decided to plant an Anglican-Baptist church.

As you might guess, there was some pushback to this novel idea. "My mentor wasn't too sure of our plan," Barry says. "I said to him, 'You are the person who taught me the theology of the kingdom of God. And this is the logical extension of your theology.'" Realizing the truth of this, he became a supporter.

Looking back on our church planting partnership, Barry says, "An Evangelical church planting an Anglican congregation is not just a conceptual construct. It works! And it gives witness to the power of living out the gospel of the kingdom. Imagine what can be accomplished for the kingdom if we move beyond models of denominational competition toward strategic partnerships. ... In the church world, our goal is not to take folks from other communities of faith. It is to have an effective strategy that seriously seeks to minister to those who do not have a relationship with Jesus Christ or have left the church for any of a number of reasons."

RELATIONAL TRUST GENERATES UNITY

Unity is not just in action, but also in relationships—in bonds steeped in trust. For North Sound to plant an Anglican church, trust had to flow in several directions. The church plant was a cooperative, mutual partnership between North Sound Church, the Baptist-initiated Converge, the non-geographical Anglican Diocese of Churches for the Sake of Others (C4SO), and the Anglican Diocese of Cascadia, as well as a number of people.

At C4SO, we often say we're not trying to build our own thing or increase the numbers in our diocese. We are willing to plant churches that we don't own and help others grow their dioceses. We're trying to position C4SO to use our charism in church planting and mission to be a blessing to anyone who wants to partner with us. Our goal is loving and ministering to the needs of as many diverse people and communities as we can.

Ryan Brotherton, who planted Holy Trinity Edmonds thanks to our partnership, notes that being able to plant on top of another church "lowers that panic mode, allowing for patience to see what the Holy Spirit is going to do and walk in it, as opposed to generating everything on the front end. ... It allows us to build a culture that is authentically Anglican, focusing on reflection, spiritual disciplines, and recognizing where God is at work, and walking in that."

WORKING THROUGH ISSUES WITH CHARITY

Imagine a Baptist sanctuary filled with flickering candles, vested clergy, and 150 people confessing sin in unison, repeating the Nicene Creed, wishing one another peace, and partaking in the *body and blood* of the Lord Jesus Christ. This was the scene at Holy Trinity Edmonds' grand opening service in 2014—a very different atmosphere than the mother church.

As you might guess, there are doctrinal areas of disagreement between Baptists and Anglicans. Are they a definitive reason for church groups not to work together? Let's consider this almost automatic behavior. Who is 100 percent right? Among the Twelve Jesus chose, there were differences about what they thought about what Jesus taught, why He did what He did, what He thought about historic Judaism, what He thought about God, etc. The churches to which Paul, John, and Peter wrote were similarly wrong on given issues.

Rightness-in-all-things cannot be the basis for practical, lived unity. But *seeking* rightness in all doctrines, attitudes, and practices can be unifying. Church planting partnerships of the kind we have been discussing is a practice, an action. It does not deny differences in baptism or Holy Communion, but it does not let those disagreements hinder the overall work of God in establishing churches who evangelize and disciple all manner of people.

Barry says, "For us, there were three issues that required the most understanding: infant baptism; the real presence in communion; and episcopal authority. I do not want to minimize what may be very different understandings of important practices, but as we learned more, we realized there could be cooperation."

I give big bragging rights to Barry and his people. They didn't ask us to negotiate our position or compromise our beliefs. They just bit the bullet as Baptists and said, "We're planting Anglican churches, and this is precisely what they do." They never once sought to make us something other than what we are. Likewise, we did not require doctrinal conformity from them.

Ultimately the reason this worked was that Barry and North Sound Church looked at their community from a kingdom point of view. Not like a McDonald's or Starbucks, making sure they have a one in every part of Seattle, but asking, "Who needs to be reached and what models would best reach them?"

Barry helped his congregation be at peace with this strange plan. He explains, "Strictly speaking, one reason an evangelical congregation can plant an Anglican church in the same facility is because there is such a dramatic difference between a contemporary service and a liturgical service. Typically, the evangelical congregation will not lose many people to the liturgical expression—other than those who are encouraged to assist in the startup. You can plant on top of yourself if you reach a different universe."

SEEK FIRST THE KINGDOM OF GOD—AND UNITY WILL BE ADDED TO YOU

From my earliest days in ministry, I have been taught to have a *kingdom* mindset, to live in the abundant riches of God's kingdom, to be a giver of one's best from the overflow of God's abundance.

I think a part of what immediately drew me and Barry together is that we have similar hearts for the kingdom of God. Church works best when loyalty is always first to God and His kingdom and never to denominations or subgroups. We are not trying to grow those institutional aspects of Christianity. Those things exist to support our goal of working with God to reach people who need Him—so the kingdom of God is always our highest loyalty.

When someone has that straight, it frees them to plant without proprietary interests. Once you have that kingdom mindset, you know that God owns the cattle on a thousand hills, and the Lord is your shepherd. When you're living in the resources of the kingdom, it allows you to give away your best people and resources. You're living from your heart, a kingdom heart.

A VISION FOR UNITY AND COOPERATION

The apostle Paul reminds us that God the Father raised Jesus from the dead and put Him in charge of *everything forever*. (See Ephesians 1:20–22.) This captures the eternal scope and divine scale of the work of God in Christ. What the Bible envisions of God's reign is a whole lot bigger than our denominations! Thinking that to be the case, there is always a question before me in my ministry: how do I, as an Anglican, be loyal to God while enjoying a fish lunch with my Baptist friend Barry? The answer is that we both center the rule of Christ, and while being happily Anglican or Baptist, we find common ground to work for the good of others in the name of God.

The church is the body of Christ, *"the fullness of him who fills all in all"* (Ephesians 1:23). The kingdom of God, His rule and reign, must be central to the task of unity for mission. It is the action of God that brings into being the church universal, the body of which Jesus is head. But today, that body, numbering about 2.6 billion members, is divided into more than 45,000 denominations. All of these church groups have some rational justification and some level of pride in holding themselves distinct from all others.

But being a part of one of these groups—as good as it can be—is not compelling enough, not big enough, and not capable of making sense of *all* the aspects of being human in the image of God, of following Jesus, of the complexities of transforming the human soul into Christlikeness. Only Jesus's gospel of the kingdom can give us an adequate notion of what *church* is.

A great attitude for living in our multidenominational reality could be based upon Paul's letter to Philemon:

> *I hear of your love and of the faith that you have toward the Lord Jesus and for all the* ***saints****. … I have derived much joy and comfort from your love, my brother, because the hearts of the* ***saints*** *have been refreshed through you.* (Philemon 1:5, 7)

When I have coffee or a meal with Barry, I do not sit with a Baptist—I sit with a saint, set apart by God in Christ. He is not a member of different denomination; he is a brother, a co-laborer in Christ.

TO MY BELOVED ANGLICANS

In your long history, you have led the way in issues of justice, repair, and reconciliation. Anglican spirituality is rooted in praying for *the other* and being sent into the world in peace to love and serve Lord—and service that implies working with the Lord as agents of healing for the least, the last, the left out, the marginalized.

It is richly commendable that Christ sits at the center of your worship. Nourishing oneself weekly in Christ via Eucharist is a spiritual treasure. We are at our best when we live the reality that *Christ the center* has boundless love for the utter reaches of the globe, for all people and for all denominations. Anglicans, enriched by Word and table, have nothing to fear in working with others. As we say, "Blessed be God's kingdom now and forever." It is the blessedness, the surety, the magnanimity of God's kingdom that allows us to see the good, the chosen-ness, the holiness, and the sent-ness of our sisters and brothers of other denominations. *They are us.* What separates us is miniscule compared to that which binds us.

Someday, from the point of view of heaven, our divisions will look as silly as thinking that the earth is flat or that the sun and the planets revolve around the earth. Someday, Revelation 7:9 (NIV) will be real: "*There before me was a great multitude that no one could count, from every nation, tribe, people and language, standing before the throne and before the Lamb.*"

We are all a part of one global church. May God breathe on our imagination such that when we ask God to bless "the one holy catholic and apostolic church," we mean it from our hearts, and we mean everyone: Baptists, Pentecostals, Presbyterians, Methodists, Anabaptists, Catholics, non-denominational churches, Amish, Orthodox—every single one of the 2.6 billion people who follow Christ. The unity that would flow from such an undivided heart is not just holy but, as my friend Barry showed us, it is a missional imperative.

Todd Hunter is founding bishop of the Diocese of Churches for the Sake of Others (C4SO) of the Anglican Church in North America. He is past president of Alpha USA. He may be reached at toddhunter.org.

22

PRESERVING HIS UNITY

Bill Johnson
| Nondenominational |

My walk with the Lord has been influenced and strengthened by many different streams of our faith. I learned from my dad, who was a champion of the whole body of Christ. He loved people and celebrated diversity. His approach allowed me to receive from many wonderful men and women of God whom I would not have had access to if I only received from those in our stream. Each of them modeled a beautiful love for Jesus as the Savior and Lord of their lives. This included Catholic and Episcopal priests, Baptist evangelists, Lutherans, Pentecostals, and many more. Exposure to them was a wonderful part of my formative years.

The language of family is used throughout Scripture. We are children of God, coheirs with His Son, surrounded by our brothers and sisters in Christ. Again and again, the Word promotes unity among the body. And if we are to preserve the unity of the Spirit, the church needs to begin to look more like a family and less like a theological social club.

If our unity is merely based on intellectual agreement, then as soon as we disagree, someone has to leave. Denominations tend to be formed around agreement; families are formed around fathers and mothers. A united family can come together at Thanksgiving, connecting Republican parents, a Democratic daughter, and a Libertarian son at the dinner table. The bonds of family supersede any division.

There are, of course, essential aspects to our life with Christ—fully God, fully man, the power of the blood of Jesus, the virgin birth, the resurrection—but most disagreements within the body have nothing to do with these foundational beliefs. We have to know what's worth taking a bullet for and what isn't. We never want to fall into the trap of dishonoring another member of Christ's body simply to prove that we're right. The church was never meant to replicate the fragile ties of agreement found in the political systems. We cannot hinge our unity on intellectual conformity.

We are called to connect and build as a family—united around fathers and mothers—who will carry the flavor of heaven into the world in the midst of conflict and crisis. The believers who can do this well are the ones who will build something lasting. When we can hear something we disagree with and turn to the face of Jesus for understanding instead of attacking one another, we can show the world an example of unity they're longing for.

THE UNITY OF GOD

One of the great mysteries, unpacked in the book of Ephesians, is the unity of God Himself. The Father, Son, and Holy Spirit reveal absolute and perfect unity. Hebrews describes the relationship between Jesus and the Father: The Son is the *"exact representation"* of the Father's nature (Hebrews 1:3 NIV). Jesus came from the Father, manifesting the Father as light that emanates from a lightbulb.

As Jesus's life was ending, He told His disciples, *"And I will ask the Father, and he will give you another Helper, to be with you forever"* (John 14:16). The word *another* can mean "an additional one of the same kind." So Jesus came from the Father exactly like the Father, in no way misrepresenting Him. And then Jesus released the Holy Spirit, who exactly represented Him, not altering His nature in any way. This great mystery called *unity,* found within the Trinity, becomes our model.

On the cross at Calvary, the blood of Jesus destroyed every legal right to separation. And it is because of the price that He paid to erase division that every form of divisiveness—racism, classism, sexism, denominationalism—has such a nauseating impact on the earth. These excuses for division wage war against the purposes of God that He revealed through His Son.

Ephesians points out that Jesus destroyed the grounds for division even between the two groups of people who had the greatest cultural and social gulfs between them imaginable: the Jews and the gentiles. His sacrifice made it possible for two cultures, once completely at odds, to become united in the same way that the Father, Son, and Holy Spirit are united.

Paul says it this way:

> *The mystery was made known to me by revelation ... that the Gentiles are fellow heirs, members of the same body, and partakers of the promise in Christ Jesus through the gospel. To me ... this grace was given, to preach to the Gentiles the unsearchable riches of Christ ... so that through the church the manifold wisdom of God might now be made known to the rulers and authorities in the heavenly places. This was according to the eternal purpose that he has realized in Christ Jesus our Lord.*
>
> (Ephesians 3:3, 6, 8, 10–11)

All people, Jew and gentile, become one in Christ in the same way that the Father, Son, and Holy Spirit are one. Here, Paul says, we have the "*manifold wisdom*" of this unity being unfolded on the earth. The word *manifold* can mean "multicolored." It reminds me of Joseph's multicolored coat. Joseph was his father's favorite, and his coat was the symbol of the delight and favor his father poured out on his life. The same delight and favor, then, can be seen in the early church's decision to operate in the divine wisdom of God. By preserving the unity of the Spirit, erasing the divide between Jew and gentile, and doing anything necessary to protect their unity, they were representing the Father well on the earth.

TUNING OURSELVES TO HIM

Before an orchestra begins to play together, they spend time tuning their instruments. Let's say I play the cello, and I spent some time tuning one string to what sounded right to me. I then proceeded to tune my other strings to that first one. In time, I got all of my strings tuned with one another in perfect harmony. Let's go on to imagine that every other musician in the orchestra tuned their instruments to mine. When we began to play, it would sound unified and in harmony—except to anyone with perfect pitch, who would notice that while we are united, we are out of tune.

My cello would most probably be completely out of tune. I could have begun with a faulty premise. But because all of my strings and subsequently every other instrument was aligned with mine, none of them would stand out as offensive. My standard would have unified our sounds with one another, but it would not be in tune. The music we made, with that foundation, would not be divine.

Instead, good musicians know that their standard must begin with perfection. They must take a single, perfect note—a tuning fork—and let that note ring out so that instead of tuning to one another, every instrument can be tuned to the one perfect sound. True unity is not the same as agreement. It is not simply uniting with one another, but being unified to Christ, with His heart and mind. It is possible to confess Christ, be unified horizontally with one another, and yet be in opposition to His purposes. We can sit in the same room, make the same sound together, and yet create something discordant if we're not carrying the note Jesus is carrying.

If we're not careful, unity can become synonymous with a desire not to rock the boat. We can allow perversion to work into our lives in the name of unity, tuning our hearts to the approval of man instead of the kingdom. Jesus rings out a note that is strong and clear. Genuine unity is found in our "Amen" to that sound. As we constantly retune ourselves to the one, true note, we will find ourselves in harmony with others. Unity is not striving to be together; it is endeavoring to live in union with the heartbeat of God. And, in that process, we connect with those around us who carry the same sound.

VISIBLE WISDOM

The wisdom of God is meant to be seen. In Paul's letter to the Ephesians, he asserts that he will preach the *"manifold wisdom of God,"* so that *"through the church* [it] *might now be made known to the rulers and authorities in the heavenly places"* (Ephesians 3:10). It's as if the church is the movie screen upon which God's wisdom plays as the entire spirit world is forced to watch. Jesus is the desire of the nations; He is the One whom every part of the created world has worshipped since the dawn of existence. When He died on the cross, it was the greatest conflict in the minds and hearts of the entire spirit world. But because of what He accomplished on the cross, the Father can now demonstrate the unity of the Godhead through His body on the earth.

Every time we yield ourselves to embrace someone from whom we would have previously kept our distance, we display His wisdom. Every time we go out of our way to love someone, stepping out of convenience and into sacrifice, we prophesy to the entire spirit world—angels and demons alike—about the unfolding plans of God. In Ephesians 3:11, Paul calls it *"the eternal purpose"* of God, telling us that this unity, being worked out on earth right now, will find its ultimate expression in eternity.

Heaven is an industrious place; it's not a place to sit around on the clouds and play harps. It is a productive city—filled with government, expansion, development, and the expression of every gift we carry here. This is who God made us to be. Learning to take authority and express the dominion of God on planet Earth is actually school for eternity. It's training ground for what we will be doing with God forever.

God extended Himself to all of the nations of the world. They rejected Him, so He chose to raise up Israel as an example of His heart for all people. He highlighted them to illustrate what He wanted to pour out on everyone. On the cross, Jesus abolished in His flesh the separation between Jew and gentile. He destroyed the enmity, every reason for conflict between any group of people, no matter how seemingly different. There is now no legal precedent for strife at any level. We can live in division, sure, but we have to step outside of God's purpose to do so.

The call we have on our lives is to protect what's valuable to God. It's not complicated. The moment we make it complicated is the same moment we are prone to making foolish decisions. Keep it simple. Jesus did: *"You shall love the Lord your God with all your heart and with all your soul and with all your mind. . . . You shall love your neighbor as yourself"* (Matthew 22:37, 39). Everything I do is unto the Lord; everything belongs to Him. And, from that place of connection with His heart, I will do all that I can to protect the unity of His body on the earth.

IN ONE ACCORD

On the day of Pentecost, 120 people gathered together to pray. Among them were Mary, the mother of Jesus, several other women, *"and his brothers"* (Acts 1:14). This was significant because one of the last times we read about these *brothers* in Scripture, they didn't believe that Jesus was the Messiah. They even tried to trick Him into revealing Himself publicly so that He would receive ridicule and opposition. (See John 7:2–5.) Clearly something later made them realize that they had, indeed, grown up with the Son of God.

Eleven of His twelve disciples were also present. They had spent three and a half years following Jesus. During that time, they not only did ministry together, they also compared themselves to one another and argued over who was the greatest. This was a group of 120 people who knew each other intimately enough to have some major relational issues. Whether their discord was resolved before the ten days of prayer or whether their issues were ironed out in the prayer meeting itself, the Bible says, *"All these with one accord were devoting themselves to prayer"* (Acts 1:14). They had kept their eyes on Jesus, and despite disagreements and differences, they operated as one.

Unity is not uniformity. True unity requires diversity in the same way that musical harmony requires different notes for that magnificent sound to be achieved. God created marriage to be a representation of this kind of coming together: *"A man shall leave his father and his mother and hold fast to his wife, and they shall become one flesh"* (Genesis 2:24). The miraculous event of marriage—two distinct people becoming one—occurs between a man and a woman. Biblical unity does not merely tolerate diversity; it requires it. It celebrates it. Our differences are what make biblical unity so beautiful.

Unity is also not something that we can create. Most human efforts toward unity, as noble as they may seem, boil down to attempts for agreement or mutual understanding. It's not an evil effort, but it is insufficient for the call of God on our lives. In Ephesians 4:3, the Bible says we are to endeavor *"to maintain the unity of the Spirit in the bond of peace."* We are to keep unity, to preserve it. We cannot create unity because it is already in existence. It is the *"unity of the Spirit."* True, biblical unity is a manifestation of the Holy Spirit's influence. Any time we see real, true unity—between a husband and a wife, a church family, a nation—it is the result of the Holy Spirit's guidance on the lives of the individuals involved. Conversely, division shows that the Holy Spirit's influence is missing.

UNITY IN HIS PRESENCE

Jesus prayed a prayer for us in John 17:21: *"That they may all be one, just as you, Father, are in me, and I in you, that they also may be in us, so that the world may believe that you have sent me."* We are only able to achieve the oneness that He speaks of because He has given us the manifested presence of God as the Holy Spirit. Jesus continues by praying, *"The glory that you have given me I have given to them, that they may be one even as we are one, I in them and you in me"* (verses 22–23). We have access to unity only because Jesus has released His glory, the fullness of His Spirit, upon us. When the power of God shows up in the room, we can see this reality become evident. All division fades away. In the face of the weighty presence of God's glory, it's hard to find someone harboring anger, hostility, or judgment toward another person. Something shifts in the atmosphere when Love arrives. The importance of any slight or offense fades quickly in His presence.

The day of Pentecost was about the demonstration of God's power. But the foundation for this manifestation of power was a group of people, united in heart, calling on heaven in one accord. Their oneness testified of the resurrection of Jesus Christ. This hungry group of early believers were united to such an extent that the Bible tells us that if one of them had a need, others would sell their possessions to take care of that need. It was unity to the point of self-sacrifice. This is what it looks like for us to maintain the unity of the

Spirit: We choose to invest in one another for the sake of the union. We don't just pray a mechanical prayer for unity; we follow our prayers with action.

One of my favorite stories occurs in Joshua 6, when Israel marched around the walls of Jericho. For seven days, they marched around the fortressed city. And on the last day, when they blew their trumpets and raised a mighty shout, the walls fell before them. Marching around the stronghold of Jericho symbolizes prayer. The intercession and mighty shout of the Israelites brought the walls down, but they still had to go in and take possession of the city. The prayer removed the obstacles standing between them and the promise, but they still had to claim their victory.

It is important that we pray for unity. Absolutely. But it's also vital that our prayers are backed up with intentional actions: communicating clearly, honoring one another, mourning with those who mourn, celebrating the favor on another's life, loving one another well. We don't need agreement on every topic, but we do need genuine love and affection for one another. We need to pursue—in action—the healing grace of God for every division that exists. So much of this is healed by the simple act of giving honor to another.

ON ALL FLESH

As the 120 prayed together in the upper room, Scripture says, "*And suddenly there came from heaven a sound like a mighty rushing wind, and it filled the entire house where they were sitting*" (Acts 2:2). All throughout the city of Jerusalem, people from different nations stopped what they were doing and gathered together because they heard their own languages being spoken. The glory of God was so present that the crowds thought the disciples must be drunk.

But then Peter, anointed by the Spirit, explained to the crowds what was happening. And he did so by quoting the prophet Joel:

> *And in the last days it shall be, God declares, that I will pour out my Spirit on all flesh, and your sons and your daughters shall prophesy, and your young men shall see visions, and your old men shall dream dreams; even on my male servants and female servants in those days I will pour out my Spirit, and they shall prophesy.* (Acts 2:17–18)

Peter knew that with this outpouring of the Spirit, all lines of division had been erased. "*All flesh*" speaks of every race. *Sons and daughters* reminds us that the issue of gender is removed. *Young* and *old* informs us that the age barrier has been removed. *Male servants* and *female servants* tells us that the socioeconomic divisions are destroyed. When the Spirit of God is poured out, when He is truly free to do as He pleases, He shatters every barrier that we tend to create. Every point of division is obliterated in the glory of God's presence. Unity is the fruit of His working in and through us. It's His idea. And now we have the responsibility and privilege to preserve it.

LOVE LETTER TO THE PENTECOSTAL CHURCH

I write to you because you are my most immediate family in the faith. My family line goes back into many diverse streams that exist in your movements and history. My mom's father and mother were baptized in the Holy Spirit in 1901 and 1903, respectively. I say that only to reinforce that claim that my family is many generations deeply involved in this movement.

You have taught me to love the Word of God and the Spirit of God. I'm so glad you made the distinction so I'd know that passion for both was essential. You have laid your lives down as some of the finest missionaries I've ever met. In doing so, you illustrated what it is like to *love not your life unto death*. You've raised the bar so high and yet helped me to understand that by grace it is doable, even by me.

I'm so thankful to my parents and grandparents for celebrating the whole body of Christ before my eyes, regardless of race, gender, or any other reason that people create to legitimize division. You showed me the heart of Jesus for people and demonstrated what it really looks like to be full of the Holy Spirit. Thank you. You illustrated the special grace given to Pentecostal churches around the world.

Our future is bright, and I'm excited, especially when we celebrate the beauty and wonder of the whole body of Christ and no longer view ourselves as superior. Those I've come to know in these many years have worked hard to destroy the notion of haves and have-nots. Such division is no longer tolerable, and you've modeled the intolerance for division well.

I pray that we will learn to celebrate who a person is without stumbling over who they are not. And in doing so, may Jesus be glorified through a united church, one that functions as a body, where every member lives under the coordinated directions given by the head, Christ Jesus.

Bill Johnson is the senior leader of Bethel Church in Redding, California, and the founder of Bill Johnson Ministries. Connect with him at bjm.org.

23

IT'S TIME FOR DARING ECUMENISM

Rev. Najla Kassab
| Evangelical |

One talk and the walls came tumbling down. At the age of eighteen, I was invited to a meeting with the Middle East Council of Churches held in Cyprus. Although I was raised in a Protestant family that was very much dedicated to the ministry of the church and grew up with friends from different churches, this was my first ecumenical meeting. As we gathered, I felt initially that I was in a strange setting; the prayers, expressions, and the way the priests looked were different. It was my first time meeting a Coptic Orthodox priest.

The setting was so new that I regretted joining the meeting until I started to hear what they were sharing. The Coptic priest presented a talk on his spiritual experience entitled "Sitting at the Feet of Jesus." That talk broke all prejudices that I had accumulated through the years about the *other*. Previously, I thought that we do not share the same belief about Jesus with other churches and even questioned their faith. Back then, to me, only Protestants knew Jesus in the right way. But the Coptic priest's talk broke all barriers of prejudice. I even discovered that he knew more about Jesus than I did. I remember that I spent most of the conference following him to hear more about his faith and experience with Jesus. This was my first step on my journey in ecumenism, where the walls that separated me from other churches came tumbling down and bridges of discovering the richness of other churches and communities were being built as I recognized God's work in every church.

That experience also helped me to discover my identity as I learned that "to be Reformed is to be Ecumenical." As a church that is called to continual reformation in the light of the Word of God, I found that through my ecumenical experience, I was challenged to closely scrutinize my faith journey and how the church is called to live the love of Christ with others, guided by the Holy Spirit.

Also, through my journey with the World Communion of Reformed Churches (WCRC), I discovered the abundant grace that we enjoy as we come together as a body in relationship to other Christian World Communions and understand our identity as an ecumenical communion that participates in God's mission for the unity of the whole church. In the light of this missional commitment, the WCRC is guided by the vision of the visible unity of the larger church in its common witness to the world.

Ecumenism is one expression on the journey of living Christ's love with others. It is rooted in our spirituality as we strive to live our faith. Ecumenism is not a mere choice but is intrinsically linked to our faith and church life. It is a call to transcend the boundaries of any church, since God is at work in all Christian traditions and the unity of the church which the Apostolic Creed testifies is already there. God gives unity as a gift and invites the church to receive this by reforming itself and its relationships to Christians of other traditions.

ECUMENISM IN THE HOUSE OF MIRRORS

Ecumenism is an act of coming together and going out to the world, to be compassionate to all those who are hungry and thirsty and struggling with all kinds of injustice, to share the love of Christ unconditionally and to preserve the dignity of the people and work together, so that all may have life and have it abundantly.

In a recent *international meeting* of *Prayer for Peace* in Rome, the Ecumenical Patriarch of Constantinople Bartholomew said, "We live in a common house. It is like the house of mirrors where whenever we look at ourselves in the mirror, we see the image of our brother and sister and we see the work of the divine Presence in every human being. As we see the image of the suffering reflected in our image, we discover hope in living together and reflecting each other's image."

I believe ecumenism is an experience where we are invited to this house of mirrors. Christ invites us to these rooms where we start to see ourselves through the image of the other. Then we can never look at ourselves without seeing the image of others. Our image coincides with the image of our brothers and sisters. In this house of mirrors, we discover anew how to live our faith together and to grow together under the care and eye of our Lord.

WE CONFESS OUR WEAKNESSES IN ECUMENISM

Still, we cannot but confess that the ecumenical movement remains *a journey with several challenges*. Some of the churches do not see ecumenism as central to their church life and do not recognize that growing in faith is linked to living the maturity of reaching out to others in humbleness. Many times, we fail to stress this in our theological institutions and in our preaching from our pulpits. Our congregations are called to grow with such teaching. We cannot grow as a healthy church with walls but are daily challenged to reach out to others, to discern how we can be Christ's church for today.

We confess that many times, *we did not strategize well* on how we can involve all members of the church in ecumenism, so that the richness of the encounter among church leaders is moved to the pews. The involvement of youth and women remains indispensable for sustenance and continuity of our ecumenical work.

We confess that our *ecumenical work is not as impactful as it is called to be*. We are called to evaluate our work in the ecumenical circles in terms of impact not merely with the number of activities. What can we do as churches to impact society and witness together as churches in the public sphere? Today the world is shaped by impact, and we are called to our common work. The youth in our churches wait to see the church leading the change in society and hope that through the church, they can live their dream of change for a more just world.

We confess that *we can do more work together around justice*. The more we join efforts on reading the signs of the times and speaking against injustice in the world, the stronger our ecumenical work is. The church has a special role that other organizations cannot fulfill. Secular organizations could speak about injustice with pragmatic thinking in mind, while the church will deal with injustices merely for the sake of the dignity of humanity, so they may have life abundant. There are lots of injustices around the world that are overlooked, and it is the role of ecumenical work to point to it. There is endangered Christian presence in several countries today and the churches are called to take this matter seriously before we lose the remnant minority left. We are called to journey with those groups and make it our priority in our ecumenical work.

We confess that *many times, we did not prioritize ecumenical work by using our financial resources*. The financial contribution of churches for ecumenism reflects the seriousness of our commitment. We are called to secure the future of ecumenism by providing resources that will encourage continuity and growth. It is not merely the contribution of those who have but a contribution of all who believe in ecumenism as central in living our faith.

DARE TO EVALUATE THE PAST

In our relations with other churches, we are shaped anew as we look at the past and evaluate the present to move toward a better future. Today we are called to reevaluate our ecumenical role and strive to bring about a continuous reform in our understanding of ecumenical work. We are challenged to recognize that the Protestant reform was radical in its beginnings, which led to the overthrow of some practices that can be revisited in the life of the Reformed Church today. Also, other churches are called to be in dialogue for closer relations. We are in a new phase, and it is time to move away from reactions and be open to the richness that exists in other churches.

DARE TO COME TOGETHER DESPITE SEPARATION

Although the Reformation historically led to the emergence of a new church, Protestant churches have been among the founders of the ecumenical movement and call for unity away from separation or division, whether in the Middle East or worldwide. This leading role in ecumenism is at the heart of our mission and vision for a better world.

DARE TO TAKE RESPONSIBILITY IN SERVICE

Also, we are called to enrich the ecumenical work with the Reformed thinking and principles that encourage healthy ecumenical work. The Reformed teaching around priesthood of all believers—where everyone who "knows Christ and unites with Him" is responsible for building the body of Christ, and believers have a role in sharing the good news with others—is an important pillar for ecumenism. Priesthood in the Reformed thinking is an office of service in which all believers participate; laity and pastors complement one another and focus on serving others. The people of God, not only clergy, are called to work responsibly in serving together as the body of Christ that is beyond one single church.

Focusing on ministry in a nonauthoritarian setting, away from hierarchical structures, opens the way for living partnership with other churches, so members who are brought up with this teaching are prepared to partner with other churches.

DARE TO LIVE THE RICHNESS OF ECUMENISM IN PLURALISM

Pluralistic expression of faith is at the heart of ecumenism and is far from working toward-withdrawal to one church or eliminating pluralism in thought and beliefs. Nor is it the hegemony of a particular church over the other churches, even if they are more numerous. Ecumenism is an enriching experience and not submission to any authority. We are all enriched as we share nonhierarchical understanding of leadership, the contribution of laity in leadership, or the role of women.

DARE TO PRESENT LIVING EXAMPLES FOR ECUMENISM

Ecumenism is about life not mere talk. Living examples of people who strive to make a difference in ecumenism is key in moving forward. Many times, we are tempted to compromise our identity, thinking that will strengthen ecumenism. I believe we are invited to share freely our identity and our rich heritage so that ecumenical encounter becomes a source of renewal for all.

DARE TO BE A LIGHT WITH A CLEAR ROLE BEYOND NUMBERS

The church role is never related to numbers; it can be a light and source of change and reform provided we live on the level of our call. Let us be a source of a shining light, in the spirit of reform, which is the work of the Holy Spirit in the church, past and present. There is no impactful church today without an active ecumenical meeting nor a renaissance without trespassing the boundaries that have separated us from the other who is different on our journey of living for God's kingdom in service together.

DARE TO CONTINUE THE JOURNEY WITH ENTHUSIASM

There is no doubt that the ecumenical work has historically been an impressive legacy, and we are called to continue working together with the same motivation, to hear the voice of the God calling us continually for unity.

A VOICE FROM TWO ECUMENICAL MIDDLE EASTERN WOMAN LEADERS

One of the blessings of ecumenical partnership that I have enjoyed is working with women leaders in churches. I am happy to share a letter cowritten with a women leader, Dr. Thouraia Bishilani, a previous general secretary of Middle East Council of Churches, addressed to the pope regarding unifying the date for Easter. Women contribute to revival in ecumenical work and will always have a special role. This letter was a sign of commitment on the journey together as women hoping for a better tomorrow.

> We are two women who hear the voices of the struggling in the Middle East, whether with the COVID-19 virus and accompanying lockdown, the economic situation, or the lack of any progress toward solving the causes of war and injustice in this region. In the midst of all the pain we come to you, trusting with the people that the church is the main source of hope for life abundant.
>
> This Easter, when people could not worship gathered in church buildings, was a time of longing to be together and to worship together as families. As never before, the people called for the need for a unified date for celebrating Easter as an expression of hope and unity.
>
> We know that many voices and concerns were raised earlier in the Middle East, namely the efforts of the World Council of Churches in "Towards a Common Date for Easter" in Aleppo, Syria, in 1997. Or in 2014, the request of Coptic Pope Tawadros II for a renewed effort to unify the date of Easter and the agreement Syriac Orthodox Patriarch of Antioch, Aphrem II.
>
> We hope that the issue of unifying the date of Easter will be revisited as a healing step and a sign of hope for the Christians in the Middle East and the world. It will be "as a gift of unity with the other Christian churches" and will encourage reconciliation and healing.
>
> As two women leaders from the Middle East—General Secretary of Middle East Council of Churches and President of the World Communion of Reformed Churches—we know that your role in unifying the date of Easter is essential and encourages us all to reflect the power of the resurrection in a broken world. When no signs of hope are clear in our sky, this step will give confidence that hope is alive, brings life and conquers death, separation and helplessness.

In the year 2025, Easter fell on the same day for both the Eastern and Western churches—a rare occurrence.

ECUMENISM IS DYNAMIC, GROWING TOWARD NEW IMAGINATION

Finally, we are *challenged for renewed imagination* in how we live our ecumenical life today. I would like to share a statement from the Wittenberg Witness proclaimed on July 5, 2017, as a voice for ecumenical commitment among the Lutheran and Reformed churches:

> Together we long for renewed imagination of what being the church in communion could mean—for our world, in our time. We need new imagination to live together in ways that would embrace our unity not only as gift but also as calling. We need new imagination to dream of a different world, a world where justice, peace and reconciliation prevails. We need new imagination to practice spiritualties of resistance and prophetic vision, spiritualties in service of life, spiritualties formed by the mission of God. Together we commit ourselves to respond to this yearning with concrete actions, convinced that God's Word leads us to deeper communion. As world communions, Lutherans and Reformed, we commit to explore new forms of life together that will more fully express the communion we already have in Christ. We commit ourselves to redouble our common efforts to embody our unity, together resisting the forces of injustice and exclusion. We call upon our member churches to make our unity more visible in their local contexts. We invite our ecumenical partners to live out our shared commitment for unity and witness to the world.

Today the situation of the world challenges us to trust that we can make a difference and we can dream together of a better world, to trust in hope that the risen Lord is capable to renew us and send us anew for a world that is broken and fallen among thieves.

MY PRAYER FOR CHURCHES

Lord of life, we pray for all the churches that strive to live and work together toward unity, as a witness to the love and strength that You provide to the world in the midst of pain and suffering. We pray for the churches in the Middle East and for the leadership as they keep the hope and trust that the

Lord will strengthen the church to be a bridge for reconciliation and healing for a broken world.

In the midst of unclarity and uncertainty, You remain with us, granting us full assurance that You are on the journey with us and You are the anchor that provides sustenance and hope for a better tomorrow

Grant us Your strength even when the numbers of Christians in the region are shrinking. Help us to trust that our role outweighs the number and remember that with twelve disciples, You changed the world. We might feel *"afflicted in every way, but not crushed; perplexed, but not driven to despair; persecuted, but not forsaken; struck down, but not destroyed"* (2 Corinthians 4:8–9) because You are with us now and forever. Amen.

—Rev. Najla Kassab

Rev. Najla Kassab is president of the World Communion of Reformed Churches and director of the Christian Education Department in the National Evangelical Synod of Syria and Lebanon. To connect with Rev. Kassab, visit wcrc@wcrc.eu.

24

SPOUSAL THEOLOGY AS A BASIS FOR CHRISTIAN UNITY

Christopher West, Th.D.
| Catholic |

I was raised a Catholic and received all the sacraments of initiation growing up in the seventies and eighties. I considered Jesus an important historical figure, but I didn't know Him personally as my Savior until, largely through the influence of evangelical Christians, I started studying the Bible in my college years and had a life-changing encounter with the Word made flesh.

Soon thereafter, I became involved in an ecumenical community of believers, Catholics and Protestants who lived and prayed in common and enjoyed a committed Christian fellowship. There was certainly much more that united us than that which divided us. Nonetheless, the lack of full communion in faith was real, and I began to long for the fulfillment of Christ's prayer that His followers *"may be one even as"* He and the Father are one (John 17:22).

LONGING FOR ONENESS

Longing for oneness, in fact, was what had started my religious quest in the first place. But it was a longing to be one with a woman. Little did I know in my teen years that God had designed that longing to draw me into what Saint Paul called the *"profound"* mystery of Christ's love for the church (Ephesians 5:32). Passing through "many dangers, toils, and snares" as noted in the beloved hymn "Amazing Grace," that's exactly what it did. In the process, I would come to discover that the original unity of man and woman in *"one flesh"* (Genesis 2:24) provided the biblical prototype for the unity of believers in *"one body"* (Romans 12:5).

The restoration of the unity of man and woman as *"one body"* in Christ provides the only solid foundation upon which we can hope for the restoration of the unity of believers. The real scandal of the divisions within the church is that, in some sense, we have made a polygamist of the heavenly Bridegroom. Unity as Christ's one bride must be built on the foundation of a proper theology of the body, and I believe that a prophetic series of biblical reflections with which the late John Paul II launched his pontificate serve as a critical contribution in that regard.

Followers of Christ everywhere recognize the Polish pope's tireless ecumenical efforts. He publicly repented on behalf of those Catholics whose sins led to divisions in the first place. He reached out repeatedly to Protestant and Orthodox leaders, even asking them to help Rome reenvision the papacy so that it could more effectively serve the needs of *all* Christians. Yet history may well recognize John Paul II's biblical study of the body as his most important ecumenical contribution. His *Theology of the Body* has already sparked an international movement that is spreading across denominational lines. It's precisely here, in fact—in the cultural battle for the meaning of the body, sexuality, gender, marriage, and the family—that committed Christians of varying professions find themselves overcoming their mutual prejudices and standing together.

SPIRIT AND FLESH

If religion in general is considered a flight from the body to reach God, Christianity presents the exact opposite movement: God taking on a body to reach us! To the degree we let that sink in, it changes *everything*.

The apostle Paul's admonitions to live *"by the Spirit"* and not by *"the flesh"* (Galatians 5:16) do not condone a rupture of matter and spirit. In his terminology, to live by the flesh means to be cut off *in both body and soul* from God's inspiration. In turn, those who open themselves authentically to life according to the Spirit do *not* reject their bodies; their bodies become the very *"temple of the Holy Spirit"* (1 Corinthians 6:19). In this way, life in the Spirit becomes at one and the same time *"the redemption of our bodies"* (Romans 8:23).

Tragically, a great many Christians today live as functional Gnostics. This ancient heresy involves a death-dealing rupture of spirit and flesh, positing the material world, including the body, as flawed and emphasizing personal spiritual knowledge.

But Christ took on a body to become the Savior of the body (see Ephesians 5:23). If I want a spiritual path and a salvation that does not involve my body and Christ's body, then my spirituality is no longer Christian. Indeed, when we are intent on divorcing ourselves from the body, we can make *zero sense* of a God who is intent on wedding Himself to it. Christian spirituality is *always* incarnational spirituality. It's a specific *spirituality of the body,* just as Christian theology is a theology of the Word made flesh.

WORD MADE FLESH

We cannot see God. As pure Spirit, God is totally beyond our vision. Yet, the Bible teaches that the invisible God has made Himself visible: "*The life was made manifest, and we have seen it*" (1 John 1:2). "*The Word became flesh … we have seen his glory*" (John 1:14). Everything about our faith hinges on the incarnation of the Son of God, on the idea that Christ's flesh—and *ours,* for it's our flesh He took on—has the ability to reveal God's mystery, to make visible the invisible.

The phrase *theology of the body* is just another way of stating the bedrock biblical truth that man and woman are created in the image of God. The human body is not divine, of course. Rather, it's a sign of the divine mystery. God speaks to us in sign language, you might say, and the main sign He uses is the human body.

Tragically, after sin, the body still speaks God's sign language, but we don't know how to recognize it. As a result, in a fallen world, we tend to consider the body merely as a physical thing entirely separated from the spiritual and the divine realms. We can spend our whole lives as Christians stuck in this blindness, never knowing that our bodies are a sign revealing the mystery hidden in God.

THE DIVINE MYSTERY

Saint Paul wrote that his mission was "*to bring to light for everyone … the mystery hidden for ages in God … so that through the church the manifold wisdom of God might now be made known …* [and] *realized in Christ*" (Ephesians 3:9–11). The biblical term "*mystery*" refers to the innermost secret of God and His eternal plan for humanity. The good news is that this mystery has been revealed in the Word made flesh. The forgiveness of our sins in Christ is wonderful news, but it's only the prerequisite to get to the even more astoundingly good news of the gospel.

The *"mystery hidden for ages in God"* that Paul wanted everyone to know is that we are destined in Christ *"before the foundation of the world"* (Ephesians 1:4) to be *"members of the same body, and partakers of the promise in Christ Jesus through the gospel"* (Ephesians 3:6). In chapter 5, Paul reveals that this mystery isn't far from us. We needn't climb some high mountain to find it. We needn't cross the sea. It's already as plain to us as the bodies God gave us when He created us male and female and called the two to become one body. The problem is, we look but do not see (see Matthew 13:13). Lord, open our eyes!

THE BIBLE TELLS A MARITAL STORY

Scripture uses many images to help us understand God's love for us. Each has its own valuable place. But the image of spousal love is used far more than any other. In fact, from beginning to end, the Bible tells a covenant story of marital love. It begins in Genesis with the marriage of the first man and woman, and it ends in Revelation with the marriage of Christ and the church. These *book ends* provide the key for understanding all that lies between. Indeed, God wants to marry us: *"As the bridegroom rejoices over the bride, so shall your God rejoice over you"* (Isaiah 62:5); *"I will betroth you to me forever"* (Hosea 2:19).

God is inviting each of us, in a unique and unrepeatable way, to an unimagined intimacy with Him akin to the intimacy of spouses in *"one body."* While we may need to work through some discomfort or fear here to reclaim the true holiness of the imagery, the truth is that Scripture describes God's love for His people using boldly erotic images (see Ezekiel 16:7–8, for example). We are probably more familiar and more comfortable describing God's love as *agape*, the Greek word for sacrificial, self-giving love. Yet one of the most astounding revelations of the Bible is that God loves His people with all the passion of a true Bridegroom. One need only think of the Song of Solomon, also known as the Song of Songs. This unabashed celebration of erotic love is not only a biblical celebration of marital intimacy, it's an image of how God loves His people, fulfilled in Christ's love for the church. And this book is not a footnote in the Bible. The greatest saints have understood this erotic love poetry as an expression of the very essence of biblical faith. Not only does God love us, He loves us so utterly that He has wed Himself to us forever in Jesus Christ. The Bible calls it the *"marriage of the Lamb"* (Revelation 19:7).

But there's more. Remember that rhyme we learned as children: "First comes love, then comes marriage, then comes the baby in the baby carriage"? We probably didn't realize that we were actually reciting some profound *theology*—theology *of the body*! Our bodies tell the story that God loves us, wants to marry us, and wants us (the bride) to "conceive" His eternal life within us. And this isn't merely a metaphor. Two thousand years ago, a young Jewish woman gave her *Yes* to God's marriage proposal with such totality that she literally conceived eternal life in her womb. This is why Christians have always honored Mary: she is the biblical model par excellence of what it means to be a believer, of what it means to receive Jesus and bear Him forth to others.

CLIMAX OF THE SPOUSAL ANALOGY

John Paul II observed that "spousal love helps us to penetrate into the very essence" of the divine mystery. And no biblical author reaches more deeply into this essence than the apostle Paul in Ephesians 5. In verse 31, quoting directly from Genesis 2:24, Paul states, *"Therefore a man shall leave his father and mother and hold fast to his wife, and the two shall become one flesh."* Then, linking the original marriage with the ultimate marriage, he adds, *"This mystery is profound* [*mega* in the Greek], *and I am saying that it refers to Christ and the church"* (verse 32). Inspired by the Holy Spirit, Paul employs the intimacy of marital union to reveal not just some aspect of the Christian mystery but the reality of our union with Christ in its entirety, the reality of salvation itself.

Could there be a more compelling demonstration of Christ's love than to make Himself *one with His bride*, even to the point of suffering as His own the death that was hers so that He might offer her His own divine life?

But let's be more specific. How does Genesis 2:24 refer to Christ and the church? Christ, the new Adam, left His Father in heaven. He also left the home of His mother on earth. Why? To give up His body for His bride, the church, so that we might enter into holy communion with Him in *one body*. In the breaking of the bread, John Paul II said, Christ is united with His body as the bridegroom with the bride.

Allow me to concretize this glorious truth with a family story. I never met my father-in-law; he died when my wife was a girl. But I admire him tremendously because of the intuition he had as a new husband. At church the day after his wedding, having consummated his marriage the night before, he was in tears as he came back to the pew after receiving Communion. When his new bride inquired, he said, "For the first time in my life, I understood the meaning of those words, 'This is my body given for you.'"

Make no mistake: when all the smoke is cleared and all the distortions are untwisted, the deepest meaning and purpose of our creation as male and female is to point us to the *"marriage supper of the Lamb"* (Revelation 19:9).

FIGHTING THE ATTACK AGAINST THE BODY

Ponder this for a moment: if the union of the sexes is the main sign in this world of our call to live in unity with God and with each other, and if there is an enemy who wants to divide us from God and from each other, where do you think he's going to aim his most poisonous arrows? If we want to know what is most important to the fulfillment of God's plan in this world, all we need do is look for what the enemy most violently attacks.

We know well that there is an all-out war raging in our world today against the divine plan for marriage and the family, and it begins with an attack against the meaning of the body in its sexual difference. The enemy knows all too well that man and woman's unity in *"one body"* is designed by God to proclaim and manifest the unity of the church in one body. Just prior to Paul's proclamation of the *mega* mystery of man and woman's unity in Ephesians 5, he proclaims in Ephesians 4:4–5 that the church *"is one body and one Spirit ...* [with] *one Lord, one faith, one baptism."* Then, in Ephesians 6:11–18, he warns us of the diabolic attack against this profound mystery, calling us to spiritual battle. And if we are to win, the first thing Paul says we must do is gird our loins with the truth (see verse 14). Only in resisting the attack against the unity of man and woman, the domestic church, do we have any hope of resisting the attack against the unity of the church at large. And, as Paul makes abundantly clear, victory for the bride (the church) comes only through union with the Bridegroom in His death and resurrection.

When Jesus prayed to the Father *"that they may all be one ... as we are one"* (John 17:21–22), He was praying for a union between God and His children. Let me pause here to point out the importance of that word *"as."* Upon this little word used by Christ hangs all the glory and all the responsibility of living our creation as male and female in the image and likeness of the Trinity, uniting in *"one body"* as a proclamation of the mega mystery of Christ's love for the church. Upon it hangs also all the glory and all the responsibility of believers working toward reconciliation as one body in Christ. As believers in today's world, we have failed in our responsibilities in all of the above, and we must be willing to seek the grace and mercy of God that alone can save us from our sins in this regard. This is the beginning of the healing that is required in both the domestic church, in our marriages and families, and the church at large.

Here we also find our way forward toward reconciliation in both the domestic church and the church at large. Because we are made in the image of the Persons of the Trinity, who live in an eternal exchange of self-giving love, we are meant to become a gift to others and receive the gift of others in a mutually enriching communion of persons. This is the basis of all genuine relationships and of the unity in the church: living in God's grace, we recognize and embrace *the gift of the other.* And that's how I would like to conclude—by recognizing and embracing the gift that my evangelical brothers and sisters have been to me.

MY DEAR EVANGELICAL BROTHERS AND SISTERS:

I owe a debt of gratitude to you for my faith in Christ. Your love for God's Word, your openness to the gifts of the Holy Spirit, and your witness to the fact that Christ wanted to have a personal relationship with me was instrumental in my life. It was your witness through which I came to discover that Jesus is not just an historical figure, but is the great *I AM*, the Son of the living God, who took flesh, died for me, and rose victoriously so that I could also experience victory over sin and death. *Thank you!* Speaking as one who knows well the average Catholic's need for the gifts of the Spirit that you bring, I ask you please to continue bearing bold witness to the risen Christ and to the power of His grace to reach hearts, heal wounds, and transform lives.

Since the early two thousands, I've been honored to have been invited to speak and teach at countless evangelical churches, conferences, and campuses. Thank you for being willing to overcome old prejudices and truly welcome me as a brother in Christ. It's been my privilege to pray and laugh and cry with you in a mutual sharing of hearts and hopes and sufferings. I've continued learning from the gifts and treasures that the Holy Spirit has poured out on you, and I've tried also to open the treasures He's shared with the Catholic Church, to which you have been so warmly receptive.

I've been heartened to see so many evangelicals studying, writing about, and sharing John Paul II's *Theology of the Body* in a language that's understandable to their own congregations and denominations. So often, what seem like causes for division stem from the fact that we use words differently. I've been so blessed by my Protestant brothers and sisters who have graciously helped me to understand better how to communicate in a language that resonates across denominational lines.

Regarding our differences, I once heard it said, by a far more learned theologian than I, that all of the major divisions in the church throughout history can be traced (directly or indirectly) to a dispute about the divine plan for marriage. It's a striking assertion, but one that, given some thought, makes biblical sense: if the union of man and woman is what Scripture proclaims it to be—a great mystery that reveals the even *greater mystery* of Christ's union with the church—it follows that fractures in our understanding of marriage will lead to fractures in our Christology and ecclesiology. For all believers, the path toward reconciliation in *"one body"* must pass through a return to the divine plan for the unity of man and woman in one body.

Again, we know well that we are engaged in a raging battle today for the truth about sex, gender, marriage, and the family. In the face of such a formidable Goliath, this is our moment to stand together on the biblical foundations of our creation and redemption as male and female! The stone that brings Goliath down is Christ. There is no other victory. But the sling that gives us the proper aim is a return to the biblical truth of the body in its maleness and femaleness as a sign revealing the truth of who Christ and the church truly are as the Bridegroom and bride of the book of Revelation.

I've been deeply inspired by how many evangelical brothers and sisters I've met over the years who have given their lives to preserving and defending the truth of our creation and redemption as male and female. If we all commit ourselves to diving ever more deeply into this profound mystery, we will be helping Christ's prayer to be answered that all may be one as He and the Father are one. And through His one body, Christ will not fall short of renewing the face of the earth. Let it be, Lord, as You desire it. Amen.

As president of the Theology of the Body Institute, Dr. Christopher West leads an international apostolate spreading John Paul II's life-transforming teaching. You may reach Dr. West at askchristopherwest.com or tobinstitute.org.

25

METHODISM AND THE CATHOLIC SPIRIT

The Rev. Dr. David F. Watson
| Global Methodist |

The spiritual sons and daughters of John Wesley are scattered throughout the world today. I am grateful to be counted among them. I love this tradition. It is my family, though like any family, we have our dysfunction. There are many kinds of Methodists, sometimes called "Wesleyans." My branch of this tradition is called the Global Methodist Church, although for most of my life, I was part of the United Methodist Church. My thoughts in this chapter will relate mainly to these traditions. Methodists of other stripes might tell this story differently. My account of Methodism and Christian unity will involve three topics: love between Christians; the faith we profess; and the gift of holiness.

First, however, I offer a few remarks about my life in Methodism. My very small part in the story of Methodism began in 1971, when I was baptized as an infant in Matthews Memorial United Methodist Church in Fort Worth, Texas. I was raised by God-fearing parents, and many of my earliest memories are in the classrooms and sanctuary of this church. I attended Sunday school each week and was given a Bible in the third grade. I learned the books of the Bible and the stories of Jesus. I learned that there was a way I was expected to live as a Christian. I learned to pray and confess my sins to God. I remember sitting in worship week after week, staring up at a large, circular, stained-glass image of Jesus above the choir loft. Around Jesus were the words, "My peace I give unto you." I would draw on the bulletin and listen to the choir sing, and even at a young age, I marveled that a small group of people could make such beautiful music. I wondered if angels were helping them. Together we would sing from the hymnal, including those masterful hymns of Charles Wesley like "O for a Thousand Tongues to Sing" and "Rejoice, the Lord is King." I remember standing beside my grandmother, whose eyesight was too bad to read the hymnal but who knew the words of our sacred songs by heart. We sang the doxology ("Praise God from whom all blessings flow…") and the *Gloria Patri* ("Glory be to the Father and to the Son and to the Holy Ghost"). We prayed the Lord's Prayer. My father would give me a quarter that I would put into an envelope to place in the collection plate. When I was a bit older, I was an acolyte. It felt like such an honor to be a part of the service, to wear a white children's robe and walk down the aisle and light the candles.

United Methodist congregations formed me, helped to raise me, and taught me to honor God. When I was baptized, the United Methodist Church was a new denomination of an older movement, having been formed by a merger of the Evangelical United Brethren Church and the Methodist Church in 1968. As a child, I didn't know I was a United Methodist, or a Methodist of any kind, for that matter. I did know, however, that Jesus loved me, and that my life should be different because of His love. He said, *"My peace I give to you"* (John 14:27). Indeed there was a beautiful peace growing up in the church. There was never a time when I did not believe in God. There have been times of doubt and wandering, but not disbelief.

Many Protestant communions in the West have gone through denominational divisions in the last thirty years. There are many reasons for this, but chief among them are differences regarding doctrine and ethics. The rise of liberal Protestantism since the late eighteenth century has involved an ongoing quest to reimagine historic Christian doctrines and ethical teachings. This process accelerated with the massive cultural shifts that took root in the West in the late 1960s. In particular, mainstream Western attitudes around abortion, sex, and gender identity have moved considerably to the left. Many churches have followed suit, having been made ready for this moment by the predominance of liberal/progressive theology among the mainline denominations. In the Global South, however, where Christianity is growing rapidly, Christians have remained far more traditional in their beliefs. Along with some in the West who are more traditionally minded, they have pushed back on these changes, and a number of denominations simply reached the point where they could no longer share the same ecclesiastical structure. Put differently, we have seen, and continue to see, denominational divisions within Protestantism. The United Methodist Church was one of the last holdouts in this schism. We resisted formal division for a long time, but that ship has now sailed.

United Methodist congregations formed me, helped to raise me, and taught me to honor this God who had given Himself for me. I will always be grateful for this. Nevertheless I am among those who have chosen to leave the United Methodist Church. In the summer of 2022, I left the denomination in which I was baptized, confirmed, and ordained. This has been no easy decision. It has put incredible strain on some of my relationships. It has been hard to explain to people I have known for years why I cannot go with them to the destination they envision. We who have been among the more theologically traditional United Methodists have been told we are dividing Christ's holy church. I certainly don't see it that way. Rather, by aligning ourselves with historic teachings and practices that have sustained the church across centuries, we are not diminishing her unity but preserving it.

THE CATHOLIC SPIRIT

Unity is a tricky subject among Protestants, but at the very least, amid our disagreements, we must love one another as Christ commands in John 13:34–35. The idea of a special love between Christians is at the core of John Wesley's sermon "The Catholic Spirit," a touchstone for Methodists as we think about our relationships with other Christians. Wesley was clear about what he expected Methodists to believe, how they should preach, and how they should live. He recognized, though, that not all Christians would believe, preach, and live just as he thought they should. He thus articulates his understanding of how Methodists should relate to other Christians without giving up their core convictions.

Wesley's first instruction in this sermon is to love without exception. Christ commands us to love both our friends and our enemies. There is, however, "a peculiar love which we owe to those that love God." In other words, while we are called to love everyone, the love between followers of Jesus is in some ways different. There should be a special bond between brothers and sisters in Christ.

Nevertheless, disobedience to this command is commonplace due to differences in beliefs and practices. Yet Wesley noted that even though these differences might prevent an "external union," they should not prevent a "union in affection." This sentiment gives rise to one of Wesley's most oft-quoted statements: "Though we can't think alike, may we not love alike? May we not be of one heart, though we are not of one opinion? Without all doubt we may." Differences of theology and practice may necessitate different ecclesiastical bodies, but we can still love one another, support each other, and do good works on behalf of one another.

Wesley encourages Christians to stand firm in their beliefs, modes of worship, and congregational affiliations and at the same time love all people, known and unknown. He was surely right that at the heart of Christian unity is a love for the other, that love Christ commanded in John 13:34–35. As He has loved us so we should love one another. At times we Christians have obeyed this commandment with the deepest sincerity. At times, we have disobeyed it, much to our shame.

THE CONSENSUAL TRADITION

Wesley is clear that while Christians are called to love all people, the special love between Christians is one in which we ask, "Is thine heart right?" He then goes on to explain what this means. For one's heart to be right, it must be right with God, which means there are certain truths we confess and certain ways in which we live. There is much that is packed into his language of being, perfections, divine governance, the supernatural perception of God, and God's eternal nature. Likewise his language about Christ is dense and meaningful, referring to Christ as the incarnation of God and His atoning work, along with the insufficiency of human righteousness to bring salvation, which presupposes a notion of sin, and alluding to salvation by grace through faith. To summarize briefly, Wesley is not asking about matters particular to the Methodist movement, or even the Church of England. His inquiry is broader. The heart that is right with God will confess those basic truths about God revealed in Scripture and confessed since the days of what he calls the "primitive church." The person of a catholic spirit "is fixed as the sun in his judgment concerning the main branches of Christian doctrine." Likewise, the character and way of life of one whose heart is right with God will meet the same standard. Put more simply, while there are clear differences between Christian traditions, if the term *Christian unity* is to be meaningful at all, the term *Christian* must have some content. This content, rooted in God's self-revelation, has been formed and refined across the centuries. In a letter dated June 20, 1789, John Wesley wrote, "In religion, I am for as few innovations as possible. I love the old wine best."

If the unity that inheres between Christians is among those whose "heart is right," this is a criterion we must apply not only to others, but to ourselves. Is *our* heart right? Do we ourselves proclaim and live out the ancient faith? We Methodists have at times been exceedingly faithful in this way, and at other times, we have fallen short. We have been prone to be blown about by every wind of doctrine and captivated by novelty. Paul instructs Timothy, "*What you heard from me, keep as the pattern of sound teaching, with faith and love in Christ Jesus. Guard the good deposit that was entrusted to you—guard it with the help of the Holy Spirit who lives in us*" (2 Timothy 1:13–14 NIV). This instruction is no less important for Christians today. We are to maintain the pattern of sound teaching, and we are to do so with faith and love. With the help of the Holy Spirit, we are to guard the good deposit that has been entrusted to us. In a culture obsessed with novelty, we Christians preserve, guard, and proclaim something very old. It is that apostolic faith "*once for all delivered to the saints*" (Jude 1:3), the consensual tradition that teaches us who God is, who we are, and what it means to be saved people. Amid the clamor of a fickle and rootless world, we are called to guard and proclaim what has been revealed to us. "*The grass withers, the flower fades, but the word of our God will stand forever*" (Isaiah 40:8).

Thomas Oden (1931–2016) was a brilliant Methodist theologian. For a good part of his professional life, he had little connection to the faith that had sustained the church over the centuries. It was a Jewish scholar, Will Herberg, who convinced Oden to take the historic teachings of his faith more seriously. Herberg challenged him to dive into the wisdom of generations past rather than to seek to be original, novel, or theologically innovative. After a particularly poignant conversation with Herberg, Oden asked himself, "Could it be that I had been trampling on a vast tradition of historical wisdom in the attempt to be original?" He soon began to consider "apostolic teachings which believers from all places and times confessed and believed with one voice and for which they had been willing to die." Oden called this across-the-board foundation *consensual Christianity*.

Consensual Christianity. The idea has been almost anathema among some circles within mainline Protestantism. Yet its rejection accounts for a great deal of our division. There are beliefs and practices that have been cherished and upheld across the ages, across denominations, and throughout the globe.

When we reject them, we diminish our unity with the communion of saints. I have worshipped with Evangelicals in Vietnam, with the Orthodox in Egypt, with Catholics in Israel, with Methodists in Cuba, and with Pentecostals in Pennsylvania. I have been blessed in both highly liturgical worship and contemporary worship complete with smoke machines and elaborate light shows. Through all of these different manifestations of the one body of Christ, however, there is a common thread. There is one God—Father, Son, and Holy Spirit. He has revealed Himself to Israel, through the Person of Jesus Christ, and in holy Scripture. He abides with us today in the Person and work of the Holy Spirit. God's self-revelation teaches us who He is, what He has done for our salvation, and how we should live. Over time, the church codified these beliefs, drawn from reflection on Scripture, in our historic creeds. We do not serve an incompetent God who is unable to communicate His identity and will for our lives. Yes, we now see only in part, as through a glass darkly (see 1 Corinthians 13:12), but there are truths that God has made clear to us, and we trample on these at our peril. There are many components to the unity of the church, but to embrace that ancient faith rooted in the truth of God's self-revelation is surely among them. It is a crucial component of a heart that is right with God.

THE CALL TO HOLINESS

I have long thought of the different Christian traditions as offering different gifts to the church universal. God has blessed the different branches of the church with their own insights, emphases, and practices—a variety of gifts, but the same Spirit. Here is the diversity of the church within its unity. Historically, Methodism's gift to the church has been to lift up and live out holiness. The early Methodists took it as their mission to "spread scriptural holiness throughout the land." In the Methodist traditions, *holiness* is a way of talking about the change that God works in our hearts, leading us out of sin and into a new, righteous life. It is, in the words of John Wesley, the "renewing our fallen nature." Welsey particularly emphasized the new birth, when "the love of the world is changed into the love of God; pride into humility, passion into meekness; hatred, envy, malice, into a sincere, tender, disinterested love for all mankind. In a word, it is that change whereby the 'earthly, sensual, devilish' mind is turned into the 'mind which was in Christ.'" The sanctifying grace of God goes to work in our lives, forming us into the people we were always meant to be. Wesley even believed that the work of holiness could grow in our lives to the extent that we would no longer inwardly or outwardly sin. He called this *entire sanctification* or *Christian perfection*. Yes, we could still make mistakes, and we could still face temptation, but the change in our nature would be such that we would not willingly commit an offense against God. Other traditions may dispute this point, but it was key to early Methodism, and it remains important to many forms of Methodism today.

Nevertheless, it is undeniable that throughout parts of Methodism, the zeal for holiness has waned. Perhaps this is only to be expected. As movements grow and institutionalize, they can gradually lose the fervor and purpose with which they began. It will be an act of love toward the church universal if we Methodists can recommit ourselves to *scriptural holiness*, the holiness that God works in the heart that is lived out in our daily lives. As we, then, pray for other traditions to pursue with zeal that work that God has given them to do, they can do the same for us. They can urge us to hold up the torch of holiness as a gift to the church, not as our special possession, but as a particular calling among the people of God.

LOVE LETTER TO THE PEOPLE CALLED METHODISTS:

My Dear Methodist Brothers and Sisters,

Thank you for raising me up in the faith. Thank you for the care you have shown me. Thank you for the sermons I've heard you preach, the teaching I have received, the friendships I have made, the worship I have experienced. I am grateful for you and for the heritage of faith in which we stand.

Alongside this gratitude, however, there is mourning. I mourn our many divisions, including the one of which I am now a part. I grieve our in-fighting and the absence of love. I lament our fascination with what is new, rather than that faith that has been refined in fire across the centuries. I am discouraged by the extent to which we have become complacent and set aside the vision of holiness that is our gift to the church catholic.

Despite the fact that our beliefs may prevent external unions, I pray that we can love one another. Family disputes can be the most bitter, and we have had plenty of these. Yet as Wesley reminds us, Christ commands that we love one another, even in the midst of disagreement. We are one part of the body of Christ, and we cannot say to one another, "I have no need of you." May we embody Wesley's "catholic spirit" also in loving Christians across the globe with a special tenderness, regardless of their faith traditions.

I pray that we will turn our eyes away from any god who is not the Father, Son, and Holy Spirit, the God who became incarnate in Jesus Christ, lived a perfect life, died an atoning death on the cross to conquer sin and death, and after three days rose again. Let us never again separate ourselves from the consensual tradition, the worship of the God of the church catholic disclosed in Scripture and proclaimed in creed. Let us recognize that we are simply a branch on the vine, and a rather small branch at that. Let us humble ourselves before the ancient wisdom of those who have gone before us in the faith.

I pray that we would return to our first love, that we would reclaim the preaching and living of holiness and share this gift with brothers and sisters across the church. I invite other brothers and sisters in Christ to provoke us to love and good works and to quicken within us the work that God has given us to do.

May God continue to build His church and may the people called Methodists become an ever more faithful and obedient people. *"Now may the God of peace who brought again from the dead our Lord Jesus, the great shepherd of the sheep, by the blood of the eternal covenant, equip you with everything good that you may do his will, working in us that which is pleasing in his sight, through Jesus Christ, to whom be glory forever and ever. Amen"* (Hebrews 13:20–21).

—The Rev. Dr. David F. Watson

The Rev. Dr. David F. Watson is president of Asbury Theological Seminary and an elder in the Global Methodist Church. He may be contacted at asburyseminary.edu or davidfwatson3.substack.com.

26

WE ARE ONE IN GOD

Sr. Dr. Mercy Shumbamhini, CJ
| Zimbabwe Catholic |

That they may all be one, just as you, Father, are in me,
and I in you, that they also may be in us,
so that the world may believe that you have sent me.
—John 17:21

I feel honored to be part of this noble project on unity. I hope and pray that in this love letter, I will be able to weave my tiny thread of ecumenical experiences and add beauty, color, healing, and life to the body of Christ's tapestry. May God help me to weave my ecumenical experiences with humility and open my writing to allow the reader in to travel through my narrative.

Father, I pray that You would grant me, according to the riches of Your glory, to be strengthened in my inner being with power by Your Spirit; and that You, Jesus, as I write this love letter, would dwell in my heart by faith, that I, "*being rooted and grounded in love,*" would be able "*to comprehend with all the saints what is the breadth and length and height and depth*" of Your love "*that surpasses knowledge* [and] *be filled with all the fullness of God*" (Ephesians 3:17–19).

Jesus prayed for unity among His disciples. The gospel creates a unity of faith with our Father, our Savior, and our fellow believers. As we live the gospel and love and serve others, we feel at one with our brothers and sisters and more in tune with the divine. Therefore, church unity is rooted in God and begins from the life and revelation of God. This unity is not to erase diversity but to embrace the oneness of faith and purpose without tension and hostility. The beauty of the church's diversity is its unity and the beauty of its unity is its diversity.

THE SIGNIFICANCE OF CHURCH UNITY

Disunity in the world is the work of the forces of evil that seek to destroy the unity of human race. This has also affected the church, but Christ has conquered the evil forces and has given the church the grace and power to live in unity. As churches, if we live in isolation from one another, we are not able to share in the ecumenical experience. The unity of the church is the essential characteristic of the body of Christ.

Saint Teresa of Calcutta, a saint of our time, diagnosed the world's problems with these words: "We have just forgotten that we belong to one another." We are all parts of the body of Christ. I see church unity as a wake-up call for unity of humanity because if the church does not find itself in unity, then the entirety of humankind will end in broken relationships. The pursuit of church unity—as well as that of all humanity through true justice—is a divine mandate. Therefore, the worldwide church must exist in fellowship and confession of one Christ as Lord. It is on this solid foundation that its mission to the world can be accomplished with greater force.

The incarnate Word of God made Himself vulnerable and if we wish to be witnesses of God's love to the world, we need to be Christlike. Ecumenical relationships should be grounded in that acceptance that we are all children of God through Christ Jesus, who died for all of us. On this basic foundation, we are called to come together, see each other as brothers and sisters, and to share our gifts and resources. As we meet and interact with each other, prayer becomes an indispensable element in the way we sustain our desire to walk together.

MY CHILDHOOD EXPERIENCES

As I write this love letter, I become aware of the multi-religious environment that I grew up in. This environment allowed me to know and appreciate different denominations. I grew up Catholic but I would also go with my grandmother to an Anglican church and with my aunt to a Methodist Church. I attended a Methodist school for both my primary and secondary education. I deeply appreciate the Methodist prayers and hymns we sang at school because they expressed deep union with God. This exposure to different denominations has given me a different perspective on church unity than many Christians who grew up firmly within one particular tradition. I found this experience very healthy for my personal, social, and spiritual growth. This also led me to take an interest in other people's religion and culture.

It is worth noting that in most cases here in Zimbabwe, when a woman marries, she joins her husband's denomination. Such was the case for all three of my aunts. Two of them joined their husbands in the Methodist Church and the third one joined her husband in the Salvation Army. However, when my mother was married, my father joined her in the Catholic Church, and they were married in the Catholic Church. My mother's brother was a Jesuit and was very close to my father. He would often visit us and share with us his religious vocation. He always encouraged us to respect other people's denominations.

From this early personal experience in ecumenism, I see the importance of preserving and deepening the experience of unity on the local level. In our village during big celebrations such as Christmas, New Year's, and Easter, we would all pray together as one family. We would not sleep on Christmas Eve or New Year's Eve, but pray, share testimonies, sing, and dance all night through. Early on Christmas morning every year, we would go around the village, singing, "In Bethlehem today a baby is born, let us all rejoice and dance together, for our Savior and Redeemer is here with us." All of us from different denominations would dance, drum, whistle, and rattle. We learned each other's songs and we would sing them throughout the night. We were all filled with joy and gratitude. By praying together, we stayed together. Prayer bonded and united us. These experiences helped us to not only develop a sense of respect for other faiths but also to learn to participate in faith-related activities with others without it being controversial or politicized.

This fellowship and commitment at the local level creates an environment where people respect each other and it preserves unity. In the community, people use the simple language of love and assist each other in times of need such as sickness or funerals, celebrations and weddings. People in the village enjoy one another's company, render service to one another, and share a commitment to the common good. Being able to work for the common good with other people from different traditions helped me develop an appreciation for diversity.

As I reflect on this experience, I can safely say that when we get to know one another on a human level, a trust is born that enables us to reconcile in the spirit of mutual respect after a tension or conflict. And the better we get to know one another, no matter how different our backgrounds, the more we recognize our similarities. The Christ in me warms to the Christ in the other. Put another way, the closer we draw to the center of our faith lives, the closer we draw to each other. I am glad this relationship between and among local church communities who frequently do this together continues to grow. I see that these faith communities respond to the gospel mandate for peace and justice by pooling their resources with other Christian neighbors and helping each other in times of great need. What I deeply appreciate in these faith communities is that, in most cases, differences are not used to divide people but are a rich resource that could help people to be creative and give a sense of purpose to our calling as children of God.

MY PERSONAL RELATIONSHIP WITH JESUS

My grandmother had a special and unique relationship with Jesus. He was her closest friend. As children, we always wanted to see and be with this Jesus. She would wake up at night and talk to her friend. When she was working in the field or in the house, she would sing love songs to her best friend. She would read to us many stories from the Bible about her friend. She would tell us that Jesus loves children, and it made us very happy to know that our grandmother's friend loved us too.

My grandmother was such an amazing woman; she respected and appreciated other people's beliefs, cultures, and traditions and because of this, she was loved by many. All of our friends from different denominations found a place in her heart. My grandmother always told us to help each other and take care of each other. She told us that we are gifted differently so we should not compete with each one but complement each other. Her faith was very much expressed in the way she treated and respected other people. She lived what she professed, and her faith was indeed expressed in her actions. My grandmother's authenticity in living for our God and her availability and generosity to others inspired me. This became the foundation for my faith and religious journey. Jesus was not only a close friend to my grandmother; He became my close friend too. As I grew up, this relationship with Jesus deepened.

UBUNTU AND UNITY

None of this is to say that people had no conflicts or tensions in my community but these were handled without blaming anyone's denomination. As I look back now, *ubuntu*, the African philosophy of *oneness*—meaning "I am because we are," "My well-being is inseparable from your well-being," and "My happiness is bound to your happiness"—cemented the unity among the faith communities. This African philosophy reminds us that we are all interconnected. It reveals a worldview that we owe our selfhood to others, we are first and foremost social beings, and no one is an island—or as the African would have it, "One finger cannot pick up a grain."

Another African proverb that inspires me is, "If you want to go fast, go alone. If you want to go far, go together." Yes, *ubuntu* is what God presses on us to work together for the common good, to make music together, to build bridges, and to bring hope to people and set the world on fire. Since God is One, humanity is also one. Therefore, a human being's individual religious vocation is not simply a mystic ascent toward unity in God but also a call to community.

Ubuntu is, at the same time, a deeply personal philosophy that calls on us to mirror our humanity for each other. *Ubuntu* describes the clear sense of living in community with others. It connotes an interdependence, so that when one member of the community suffers, everyone suffers. It is a word that is so very descriptive of the biblical concept of unity. No matter how diverse our denominations or religions may be, as children of God, we have an unmistakable bond that breaks down barriers and binds us together. And I experienced this *ubuntu* in the faith communities in my village.

It is noteworthy that *ubuntu* widens the notions of interdependence and connectedness. It goes beyond "fellow humans" to Mother Earth. For example, "My well-being is inseparable from your well-being" refers not just to other human beings but also to the whole of creation.

In this philosophy, the church or faith community is the nesting and nourishing place from which each member springs and gains life, healing, and hope. The individual member is the medium through which the talent, gift, and genius the church needs to develop and grow. The relationship of the individual member and the church or faith community promotes the well-being of all, including Mother Earth, promotes cooperation rather than competition, and above all serves everyone and leaves no one behind.

Ubuntu affects my way of being, my friendships, relationships, and encounters. I have very close friends from all traditions and religions. My Hindu and Muslim friends from Kwekwe have supported our mission with the vulnerable children at our Mary Ward Children's Home; my Protestant friends from Sweden have helped us build the children's hall; my Catholic friends from Germany and the United Kingdom continue to support our mission with the needy; my Buddhist friend from Hong Kong taught me that compassion means to be with, feel with, and suffer with others; and I share many close bonds with the Jewish friend I met in the Holy Land. We are all humans with the same dreams, fears, joys, hopes, and worries. I believe that if we embody this philosophy of *ubuntu*, we can create unity in our church and the world while also bringing healing and hope.

CLINICAL PASTORAL EDUCATION (CPE) IN SOUTH AFRICA

In 1998, as part of preparation for professing my perpetual vows in religious life as a member of the Congregation of Jesus, I went to Groote Schuur Hospital in Cape Town, South Africa, for Clinical Pastoral Education. CPE is an educational process for people involved in any form of pastoral care or pastoral ministry. It is open to people of all faiths and spiritualities who desire to learn more about what it means to practice pastoral care. My group included members of different religions, and our supervisors were from different denominations. I had a number of meaningful ecumenical and interfaith experiences. My personal supervisor was a layperson from the Anglican Church. She was superb in helping me to get in touch with my feelings and making sure they were not displaced.

This clinical placement offered me the opportunity to develop skills in pastoral and spiritual care with people across the spectrum of society and to integrate my own operational theology to offer care in different stages of life transitions, including birth, aging, trauma, rehabilitation, mental health issues, dying, and death. I visited and prayed with patients of diverse faith backgrounds. After every visit to the assigned hospital ward, I took some time for reflections. This experience was both faith-stimulating and challenging. The reflection process transformed me as a person; I saw being human as a foundation to becoming Christian. It gave me space to totally reevaluate not only my vocation journey as a religious sister but also my spiritual journey as a Christian.

Two members from my CPE group richly blessed me as they came all the way from South Africa to celebrate with me as I professed my perpetual vows to serve God and God's people as a member of the Congregation of Jesus. This friendship with ministers and laypeople from other faith and religious traditions is one of the greatest joys and gifts of my ecumenical life.

MY STUDIES AT THE UNIVERSITY OF SOUTH AFRICA

Having worked at Mary Ward Children's Home in Kwekwe, Zimbabwe, as a social worker for seven years, I began master's degree studies in practical theology with a specialization in pastoral therapy at the University of South Africa (UNISA) and then went on to receive my doctorate there. The training was aimed at respecting the spiritual and religious values and ethics of a person in therapy or counseling. *This was one of the most amazing learning and enriching experiences of my professional life.*

In my program, I interacted with many people from different faiths. I greatly appreciated this experience. My supervisors were both Dutch Reformed Church ministers. They were indeed first-rate scholars, educators, and well-seasoned pastors. Through these studies, not only did I discover a new and authentic way of being a pastoral therapist, I also learned a whole new and liberating way of doing theology since doing is more important than knowing or speaking. I also learned that commitment is the first act of theology, especially commitment to the poor and marginalized. Theology or spirituality cannot be done from above or even from below, but mostly from within, by walking with those who suffer, or "smelling like the sheep," as Pope Frances once put it.

MY EXPERIENCES AT TANTUR ECUMENICAL INSTITUTE IN JERUSALEM

I never realized that these seeds of hope that have been nurtured in my heart over the years would help me in my faith journey, expressed in my love for other faiths in the Holy Land. In 2019, after eight years of leadership in the Congregation of Jesus here in Zimbabwe, I went to the Holy Land for my sabbatical. I was living at Tantur Ecumenical Institute. Here I encountered the rich sacredness of others and their faith traditions while experiencing a personal renewal. Tantur welcomes all people from different Christian denominations, religions, nationalities, and ages to study, pray, explore, and live in community. The Tantur experience includes classroom instruction on such topics as Hebrew Scriptures and the New Testament, Biblical Geography, Eastern Christianity, the History of the Middle East, and Spirituality. Classroom instruction is also woven into guided tours and excursions to religious and historical sites in the Holy Land, as well as engagement with the people of the region. I was able to reach out to more people. These activities at Tantur gave me numerous significant ecumenical and interfaith experiences I will never forget.

I was very much inspired by the ecumenical evening prayer. Tantur has formed partnerships with several communities—such as Taizé, Bruderhof, and Chemin Neuf—to assist the institute in providing enriching ecumenical prayer styles and formational experiences. I looked forward to participating in these evening prayers and brought in my African taste while also building up my own faith by encountering the faith of other Christians and other religions. It was such a great joy to see people from different backgrounds and religions working together for peace and unity. This experience touched me deeply. Such an experience can help us bring about that love that Jesus calls on us to develop in our hearts. My experience at Tantur renewed and deepened my faith; it felt like a *refreshing blowing of God's love and Spirit in my life. It gave me hope for the renewal of our world.* I commend Tantur for creating an environment that makes peaceful coexistence possible. This is very important in healing the body of Christ.

TO MY DEAR BROTHERS AND SISTERS IN CHRIST,

May *"the grace of the Lord Jesus Christ and the love of God and the fellowship of the Holy Spirit be with you all"* (2 Corinthians 13:14).

My dear friends in the Lord, let me take a few moments to thank you for your contribution toward unity and healing in our world. In the body of Christ tapestry, each thread or voice has beauty and can stand alone and yet it makes an important contribution to the whole tapestry. It is in this careful positioning of each thread and piece of fabric that the tapestry is created. In the weaving process, there are many threads that remain unseen but still have a part to play in the finished product. Many of you are weaving many threads into the colorful tapestry of unity in our church and world today. These include the threads of strength in adversity; threads of sisterhood and brotherhood; the way we reach out and support and embrace our suffering brothers and sisters; the threads of healing that we gather together as we pass through and beyond the pain of pandemics, wars, crises, floods, drought, and earthquakes; the threads of love that we weave through our families, friends, society, the world, and ourselves; the threads of joy and laughter that add color to our weaving; threads of culture that brings uniqueness and depth to our weaving; threads of mercy and compassion that enable us to reach out to others; and threads of sorrow and grief. Our weaving is testimony to all of our ecumenical experiences. Thank you for adding depth, color, energy, light, life, vibrancy, beauty, peace, courage, healing, hope, and strength to this tapestry.

These threads speak to us and others of who Christ is and who we are. Our tapestry is forever growing with the help of Christ. Let us continue to weave together our threads for unity and healing for the honor and greater glory of God.

I encourage each and every one of us to pause for a few moments and thank God for being a member of the body of Christ, which is the church of Christ. I pray that our God of mercy and love may bless our efforts toward unity in our churches and the world. Please keep this good spirit of working together for unity, healing, and peace.

Dear Lord Jesus, unite us and bring us together as one family, bind us together in love, in the unity of spirit and the bond of peace. Lord of peace and unity, You prayed for unity, that we may be united in love just as You are united with the Father in love. Enkindle in us Your Spirit of unity and teach us how to live together in peace and unity.

Awesome *Creator,* I pray for the whole human family that a new sense of shared humanity will inspire us to live peacefully and sustainably on this fragile planet. I pray for the worldwide Christian community, that all the baptized will treasure the blessings bestowed on them and radiate the joy of the gospel.

Eternal God, You are worthy to be praised because You are able to bless others abundantly. I praise You for You are worthy all the glory, the honor, and the praise. Amen.

Glory be to Him whose power working in us can do infinitely more than we can ask or imagine. Glory be to Him "*in the church and in Christ Jesus throughout all generations, forever and ever. Amen*" (Ephesians 3:21).

My dear brothers and sisters, may God bless each one of you and may God's love enfold you. May the God of unity keep you. May God bless you in all areas of your life. May the God of mercy and forgiveness bring healing to each one of you.

"*May the God of hope fill you with all joy and peace in believing, so that by the power of the Holy Spirit you may abound in hope*" (Romans 15:13). Amen.

Sr. Dr. Mercy Shumbamhini, CJ, is a member of the Congregation of Jesus in Zimbabwe. Connect with her at www.congregatiojesu.org.

27

SEEKING COMMUNION WITH CHRIST AND WITH EACH OTHER

Archbishop Ian Ernest
| Anglican |

From [Christ] *the whole body, joined and held together by every supporting ligament, grows and builds itself up in love, as each part does its work.*
—Ephesians 4:16 (NIV)

In 2013, I read the following words in a church magazine: "The body of Christ seems not a reality, but an ideal hardly to be grasped." They posed a challenge to me as they brought back questions I had as a child about the church and its institutions. In the same breath, these words enlightened me on my own experience as I daily strived to seek a greater spirit of understanding and acceptance among those who are part of the body of Christ.

So, as I write this love letter, my questions and my experience as a child of God urge me to go deeper in my understanding of what it means for me to act responsibly as I long for a greater spirit of unity in the body of Christ. I know that my childhood exposure to the harsh reality of division within the church has offered me a unique opportunity to tread on a pathway that would lead me to gradually establish genuine relationships across a range of disputes and to reach out to the other. In the course of this journey, I discovered day by day that God is always guiding us to something greater than ourselves.

As a child, I grew up in an atmosphere that allowed me to know and appreciate that love is the basic foundation for human development and acquiring self-respect. Each time that love was out of sight, I felt that I was losing part of my humanity and my identity. I feel privileged being born into a family whose lifestyle was grounded in the Christian faith. As we were living in a multireligious and multicultural society and belonged to a minority church, there was a temptation to exclude ourselves from others out of fear and because of the perceptions that they may have had of us. But growing in a family experience where one felt loved and able to love, I was overwhelmed with a thirst for being in communion with the other irrespective of who we were. It was quite a risky road to embark on, as one could be disillusioned because of divisive, irrational situations that were prevailing.

CHILDHOOD QUESTIONS

Since my early childhood, I was profoundly disturbed by the divisions that I witnessed as a result of irrational behavior on the part of those who were members of the church. I could see my own family being seriously damaged by a spirit of division and by judgmental comments because of religion. It was clear that people acted in this way because they were asked to follow a set of unquestioned principles. Tensions within the family network were therefore fueled by the nurturing of erroneous perceptions of the *other* because of religious differences.

As children, we always looked forward to family weddings, but we were not able to attend some of them because of confessional differences, which strained family ties and relationships. For example, I could not be present at my own uncle's wedding because he married a non-Anglican woman. I therefore grew up with this erroneous notion that we were different and thus not able to be and walk together, even though we had the same Master and Lord.

But in the depth of my heart, I knew that there could be a way that would help us to overthrow the erected barriers that prevented us from being together. As I grew up, I came to learn of the love of God as revealed by Christ, a love that conquers everything, even the death of family relationships. It can give life to our bruised and broken relationships. From this love, hope embraced me, and it sustained my dream that we can be and walk together. Differences are not to be used to divide us but are rich resources that can help us to be creative and give a sense of purpose to our calling as children of God.

> *See what great love the Father has lavished on us, that we should be called children of God! And that is what we are!* (1 John 3:1 NIV)

VATICAN II: THE SEEDS OF HOPE

I grew up, implicitly, with this dream for unity. It was consolidated by my early formation in an ecumenical setting. I attended Roman Catholic institutions for my primary and secondary schooling, and it was during that time that my father, an Anglican priest, met the chaplain of my school, Father Henri Souchon. From this encounter, they were able to engage in conversations that led our two churches to collaborate after the Second Vatican Council. This initial conversation between two priests from different denominations gave birth, years later, to a National Working Committee for Ecumenism, and my father became the first Anglican priest to preach in a Roman Catholic Church in Mauritius. As a result of this, my thirst for a living and loving church intensified as I thought that God's love was at work. It is only now that I think of the pathway traced for me as a child of God but I never realized that this seed of hope, nurtured in the heart of a child, would help me in my faith journey to discover God as a God of surprises. Indeed He is.

Nourished by the commitment of those who believed that the Christian faith has a responsibility to witness to the life and love of Christ, I started to build up my own faith by encountering the faith of other Christians. I still remember, with gratitude in my heart to God, the historic visit in 1966 of the Most Reverend Michael Ramsey, archbishop of Canterbury, to Saint Pope Paul VI. This ignited a fire within my heart that in time would envelop my whole being with a desire to burn down the barriers to unity with the flames of love. However, nothing can happen without due sacrifice. We need to lay down our own selves and perceptions in order to give room to the sanctifying, liberating, and unifying presence of Christ. This is how the seeds of hope sown deep within my heart have grown over time. It was not a naïve expression of a form of altruism, but one which is and should be grounded in the sacrificial love of Christ, who emptied Himself so that we can be reconciled to God our Father.

> *If you have any encouragement from being united with Christ, if any comfort from his love, if any common sharing in the Spirit, if any tenderness and compassion, then make my joy complete by being like-minded, having the same love, being one in spirit and of one mind. Do nothing out of selfish ambition or vain conceit. Rather, in humility value others above yourselves.* (Philippians 2:1–3 NIV)

THE FRUITS OF FAITH AND PRAYER

In the turbulent period of my adolescence, I questioned the validity of the religious instruction I had received. I never could see Christians walking the talk of love, so I was disillusioned. But the whole process of questioning helped me. As I embarked on this journey of reflecting on my life with God, I was influenced by Friedrich von Hügel, the Roman Catholic layman who wrote *The Mystical Element of Religion*. Hügel said religion has three essential components: the institutional, the intellectual, and the experiential. My questioning brought me to a wider understanding of my faith based on these three elements. I gradually discovered that my perceptions of the church were not appropriate, but it took me years to realize this fact.

In the course of this voyage of discovery, I was given the opportunity to pursue further studies in Chennai, India, in the mid-seventies. I attended the Madras Christian College, an educational tertiary institution of the Church of South India. Gradually, some of the ideas I had formed of the church faded away, as the Church of South India, in spite of the challenges and difficulties it was going through, embodied that spirit of communion I was longing for: fellowship and communion in diversity. People from different walks of Christian life happened to be walking together. Differences were channeled in such a way that the pioneers of the Church of South India and Church of North India thought that all the Christian denominations who came together possessed an abundance of riches on which to build a togetherness in faith and the worship of the one Lord. These churches did not become a mixed fruit jam but a fruit salad in which each ingredient preserved its flavor, color, and taste, as Cardinal Jean Margéot noted in one of his pastoral letters to the Roman Catholic Diocese of Port Louis, Mauritius. I came to know, by God's grace, that I actually belonged to a greater family.

This is how the taste of God's love came to my mouth. This experience forged the distinctive character of my own calling—the urge to build up a genuine relationship of friendship, brotherly love, and a collaborative ministry with other Christian brothers and sisters. This goes beyond ecumenical theories or endeavors. This route toward a greater spirit of collaboration among the Christian denominations is filled with stumbling blocks but with a prayerful life and the commitment to empty oneself for the sake of God's love, one can work for the victory of a living love over the death of relationships.

A faith grounded in love has brought me to understand that it is possible for Christians to foster a greater spirit of mutual acceptance. This faith, if nurtured in prayer, brings about a restored relationship. Prayer is the key that Christians engaged in ecumenical mission are called to use if any fruit is to be borne.

> *A new commandment I give to you, that you love one another: just as I have loved you, you also are to love one another.* (John 13:34)

PAST ECUMENICAL EXPERIENCES

When I joined the Anglican seminary in the eighties, my exposure to theological learning came as an eye-opener: the participation of other Christians from other denominations as our guides and teachers gave flesh to my yearning to liberate myself from the erroneous thoughts I may have had of others. This granted me the ability to respect others and know that they also had an experience with the Lord that I am called to receive. I became interested in entering into dialogue and establishing friendships with people of other faiths. It helped me to discover the rich nature and culture of the multireligious society that I belonged to.

As I began my ministry in Mauritius, I came to discover that the same thirst was at work in others, and that the love of God was always present, even though it had been hidden from my eyes. God's living and loving presence, rooted in the faith of God's people, could never leave the church.

In my increasing exposure to church life in Mauritius, I realized that there were various projects of an ecumenical nature that were already in place. I discovered that theological education was a springboard to foster a true spirit of ecumenical collaboration.

Later, as a priest, my thirst for ecumenical collaboration was quenched by the invitations I received to support Christian education in other churches. I was asked to equip teachers at an Adventist school with counseling skills. I was also given the opportunity to share the riches of the Anglican tradition as a guide to those who were trained by the Roman Catholic diocese to be catechists in schools. The process of mutual recognition was well on its way.

Years later, as a diocesan bishop, the exposure I received during my formative years sustained the desire to work relentlessly with other church leaders so that our witness in a pluralistic society might bear the compassionate and redeeming love of Christ. There was always an opportunity, because of a common vision spelled out in the conversations the church leaders had, to address matters of national importance, including moral, environmental, and educational issues. The call to defend justice and build up a spirit of solidarity was always at the heart of our intervention. This certainly helped our Christian witness in the diverse Mauritian context.

With the apostolic vicar of Rodrigues Island, an autonomous dependency of Mauritius, the Diocese of Mauritius, through my episcopal commitment, consolidated the ecumenical task of jointly managing a secondary school. This secondary educational institution was created by Anglican and Roman Catholic priests in the early seventies. This initiative greatly contributed to unlocking the potential of the young people on this very small island of forty thousand inhabitants. This ecumenical collaboration gave the church the opportunity to mold a society where mutual respect continues to lie at the heart of daily living. This special relationship was always grounded in prayer.

At a farewell dinner given on the occasion of my departure to Rome in 2019, Cardinal Maurice Piat, the bishop of Port Louis, said that I, the Anglican bishop, was no more a friend but had become his brother. Friendship in ecumenical relationships can forge genuine brotherhood if there is mutual respect and love.

TOWARD THE FUTURE

The God of surprises led me to Rome, where I was interacting with the hierarchy of the Roman Catholic Church. It was an experience I never expected to live. At its heart was the need to listen, to share, to work with, and to establish collaboration that seventy years ago was believed to be impossible task. As time goes by, we come to discover that friendship and mutual hospitality can be the only threads that knit together who we are as disciples of Christ.

Ecumenism calls us to be vulnerable and take risks. The incarnate Word of God made Himself vulnerable, and if we wish to demonstrate God's love to the world, we need to be Christlike. Ecumenical relationships should be grounded in the acceptance that we are all children of God through baptism. On this basic foundation, we are called to come together, see each other as brothers and sisters, and share our gifts. As we meet, prayer becomes an indispensable element in the way we sustain our desire to walk together.

At the Anglican Centre in Rome, members of the clergy from different denominations meet and pray. This is the leaven that raises relationships into concrete friendships. Theoretical dialogue is important but the practice of praying together is essential.

It is exciting how this life can help us to bring about that love that Jesus calls on us to develop in our hearts. As a child I was disillusioned, as an adolescent I was questioning, and as an adult I have found the grace to grow in Christ with others, regardless of our different church traditions.

CONCLUDING WORDS

Dear brothers and sisters in Christ, the future lies in a living faith that opens our hearts to offer our hands to the other in fellowship for the sake of God's kingdom. This brings us to the role of the church in the world. It is a world created by God intended for great purposes. We may have heard this before, but it is good to remind ourselves that the church exists for God's mission. Both the church and the world belong to God. In spite of the awareness of the problems that threaten our unity as the body of Christ, it is good for us to trust the Holy Spirit and let Him bring Christ into the situation to make a Christlike difference.

We are people called by God to be His servants and His disciples. May He guide us in our quest for unity, illuminate our understanding, and inspire our lives to be instruments of His love.

PRAYER FOR THE CHURCHES

Almighty God and Father, since creation, You have loved us and established us as the crown of creation. The love that You have always manifested to us goes beyond human imagination. The Psalms exalt Your holy name and the wonders You have performed; they have expressed Your love to us in spite of our fragility, our sinfulness, and our weaknesses. As we exalt Your name, we bow down to You to ask for Your forgiveness and mercy toward us.

You have so loved the world that You have given us Your Son, Jesus Christ. Through Him, we receive Your compassionate love, which redeems, gives life, and offers the grace that brings about the transformation of our minds and hearts. We are thankful that on the eve of His death, He prayed for us and declared to You how precious we are. This makes us recipients of Your mission. By Your Spirit, help us O Lord to see the church as Your living body, to show the world that true love is possible. Amen.

Archbishop Ian Ernest served as the archbishop of Canterbury's personal representative to the Holy See and director of the Anglican Centre in Rome until his retirement in January 2025. Connect with him at www.worldanglican.com/mauritius.

28

RADICAL ECUMENISM AND A PENTECOST OF MERCY

Edgardo A. Colón-Emeric
| Methodist |

Early in the morning of October 5, 2022, a small band of Catholics and Methodists gathered in a room behind the Paul VI Audience Hall in the Vatican to meet with Pope Francis. The room was called an *auletta*—literally, a "little hall"—but it was only little in comparison to the 6300-seat-capacity room next door. While we waited for the pope, a member of our group spoke of having "happy legs," which was a more original way of naming what I experienced as butterflies in the stomach as I prepared to present the most recent report of the Methodist-Roman Catholic International Commission.

MY JOURNEY

My journey to the *auletta* began at Duke Divinity School in the mid-1990s, when I studied theology under the great Methodist ecumenist Geoffrey Wainwright. From him, I learned the journey toward Christian unity has deep roots in church history and Scripture. The word *ecumenical* comes from the Greek *oikoumene,* which the New Testament and the Greek version of the Old Testament use to refer to the whole inhabited world. For instance, Luke 2:1 says that around the time of the birth of Jesus, *"a decree went out from Caesar Augustus that* ***all the world*** [oikoumene] *should be registered."* When Christian leaders met in Constantinople in AD 381 to argue for the true humanity of Jesus against detractors, they referred to the previous gathering of bishops in Nicaea in AD 325 as an "ecumenical synod." For many centuries since, the adjective ecumenical has been used for particular church offices, such as the patriarch of Constantinople, and for statements that represent the teaching of the entire Christian world, such as the Nicene Creed and the Apostles' Creed.

Wainwright helped me understand the abiding significance of the historical ecumenical councils and the creeds that came from them. From him I learned that, in the context of the First World War in the twentieth century, a new longing for church unity emerged for the sake of evangelism, peace, and justice, receiving the venerable name "ecumenical" but in new ways. Today, the term ecumenical encompasses more than geographical scope or historic landmarks; it names a way of being the church that affirms diversity, rejects division, and works for unity. It denotes a new posture before God and fellow Christians, a posture of dialogue (sitting ecumenism), service (walking ecumenism), and prayer (kneeling ecumenism). This last one most of all, for at the heart of the ecumenical way is Jesus's prayer on the eve of His passion for His followers throughout the ages: "*That they may all be one ... that the world may believe*" (John 17:21).

Wainwright introduced me to landmark ecumenical documents from the World Council of Churches such as *Baptism, Eucharist, and Ministry*, ecumenical heroes like Lesslie Newbigin, and the gift of Wesleyan hymnody for the church universal. Wainwright's teaching on the true nature of the church—which stands in stark contrast to a visibly divided Christianity—provoked a kind of existential ecclesial crisis in many of his students. Some resolved the crisis by joining denominations that appeared to represent the whole better than others, such as Roman Catholicism and Eastern Orthodoxy. Others became busy in their own ecclesial settings and limited ecumenical work to interdenominational cooperation. Still others, like me, were swept up by the ecumenical movement.

After graduation from Duke Divinity School in 1997, my bishop appointed me to start a new Methodist church among the Hispanic community in Durham, North Carolina. Engaging in this ministry raised all kinds of questions. Was I not contributing to church division by starting yet one more congregation? After all, there was not a shortage of churches in Durham. Within the small three-block radius of where my congregation gathered, there were nine churches, three of which were sharing the same building. The more I visited door-to-door, offering Christ and inviting people to church, the more resistant people became because another evangelist had just been there ten minutes earlier. To be sure, in these encounters, I sometimes heard Spirit-inspired cries of, "What should we do?", echoing the assembly that heard

Peter's Pentecost sermon in Acts 2:37. More frequently, I heard questions like, "What does your church offer me?" Witnessing to Christ from divided congregations too often turns people into hagglers and preachers into *"peddlers"* (2 Corinthians 2:17). At times, I felt more like a hawker of supernatural wares than a steward of God's mysteries. Even so, I never abandoned my ecumenical formation and longing for unity but carried these with me into my doctoral studies and my participation in official ecumenical dialogues.

Since 2008, I have had the humbling privilege of representing Methodists in bilateral dialogues with Roman Catholics nationally and internationally. In these years, I have been blessed by the exchange of gifts that comes from walking toward Christian unity. There is something truly remarkable about travelling, reading, discussing, eating, and praying together with fellow Christians with whom one has substantive disagreements.

REFLECTIONS ON DOCTRINE, BAPTISM AND RADICAL ECUMENISM

One characteristic of these dialogues I greatly appreciate is their unabashedly doctrinal character. After all, historically, one reason why Christians part ways and remain divided is doctrine. Differences between how Catholics and the Orthodox understand the Person of the Holy Spirit and how Protestants and Catholics understand the role of Mary all promote and sustain separation. The unity Christians seek cannot downplay doctrine's importance because faith involves thinking. A unity that papers over questions of truth is, at best, toleration and, at worst, indifference.

Clearly, what unites Christians at the deepest level is not doctrine, but Christ, with whom we are one through baptism. Scripture testifies to baptism's significance when it says, *"In one Spirit we were all baptized into one body—Jews or Greeks, slaves or free—and all were made to drink of one Spirit"* (1 Corinthians 12:13). The church is already one. Ephesians 4:4–6 declares this in a beautiful way: *"There is one body and one Spirit—just as you were called to the one hope that belongs to your call—one Lord, one faith, one baptism, one God and Father of all, who is over all and through all and in all."* This oneness does not erase diversity. Indeed, *"Grace was given to each one of us according to the measure of Christ's gift"* (verse 7). The waters of baptism do not wash away difference. Instead, they cleanse difference and prepare it for sanctification.

Even so, ecumenical dialogues often focus on doctrine. Ecumenical doctrinal statements claim baptism as the common ground for Christian unity. It is, however, a contested claim. Some fail to recognize the validity of baptism if administered to the very young (infants rather than youth), or with little water (sprinkling rather than immersion), or without invoking the name of the Father, Son, and Holy Spirit (Trinitarian rather than Jesus only). Others recognize the full implications of baptismal recognition for Christian communion. One of the most painful moments in Methodist-Catholic dialogues comes when we celebrate the Eucharist and fail to share the body and blood of Christ. It is a scandal to see people who have been spending intense time together and share so much in common part ways at the Lord's Supper. For some, the contradiction is infuriating; for others, it is stimulating. In either case, the ideas of collegiality and conviviality crash against the harsh realities of imperfect communion with each other. The ecumenical journey is not a yellow brick road but a *via dolorosa* (sorrowful way). We are bound to fall against the stumbling blocks of divided doctrines and practices. However, on the ecumenical journey, there are also glimpses of God's promised unity.

In 2017, I visited Rome as part of a delegation of Methodists and Catholics who met with Pope Francis to celebrate fifty years of ecumenical dialogue. Before our audience, we visited the Scavi, a network of catacombs beneath the Vatican that include what many believe to be the true resting place of Peter. In a small grotto by this grave, in sight of Peter's jawbone, our delegation paused to pray the Lord's Prayer. In that dark, cramped room, beneath the weight of marble, gold, and centuries of conflicted histories, we witnessed a small miracle. We saw more than Catholics or Methodists, bishops or theologians. We saw Christians standing before *our* Peter, calling on *our* Father, begging for *our* daily bread, and confessing *our* sins. The Borgias were *our* popes, *our* crusades, *our* inquisition. Prayer opened my eyes to see again an important truth—we are radically one.

Ecumenism is radical work. Radical change goes to the root. This is why some of the most radical changes can go unseen for a long time. It took decades for the revolution initiated by Christ's crucifixion and resurrection to reach Rome. Our unity is radical because its roots go deep. We are one because there is one baptism, one church, one Christ, one Spirit, one God. Because the roots of Christian unity lie mostly underground, the most important work in ecumenism may escape notice.

CHALLENGES TO ECUMENISM

The radicalism of the ecumenical way is not easy to sustain. Millennia of splits and separations has carved a challenging ecclesial landscape. The tectonic shifts occasioned by the Great Schism of 1054 or the Reformation of the sixteenth century have opened up doctrinal, liturgical, and spiritual chasms across which Christians struggle to recognize each other as fellow Christians. Building bridges and paving paths toward Christian recognition and reconciliation is long, arduous work.

One challenge facing ecumenical work is disagreement about its goal. Jesus prayed that His disciples may be one as He and the Father are one but did not offer a blueprint or model for unity. The statement from the World Council of Churches assembly in New Delhi in 1961 perhaps comes closest to a common vision of the goal. It highlights unity as "both God's will and His gift to the church." Unity does not mean uniformity. There is legitimate diversity within Christian life. Nevertheless, beyond this broad level of agreement, differences emerge. The earliest Protestant expressions of the ecumenical movement aimed for organic union as the goal, the merging of diverse churches under one common structural arrangement. For instance, the United Methodist Church was born in 1968 from the merger of the Evangelical United Brethren and the Methodist Episcopal Church. Prior to the Second Vatican Council, the Roman Catholic model for unity was simple—return to Rome. More recently, the Catholic Church has rejected this ecumenism-of-return and instead committed itself to the "reintegration of unity" (as the Vatican II document on ecumenism was called) whose form is more mysterious because there is more to the church than the communities in communion with the bishop of Rome. Other models have emerged over time like that of unity-in-reconciled-diversity, which makes room for particularities from the variety of Christian communions to be received as gifts. Some speak of different ecclesial forms like the Pauline (Protestant), Petrine (Roman Catholic), and the Johannine (Orthodox). Multiple models suggest multiple paths and may provoke even more estrangement.

POSTURES THAT CHALLENGE ECUMENISM

In addition to the lack of a common vision of Christian unity, there are attitudinal postures that challenge the ecumenical movement:

ECUMENICAL SKEPTICISM

In Latin America, many Protestant churches experience deep misgivings about the work for Christian unity. Interdenominational cooperation is one thing, but a movement that embraces Roman Catholics as sisters and brothers is something else. The language itself is telling. In Latin American communities, it is still common to hear people distinguishing Christians from Catholics. The word *ecumenism* carries the baggage of sounding like communism and evokes external hegemonic forces. Latin American history does indeed bear the marks of a Roman Catholic ecclesial monopoly, which has only broken up in recent decades. The idea of sitting down with Roman Catholics for fraternal dialogues strikes some as a betrayal of the Gospel and of the witness of hard-fought battles for social recognition.

NOSTALGIA FOR A GOLDEN AGE

It is common to hear that the most exciting days for ecumenism are past. The early decades of the twentieth century witnessed stellar signs of hope for Christian unity: the formation of the World Council of Churches, the invitation of Protestant observers to the Second Vatican Council, the Joint Declaration on the Doctrine of Justification, and many more. The abundance of signs of unity moved Pope John Paul II to look to the twenty-first century as inaugurating a millennium of Christian unity that would heal the wounds of division from the second millennium. However, the agreements achieved through official dialogues have not changed much in daily Christian life. The Joint Declaration on the Doctrine of Justification may have bridged gaps opened by the Reformation, but the churches have yet to cross these bridges.

APATHY TOWARD DIVISION

Simply put, we do not miss each other enough. In the international Methodist-Catholic dialogue, the parable of the prodigal son in Luke 15:11–32 mirrored the reality of this unrealized estrangement. Both sons abandoned the father's house. The younger one lost himself in licentious living in a far country. The older one lost himself in work close to home. When Methodists and Catholics read this together, we saw ourselves. Both of us were the younger son. Both of us were the older son. Both of us long to return to the father's house and be embraced. In Scripture, the parable ends without resolution. The older son refuses to celebrate with the father. One detail that interests me is the two brothers' relationship—or the lack thereof. In his journey to and from the far country, the younger son spares no thought for his older brother. The older son only bears contempt for the younger one. Neither refers to the other as brother; neither longs for the other.

DREAMS OF AN ECUMENICAL MOVEMENT

The challenges facing the ecumenical movement are not cause for despair but for dreaming. In Scripture, we find hints of an eschatological dimension to ecumenism. In Hebrews 2:5, we read of "*the world to come* [oikoumene]." Difficult experiences with the edicts (dogmas) of Caesars and the ecumenical pretensions of Rome pushed Christians to distinguish the *oikoumene* of the empire from the *oikoumene* of the church. The unity of the coming world will not derive from homogenizing cultures or subjecting differences but from purifying and perfecting them. The promise of this coming world guides the ecumenical movement and inspires Christian dreams of unity. Here I share a few dreams I believe are not simply my own but reflect the aspirations of many.

I dream of an ecumenical movement that goes out to the world. Ecumenism and evangelism cannot be separated. The event most frequently credited with the launch of the ecumenical movement was the Edinburg Missionary Conference of 1910. The call to unity came from the mission field, where the denominational differences among Christians paled in comparison to the differences between Christians and non-Christians. Interestingly, in the lead up to the gathering, they called it the Ecumenical Missionary Conference, but the organizers judged that the absence of Catholic and Orthodox participants stretched the definition of "ecumenical" beyond the breaking point. Christian unity matters, but it does not exist for its own sake. Unity is the goal of the ecumenical movement, not the goal of the church; the church seeks unity for the sake of its credibility in its mission to the world.

I dream of an ecumenical movement that goes down to the margins. The church has gone south, in the sense that the majority of its members are now found in what is often called the Global South. As the church has changed, so too must the movement toward Christian unity. The ecumenical questions emerging from the Global South are not identical to those of the Global North. Doctrine matters, but the pressures on the churches are not simply those coming from the secular age; they come from the heavy legacies of colonialism. Moreover, in the movement to the margins, we might rediscover the power of Jesus's high priestly prayer by joining His journey of descent. Jesus voiced His prayer not from a temple or throne but from the place of rejection and suffering.

I dream of an ecumenical movement that draws in the youth. Before the Edinburg Missionary Conference, the movement toward Christian unity was a youth movement. The contributions of interdenominational groups such as the YMCA, the YWCA, and the World Student Christian Federation are underappreciated today. Youth and student groups committed themselves to Christian unity and "the evangelization of the world in this generation." Along with recovering the role of youth, the ecumenical movement needs to place laity at the center. Clericalization has rendered the movement the work of specialists rather than the work of the people of God.

I dream of an ecumenical movement that draws in the theological academy. In its list of "instruments of unity," *The Oxford Handbook of Ecumenical Studies* does not mention theological schools, yet these have long served as signs of and instruments for Christian unity. In seminaries and divinity schools, future Christian leaders deepen their understanding of the faith by studying, worshipping, and serving next to Christians of different traditions. There is an old saying that guides the Christian journey toward unity: "In essentials, unity; in nonessentials, liberty; in all things, charity." In seminaries, many learn there is a hierarchy of doctrines, and this hierarchy clarifies the terms for the theological pluralism coherent with Christ's gospel. Ecumenical seminaries and divinity schools are fragile institutions, stressed by the forces of secularization and polarization. However, God's promised vision of the church is ecumenical, and a school that forms people for strictly denominational (or even non- or post-denominational) leadership will fall out of step with the richness of Christ's prayer.

A PENTECOST MOVEMENT

Returning to the *auletta,* Pope Francis walked slowly into the room. Aided by a cane, he made his way to his chair and sat down. Official greetings from the Methodist-Roman Catholic International Commission followed. In contrast to our scripted remarks, the pope spoke off the cuff. He fondly reminisced about his connections to Methodist pastors in Argentina before turning to talk about ecumenism and the parable of the prodigal son. He alluded to a popular staged rendition of the parable. In this play, the prodigal longs to return to his father's house but fears rejection or worse. He asks a friend to carry a letter to his father asking him to drape a white handkerchief from a window if he is welcome to come home. When he draws near to the house, he sees not one but hundreds of little handkerchiefs.

The message was clear. God's mercy is extravagant. God sends the church, as the body of Christ, into the world as the face of mercy. The signs of mercy may be as small as little handkerchiefs, but they can overwhelm those who have eyes to see. In this connection, I find it fitting that one of the names for the feast of Pentecost is Whitsunday. The name comes from Pentecost's association with baptism and the practice of wearing white for that occasion. This is the ecumenical movement toward a new Pentecost of mercy.

DEAR HISPANIC AND LATIN AMERICAN PROTESTANTS,

On the eve of His death, Jesus prayed to the Father for His followers in the generations to come, *"That they may all be one, just as you, Father, are in me, and I in you, that they also may be in us, so that the world may believe that you have sent me"* (John 17:21). Unity is Christ's prayer for the sake of the church's integrity and its mission in the world. Christ's prayer is the church's commission. The answer to this prayer will come from God and yet not without us. We are called to do more than say "Amen" to this prayer. We are called to be instruments for its fulfillment. This is one reason why Paul begs the Christians in Ephesus to make every effort *"to maintain the unity of the Spirit in the bond of peace"* (Ephesians 4:3). Jesus *"is our peace"* (Ephesians 2:14), but if Christians break the bond of peace and fight each other over doctrines or disciples, the world will have a hard time believing this. The ecumenical movement is not born from a desire to water down truth or paper over differences. It is born from Christ's prayer and its stated correlation between the Gospel's credibility and Christian unity.

I know some of you may have questions about the ecumenical movement. Indeed, some of you expressed concerns about my visit to the Vatican in October 2022. This visit happened in the context of a new round of ecumenical dialogue sponsored by the World Methodist Council and the Roman Catholic Church. These dialogues have proceeded uninterrupted since 1967. You may wonder about the purpose of these encounters and whether the name of a bilateral dialogue like the Methodist-Roman Catholic International Commission signals denominational merger as the goal. Some have even asked whether those who engage in ecumenical dialogue as I do are "closet Catholics." The answer to these questions is an unequivocal "No."

The official goal of these dialogues is full communion in faith, mission, and sacramental life. The attainment of this goal is not something we can do on our own, and it cannot be completed in this life. Christian unity is the work of the Spirit. Fullness of communion among Christians is inseparable from fullness of communion with Christ. This fullness will be attained in the life to come, when people from every church community gather around the throne not as separate denominations but as one people of God "lost in wonder, love, and praise," as Charles Wesley sang. We experience foretastes of this fullness along the way when we worship and witness together. Paradoxically, ecumenical dialogue helps me become more Methodist, not less.

My participation in ecumenical dialogues such as that with Roman Catholics comes not from a desire to become Roman Catholic but from a longing to restore the bond of peace among us. Even Peter got it wrong, and when he did, Paul confronted him and corrected him. (See Galatians 2:11–14.) The pope is not beyond reproach, and neither is any follower of Jesus. What are we Protestants protesting? Is it not time to reframe our posture to one that is more evangelical, that announces good news? At the heart of the ecumenical movement and the search for Christian unity is seeking the mind of Christ and walking as He walked. In John Wesley's terms, the goal of ecumenism is nothing less than perfection in love.

My dear *protestantes, evangélicos, evangélicas,* and *metodistas,* if you are walking in the way of Christ, whether you know it or not, you are on the way to Christian unity, you are an ecumenical pilgrim. May God guide our steps and keep us from falling, that we may stand "*blameless before the presence of his glory with great joy*" (Jude 1:24).

Edgardo A. Colón-Emeric is dean of Duke University Divinity School, where he is also director of the Center for Reconciliation. Connect with him at divinity.duke.edu/faculty/edgardo-colon-emeric.

Editor's note: *Portions of this chapter are drawn from Dean Colón-Emeric's blog post "Christian Ecumenism and Extravagant Mercy: The case for Christian unity and dreaming in line with Pentecost," March 6, 2023, dukedivinity.medium.com/christian-ecumenism-extravagant-mercy-c11c4680352c.*

29

UNITY THROUGH THE CROSS

Dr. Mary Healy
| Catholic |

What was on the heart of Jesus on the night before He died? His deepest prayer was that His followers would be united—not with a superficial conformity of outlook or behavior or structure, but with the fire of divine love that burns eternally in the heart of the Trinity. "[Father,] *that they may be one even as we are one*" (John 17:22).

I was never more struck by the scandal of Christian disunity than when I first visited the Church of the Holy Sepulcher in Jerusalem, built over the place where Christ died. This church is a microcosm of the Christian world, and there, the sin of disunity is most clearly on display. The church is divided into six areas: three main areas controlled by the Catholic Church, the Greek Orthodox Church, and the Armenian Apostolic Church, and three smaller areas controlled by the Syrian Orthodox, the Coptic Orthodox, and the Ethiopian Orthodox. Any encroachment by one group on the area of another is considered a serious offense. These Christian churches have such a hard time getting along that for several centuries, the key to the main door has been held by a Muslim family, whose members are responsible for unlocking and locking the church every morning and evening. So bitter are the disputes that for over a hundred years, a workman's ladder has stood on the facade just above the main door, since no one can agree on who or how to remove it. Here is the most sacred site in the whole Christian world, where Christ died for our sins, and we cannot even be united enough to hold the keys.

It is impossible to visit that church and not feel the heartbreak of Jesus over the brokenness in His body. At an ecumenical conference in Kansas City in 1977, my friend Ralph Martin gave this prophetic word: "Come before Me with broken hearts and contrite spirits, for the body of My Son is broken. Come before Me with tears and mourning, for the body of My Son is broken. ... I would have made you a light on a mountaintop, a city glorious and splendorous that all the world would have seen, but the body of My Son is broken. ... Turn from the sins of your fathers and walk in the ways of My Son. Return to the plan of your Father, return to the purpose of your God. The body of My Son is broken." Those who were present say that as Ralph gave this word, sobbing could be heard around the stadium as people's hearts were pierced with contrition.

This sense of Christ's grief at the sin of disunity is part of the reason that when I consecrated myself totally to Jesus, in the place of the crucifixion in the Church of the Holy Sepulcher on March 7, 2000, I included a commitment to pursuing unity in the body of Christ as an essential part of my consecration.

I grew up Catholic, in a family that was at first nominally Catholic and then deeply converted. But from an early age, I experienced the richness and beauty of other Christian traditions. At age ten, I attended an Evangelical summer camp on Lake Winnipesaukee in New Hampshire. Every morning, before all the fun outdoor activities, we had "devotions"—something I'd never heard of—in which a counselor gave a short teaching, and then every child had some time alone with Jesus, to read the Bible and pray. I loved this intimate and familiar way of relating to the Lord. I also loved memorizing Bible verses painlessly through catchy songs.

After college, I spent a summer in the Soviet Union, where tens of thousands of believers had paid the ultimate price for their faith. Most churches back then were closed or converted into museums, but a few times, I was able to attend the Russian liturgy with its repeated prostrations, icons, candles, and haunting chant. I saw the ravages of seventy years of brutally imposed atheism, but also the way ordinary people had held on, baptizing their children in secret and attending church when they could, even at risk of arrest and torture. I was deeply inspired by the life of Father Walter Ciszek, a Catholic priest, and Piotr Andreyevitch Streltzof, better known as Father Arseny, an Orthodox priest, both of whom spent decades serving God as prisoners in the Soviet Gulag.

Later, when I became involved in pro-life activity, I had the privilege of praying and protesting at abortion clinics shoulder to shoulder with

Evangelicals and other Christians, and sometimes being arrested with them. It was evident that our common love for the Lord made us equally passionate about speaking up for little ones who had no voice.

As a young adult I became a member of Mother of God Community, a Catholic and ecumenical lay community in Gaithersburg, Maryland. Every week, we gathered for praise, worship, prophecy, and teaching. We studied Scripture together and supported each other in living radically the new life in Christ. One of the highlights every year was the Easter Vigil liturgy, celebrated from ancient times on the night when Christ rose from the dead. By permission of the bishop, we would be all together for the first part, with the lighting of the Easter candle, the chanting of the Exsultet, the Scripture readings and homily, and thunderous praise. Then we would separate, with a Catholic priest presiding over the liturgy of the Eucharist for the Catholics and an Anglican priest presiding over it in another room for the Protestants. It was a powerful experience of unity, but one that also allowed us to taste the pain of division. We are not yet fully one to the point of being able to celebrate the Eucharist together.

In the community, we read about the lives of Catholic saints as well as works from Christian authors like Watchman Nee, Andrew Murray, and A. W. Tozer, who had a profound impact on me. From Merlin Carothers' book *Power in Praise*, I learned the amazing secret of the power of praising God in all circumstances, especially the most difficult. I was deeply moved by the testimonies of Protestant evangelists, martyrs, and confessors of the faith.

While studying for my doctorate in biblical theology, I saw firsthand that much of contemporary biblical scholarship was spiritually barren and lifeless. All too often, it treated Scripture as if it were a merely human ancient document and ended up undermining faith in the Word of God rather than strengthening it. But shortly after I got my doctorate, I was invited to join a remarkable group of biblical scholars that met every year, led by Anglican minister Craig Bartholomew. Craig's vision was to renew biblical studies on a foundation of faith, in an attitude of truly listening to God's voice. It was deeply inspiring to study, interact, and pray at these meetings with top-notch scholars (Protestant, Orthodox, and Catholic) whose faith in Christ shone out of everything they said and wrote. I found I had more in common with them than with some Catholic scholars who held that faith should have no place in biblical research or who seemed uncomfortable talking about Jesus.

Years later, after becoming a seminary professor, the Lord gave me a surprise of the Spirit. In the fall of 2013, I had a sabbatical semester, a time for extra research. I felt the Lord leading me to deepen my understanding of the supernatural gifts of the Holy Spirit, especially healing. During that semester, I went on a two-week mission in Brazil with Global Awakening, led by healing evangelist Randy Clark. It was two weeks of living in the supernatural. We witnessed miracles every day—people with tumors, crippling arthritis, blindness, deafness, and severe injuries sovereignly healed by the Lord. One of the most striking aspects of that mission was its evangelistic focus. It was very clear that the primary goal was not healings for their own sake, but salvation—that unbelievers would come to know the Lord Jesus and give their lives to Him. Every evening, we would visit a church packed with people, many of whom were not churchgoers but had been dragged there by their friends. After a time of worship and preaching, the Lord would work miracles. Then around midnight, the service would conclude with an altar call. People would come forward weeping to surrender their lives to Christ. The members of the local church would be on hand to receive them and introduce them into life in the church. After that mission, I could not but speak of what I had seen and heard! I was deeply convinced that *God wants this in the Catholic Church*—that this manifest power of the Holy Spirit, convincing the hearts of unbelievers through signs and wonders, is not something novel or peripheral but is a restoration of something that belongs to our apostolic heritage.

I was also greatly blessed numerous times by visiting Catch the Fire Church in Toronto, where the "Toronto Blessing" originated in 1994. Some have criticized the manifestations that have occurred there, but what I've seen most prominently is the fruit of holiness: lives radically given over to Jesus and the spread of His kingdom; godly marriages and families; and generosity, humility, and love. I've been deeply moved by the testimonies I've heard there of conversions, physical and emotional healings, reconciliation of marriages, deliverances from drug addiction and demonic bondage, people renewed in faith and deepened in zeal for God, and people catapulted into missions of evangelism and service to the poor, still bearing great fruit in some of the most challenging mission territories of the world. It is good to remember that some lives of the saints also include rather strange phenomena that were misunderstood or criticized at the time.

For several years, I had the privilege of participating in the International Pentecostal-Catholic Dialogue, which meets in a different location for a week every year. The task for our five-year phase of the dialogue was to discuss the charisms of the Holy Spirit and come to as much theological agreement as possible. It was sometimes amusing to see how the same words, such as *prophecy* or *discernment*, were being used on both sides with very different meanings. As the only charismatic Catholic on the dialogue at the time, I was sometimes able to serve as a "translator" of sorts between Catholics and Protestants. By the end of our discussions, I think all the participants were amazed at the degree to which we could agree that gifts of the Holy Spirit "are essential both for the life of the church and for her evangelizing mission."

So how can we pursue greater unity in the body of Christ? In some settings, I have witnessed the problems that can be caused by misguided attempts at unity. One of these could be called "lowest common denominator ecumenism." In this view, drawing closer to other Christians means dropping or downplaying what is distinctive to one's own tradition. For Catholics, this means we avoid speaking of Mary and the communion of saints, the priesthood and sacraments, or the real presence of Christ in the Eucharist. But a unity not based on truth is an illusory unity that will not last.

Another misguided attempt at unity is the opposite view, what might be called the "just come home to Rome" mentality. This one insists that everyone just needs to discover that the Catholic Church is the one true church and convert. But this ignores the fact that the divisions in Christ's body were usually not due to a sincere pursuit of truth but to sins on both sides—pride, arrogance, stubbornness, self-righteousness, anger, vengeance, pettiness, and other failings. The deep fissures and clefts in the body of Christ occurred over long periods of time, and they cannot be healed superficially. The long road back to unity will only be traversed by repentance, humility, prayer, and deeper conversion on both sides.

I have gotten to know two amazing examples of lived ecumenism that manage to avoid these two pitfalls, no doubt after having learned from mistakes along the way: the Chemin Neuf Community in France and the Alleluia Community in Augusta, Georgia, USA. Both of these communities have members (including priests and pastors) from numerous Christian traditions—Lutherans, Pentecostals, Baptists, Reformed, Mennonite, Messianic Jewish, non-denominational, Anglican, and Catholic. They have a tight-knit, deeply committed community life, yet every member is taught and encouraged to be a loyal and practicing member of their own church family as well. If they were not, then the community itself would become just one more Christian denomination among the tens of thousands that already exist. But as it is, they are a force for unity. It's as if each member with one arm holds on tightly to their church family and with the other arm holds on tightly to their brothers and sisters in the community. This does not happen easily or automatically. They have to learn how to speak about the faith in a way that respects one another and doesn't offend or confuse those of a different tradition. They have to learn to confront one another when needed, to repent, forgive, forbear, and love more deeply. Ultimately, to have one's arms held out that way, pulled in two directions, is to be crucified. It cannot be done without dying to self and becoming more closely united with Jesus in His self-giving love on the cross. Ironically, the cross, the sign of contradiction with two bars at perpendicular angles, is the sign and way toward unity.

As we draw closer to the two-thousandth anniversary of the event at the center of world history, the passion of Christ, we cannot ignore the signs of the times. The times are urgent, and we can no longer afford to be divided. The enemy is on the move, and he is drawing many souls into deception, darkness, and destruction. The battle is far too big for us to keep fighting separately. But the Lord is also on the move. As many have prophesied, God is preparing to bring about a massive harvest of evangelization in our time. *"I tell you, look up and see the fields ripe for the harvest"* (John 4:35 NAB). The Lord wants to sweep as many people into the arms of Jesus as will listen to the gospel, while there is time. We need to learn to proclaim it with one voice, with hearts united, even while we still await the day when we will be fully and visibly united. In the words of my good friend Fr. Peter Hocken, "The Lord is coming for His bride. Without the work of the Holy Spirit in every tradition, the bride is not prepared. She is only half clothed."

DEARLY BELOVED EVANGELICAL AND CHARISMATIC PROTESTANT BROTHERS AND SISTERS,

Whenever I am with you, my heart is touched in a deeper way by the love of the Father, my love for Jesus increases, and my awareness of the presence and power of the Holy Spirit grows.

You have shown me what it looks like to believe and obey the Word of God radically, without any watering down, hedging, mixing, reinterpreting, soft-peddling, or over-complicating. As the great Holiness Pentecostal healing evangelist Smith Wigglesworth used to say, "God said it, I believe it, and that settles it."

Because of your preaching and the dozens of your testimonies that I've read and heard, I've experienced the power of God's Word to pierce to *"the division of soul and of spirit, of joints and of marrow, and discerning the thoughts and intentions of the heart"* (Hebrews 4:12).

You've stirred my heart with the simplicity and intensity of your love for Jesus. Most of your songs for worship are love songs. Gregorian chant and doctrinally rich traditional hymns are beautiful too, but there is something about those love songs that awakens the heart. They can bring a group of worshipping people right into the throne room of God, the holy of holies. I've worshipped with you at times when the things of earth fade away and the glory cloud of God's presence comes down upon us. Your worship has lifted my heart countless times.

You've deeply challenged me with your commitment to evangelizing the lost. Years ago, I got to know a dear elderly pastor, Ray Bringham, whose goal was to lead at least one person to Christ every day—and for most of his days, he had done it! I'm continually amazed when I witness that personal conviction of our responsibility to lead the lost to salvation. That conviction is also deeply rooted in our Catholic tradition and is modeled by many saints, like Patrick, Francis Xavier, and Thérèse of Lisieux, yet somewhere along the way, we Catholics lost sight of it. So we need your help in relearning the art of evangelism and making it a part of our culture.

You've shown me a level of faith in the mighty working of God that I didn't know was possible—the supernatural as the normal Christian life. Some of your conferences and events are amazingly high voltage, with the power of God breaking out everywhere, radically changing lives and history. So many of you are models of the fact that the power by which the Holy Spirit does miracles is the same power by which He makes us holy, capable of pouring ourselves out in love for others.

Thank you for being who you are and generously sharing your gifts. We need you. When asked why the Holy Spirit has allowed so many divisions among Christians, Pope John Paul II said, "Could it not be that these divisions have also been a path continually leading the church to discover the untold wealth contained in Christ's Gospel and in the redemption accomplished by Christ? Perhaps all this wealth would not have come to light otherwise."

And dear fellow servants of the Lord, please forgive us Catholics for the ways we have sometimes nurtured attitudes of spiritual smugness, superiority, arrogance, disparagement, or even contempt for other Christians, as if we have nothing to learn from you.

Please forgive us for the times we have harbored a sectarian, us-versus-them mentality, for the times we have judged or looked down on you, forgetting what Scripture says: *"Who are you to pass judgment on the servant of another? It is before his own master that he stands or falls. And he will be upheld, for the Lord is able to make him stand"* (Romans 14:4).

Please forgive the poor example we have sometimes given, having a complacent satisfaction in the fact that we belong to the Catholic Church while actually living in Christian mediocrity, an outward religiosity without a heart burning for Christ.

Please forgive the imbalanced theology and catechesis that has led many Catholics to think—contrary to our own church's doctrine—that salvation is earned by our works.

Please forgive the ways we have simply been indifferent to the scandal of Christian disunity, not weeping as Christ weeps over the divisions in His body and over the unbelievers who are repelled instead of attracted to the gospel when they see our divisions.

May the Lord wash away all these sins and failings in His own precious blood. May the walls of misunderstanding and division come crashing down and may the Holy Spirit reunite us in truth and love by His divine power. Together may we lift high the cross, the world's only hope, and glorify Jesus together.

Your sister in Christ,

Mary Healy

Dr. Mary Healy is professor of Scripture at Sacred Heart Major Seminary in Detroit. Connect with her at www.drmaryhealy.com.

30

THE ORTHODOX CHURCH'S QUEST FOR CHRISTIAN UNITY

Metropolitan Job of Pisidia
| Eastern Orthodox |

Contrary to what some may think, the Orthodox are neither opposed nor indifferent to the quest for Christian unity. Indeed, for centuries, at every church service, the Orthodox pray "for the stability of the holy churches of God and for the union of all."

In fact, Orthodox were pioneers and architects of the ecumenical movement of the twentieth century. Already in 1902, the encyclical of Ecumenical Patriarch Joachim III sent to the primates of the autocephalous Orthodox churches raised the question of relations and theological dialogue with non-Orthodox churches, stating, "The union of them and of all who believe in Christ with us in the Orthodox faith is the pious and heart-felt desire of our church and of all genuine Christians who stand firm in the evangelical doctrine of unity, and it is the subject of constant prayer and supplication."

Two decades later, the famous encyclical of the Ecumenical Patriarchate of January 1920 "unto the Churches of Christ everywhere" stressed the "necessity for establishing a contact and league (fellowship or κοινωνία) between the churches," by analogy to the League of Nations created in 1919. This encyclical is often seen as a prophetic call for the creation of what later would become the World Council of Churches (WCC), established in 1948.

On January 5, 1964, Patriarch Athenagoras met Pope Paul VI during their common visit to the Mount of Olives in Jerusalem, where they exchanged the kiss of peace. There, they took the prophetic risk of moving the Christian world from the night of division toward the shining day in which Christians ought to be reconciled. After their historic meeting in Jerusalem, Patriarch Athenagoras and Pope Paul VI agreed to "remove from memory and from the midst of the church the sentences of excommunication" leveled against each other in 1054, which had divided the churches for centuries. The lifting up of the anathemas of 1054 between the churches of Rome and Constantinople at the end of the Second Vatican Council, on December 7, 1965, is of extreme importance, since it brings back the two churches of Rome and Constantinople to the situation they were before their imposition, at the beginning of the eleventh century: they do not stand in an accomplished schism but are rather in a state of rupture of communion (*akoinonesia*), due to historical events and theological disputes, which must be clarified and overcome through theological dialogue in order to restore today the full ecclesiastical communion.

Ecumenical Patriarch Athenagoras always stressed the importance of meeting with other Christians. As he often used to say, "Come, let us look one another in the eyes, and let us then see what we have to say to one another." He is the one who has contributed the most to open the eyes of the Orthodox to a broader ecumenical family.

THE FUTURE OF THE MOVEMENT FOR CHRISTIAN UNITY

In our days, we often hear that the ecumenical movement is in crisis. It is well known that the practice of ordination of women and same-sex marriages that have been introduced within some Christian confessions have jeopardized the goal of the bilateral dialogues conducted with them, making unrealistic the restoration of communion with them and the achievement of Christian unity. Nevertheless, dialogue still continues in a warm and friendly atmosphere and is making progress in mutual understanding.

If we look more closely, we will notice a certain dogmatic relativism among some Christian confessions, which are either indifferent or lax toward doctrinal and ethical questions and therefore consider that the ecumenical movement should not be preoccupied by the quest of Christian unity but should focus on common action, either on charity or on social, environmental, and political issues.

Some Orthodox coming from countries where Orthodoxy is the dominant confession also consider that there is no point searching for Christian unity with other Christians who express dogmatic and moral relativism. They are tempted to reduce the ecumenical movement to a common Christian block against secularism, Islamization, and Christianophobia.

Often, many challenges emerge on unity not only between the churches, but even within the same Christian family. Matters of faith and order are not only stumbling blocks between the different Christian churches; sometimes, ethical, social, or political questions are causes of divisions within the same church or Christian denomination. The most eloquent example is certainly the questions relating to human sexuality, which create divisions not only between the various Christian churches, but sometimes even within the same family. Confronted with internal tensions within different Christian churches or denominations, the World Council of Churches has, perhaps even more than ever, the mission of leading divided Christians toward unity by facilitating their reconciliation.

Therefore, it is evident that the most urgent and relevant question for the future of the ecumenical movement is the reconciliation of Christians, both the reconciliation of the churches among themselves and the reconciliation within each ecclesial family. To this, one may also add genuine solidarity not only with our fellow human beings, especially those in need, but also solidary with the entire God's creation, by taking the proper urgent actions for the protection of the environment.

Fr. Georges Florovsky had already noted in 1971 that the reason of the decline of the ecumenical movement in general, and of the World Council of Churches and its commission on Faith and Order in particular, was the result of "decisions made by men who are ignorant of dogma and ignorant of church history, tradition, Christian culture. Hence, they feel that what we need to do is find what we have in common, then forget the rest."

ORTHODOX CHALLENGES ON THE WAY TO CHRISTIAN UNITY

The Orthodox participation in the ecumenical movement is being challenged today by different problems. One of them is religious fundamentalism, observed not only in countries where Orthodoxy is the main Christian confession, such as Greece, the Balkans, Eastern Europe, and the Caucasus, but also in countries of the Orthodox diaspora, such as the USA. These *Orthodox fundamentalists* condemn the so-called "heresy of ecumenism" and reject ecumenical common prayer and even the possibility of inter-Christian marriages.

They have orchestrated an aggressive campaign against the Holy and Great Council of the Orthodox Church of Crete in June 2016. For this reason, the council condemned "all efforts to break the unity of the church, undertaken by individuals or groups under the pretext of maintaining or allegedly defending true Orthodoxy." This statement is a very important one at an epoch when fundamentalism is growing among some Orthodox believers who very often out of ignorance are promoting anti-ecumenical views that contradict the ethos and the vision of Orthodoxy.

Besides encouraging inter-Christian dialogue, the Holy and Great Council has indicated inter-religious dialogue as an antidote to religious fundamentalism, noting, "Honest interfaith dialogue contributes to the development of mutual trust and to the promotion of peace and reconciliation."

Theological fundamentalism is essentially due to ignorance of the progress of the theological dialogues and, above all, of the documents produced by these dialogues over the last forty years. In order to overcome this fundamentalism, it is urgent that these documents be studied in theological faculties so that the future pastors of the churches be informed properly. But this is not enough. These documents, most often incomprehensible to the basic faithful, should be explained and summarized for the laity. Perhaps the national committees for bilateral dialogues could take this responsibility of popularizing the results of the Joint International Commissions.

Very often, fundamentalism exists where there is an ignorance or a fear of *the other*. As the late Metropolitan of Pergamon, John Zizioulas, has pointed out, we often feel threatened by the other, whom we often see first as an enemy before we can consider him a friend. Communion with the other is not spontaneous. It presupposes overcoming barriers. In order to overcome these barriers, local dialogue is necessary so that former enemies might become friends. For this reason, there is a need for regional inter-Christian dialogues to foster the encounter of former enemies and create new friendships and thus overcome the fear of the other and religious fundamentalism.

Another problem is the revival of ethnophyletism (religious nationalism) that not only threatens the unity of the Orthodox Church but the ecumenical movement as well. The Orthodox religious nationalist considers that he does not need the *other* Christians and therefore does not care about them. The Orthodox in the *diaspora* can show how to overcome this nationalistic temptation by witnessing that Orthodoxy is much broader than one's national identity and that Christianity rather calls humanity toward unity rather than fragmentation.

DEAR BROTHERS AND SISTERS IN CHRIST,

The quest of Christian unity is not merely the purpose or, as one would say, the dream of the ecumenical movement, but a norm that derives from the very definition of the church as being *one*. All Christians believe and confess their faith in the "one, holy, catholic, and apostolic church." In the structure of the church, the bishop is the guarantor of its unity and therefore one can define his ministry as being at the service of church unity.

Indeed, in what we call the local church, which is the diocese, the clergy and the faithful are united under one bishop. Thus is manifested their communion as being the one body of Christ in a particular locality. The bishop is not only the head of his local church but assures the communion of his church with all the churches throughout the universe. This is a fundamental principle of ecclesiology and a fundamental role of the bishop as the minister of the unity of the church: assuring the internal and external unity of his local church.

But already, the Apostolic Canon 34 underlined the correlation between the first bishop of a region with the other bishops of that region, stating that the bishops of a region must recognize the one who is first among them and not do anything important without his consent, as the first cannot do anything without the consent of all. The seven ecumenical councils in AD 325–787 attributed certain prerogatives to the first bishop of the region, which was called metropolitan and who ought to minister the regional communion between the different local churches. From this principle subsequently emerged the patriarchates. Between the fourth and the seventh centuries, an order appeared among the five patriarchal sees (Rome, Constantinople, Alexandria, Antioch, and Jerusalem), with the see of Rome occupying the first place, exercising a primacy of honor (*presbeia tes times*). This *diakonia* of the ecclesial *koinonia* is both internal and external. It presupposes serving unity at the local, regional, and universal level. It presupposes serving unity within our church and among the churches.

Despite all problems that we may encounter on the way toward Christian unity, the Orthodox Church believes that it is the main goal of the ecumenical movement and always underlines that unity of doctrine presupposes ecclesial unity and unity in the sacraments. During his visit to the headquarters of the World Council of Churches in Geneva in April 2017, Ecumenical Patriarch Bartholomew affirmed, "We Orthodox strongly believe that the aim and the raison d'être of the ecumenical movement and of the World Council of Churches is to fulfill the Lord's final prayer, that *'all may be one'*," citing John 17:21. "The Holy and Great Council stressed that 'Orthodox participation in the movement to restore unity with other Christians in the one, holy, catholic and apostolic church is in no way foreign to the nature and history of the Orthodox Church, but rather represents a consistent expression of the apostolic faith and tradition in new historical circumstances.'"

In fact, the Holy and Great Council of the Orthodox Church, convened in Crete in 2016, reaffirmed what the Orthodox already stated during the first Conference on Faith and Order in Lausanne in 1927, that goal of the participation of the Orthodox Church in the ecumenical movement is "seeking the unity of all Christians on the basis of the truth of the faith and tradition of the ancient Church of the Seven Ecumenical Councils."

But the council has also underlined the necessity in the ecumenical movement for the synergy between human efforts and the grace of God, reminding us, "While the Orthodox Church dialogues with other Christians, she does not underestimate the difficulties inherent in this endeavor; she perceives these difficulties, however, on the path toward a common understanding of the tradition of the ancient church and in hope that the Holy Spirit, '*Who holds together the whole institution of the Church*,' will '*make up that which is lacking*.'"

Therefore, our thirst for Christian unity cannot be only the result of human efforts through theological dialogues and business meetings, but of the grace of God, which we seek through humble prayer. In this sense, let us never forget that the final words of Christ that "*they may all be one*" (John 17:21) were in fact not a commandment, but a prayer!

Lord Jesus Christ, look down from heaven, visit and fortify Your church, which You bought with Your own blood (Acts 20:28). Prevent in her schisms and divisions and stop the uprisings of heresies by the power of Your Holy Spirit. You who have established repentance as the way of salvation, grant us the spirit of contrition for our sins and of reconciliation between ourselves. Grant us to be one and remain in unity, as You are one with Your Father, so that with one voice and one heart, we may glorify and praise Your most honored and majestic name, of the Father and the Son and the Holy Spirit, now and forever and to the ages of ages. Amen.

Metropolitan Job of Pisidia is co-president of the Joint International Commission for the Theological Dialogue between the Roman-Catholic Church and the Orthodox Church. He is a member of the Commission on Faith and Order of the World Council of Churches. His church website is pisidia.church.

31

LESSONS FROM A FRIENDSHIP THAT WENT SOUTH

Avi Snyder
| Messianic Jew |

Division.

An ugly word to the apostle Paul. So ugly, in fact, that he exhorted the believers in Corinth:

> *I appeal to you, brothers, by the name of our Lord Jesus Christ, that all of you agree, and that there be no divisions among you, but that you be united in the same mind and the same judgment.*
>
> (1 Corinthians 1:10)

I can't help but wonder whether memories of his split with Barnabas flashed through Paul's mind when he wrote those words to the Corinthians. And in Philippians 4:2–3, when he implored believers to help Euodia and Syntyche to become reconciled to each other, is it possible that Paul thought to himself, "If only someone had been there for Barnabas and for me." What went wrong between Barnabas and Paul? The two of them had started off so well.

It was Barnabas who stood up for Paul in Jerusalem and brought him into the company of the other believers when they shunned him. They just couldn't believe that this virulent persecutor of the church had become a genuine proclaimer of the faith. But Barnabas believed, and Barnabas brought unity between them and Paul. Years later, Paul would tell the Corinthians that love bears all things, believes all things, endures all things, and hopes all things. Did he learn that from Barnabas?

It was Barnabas who fetched Paul from Tarsus and brought him back to Antioch to minster to that fledgling church. We can only imagine the intimate fellowship that they enjoyed, not just as they served together day in and day out, but when they spent days and nights together in prayer.

It was Barnabas and Paul whom God called *together* and who set out *together* to bring the gospel to the gentiles in Cyprus, Pamphylia, and lower Galatia. God's Spirit must have used their mutual love and companionship to bolster one another as they ventured into totally unknown fields of ministry.

And when misguided or counterfeit believers began to teach gentile converts that they needed to be circumcised and observe the Law of Moses along with the non-biblical oral law in order to be saved, it was Barnabas and Paul who to traveled to Jerusalem to dispute those fraudulent claims. True, Peter's testimony put the defining word on the dispute. But it was Barnabas and Paul who gave weight to Peter's words by describing the miraculous ways in which the Lord had worked among the gentiles during their missionary trip.

So, quite naturally, they planned a second trip together.

Then matters went south.

Barnabas wanted to take his nephew John Mark along with them, but Paul objected because the young man had deserted them in Pamphylia. This was no minor disagreement. The dispute grew so fierce that Paul and Barnabas split and went their separate ways.

Division.

How could they have split? As Jewish men, they certainly understood the need for unity and the strength that comes from laboring as one. That sense of unity and collective identity punctuates our entire history. We consisted of twelves tribes, but we constituted one people: Jacob, Israel.

A HEALTHY DIVISION

Early in his letter to the Philippians, Paul gives a virtual table of contents for a treatise on unity. But he prefaces his words with a reminder that a healthy division must occur between true believers and those who oppose the spread of the good news. A blanket, indiscriminate unity with all people, regardless of their views about the gospel, can only come about through a compromise at the cost of truth. It should come as no surprise, then, that Paul starts off his word about unity within the body of believers with a reminder of the opposition that will be encountered from without. He tells the Philippians that it's been granted to them not only to trust in Yeshua (Jesus), but to *"suffer for his sake"* (Philippians 1:29). Opposition should be expected, because whenever the gospel message is clearly proclaimed, division and polarization always occur. That's one of the reasons why the gospel must be presented in love. The message itself is so cutting that it hardly needs any additional sharpening from its advocates.

Division that comes out of a clear and loving presentation of the good news is healthy, even good, because it proves that the gospel message is getting through. To those who are perishing, we're the smell of death unto death. To those who are being saved, we're the fragrance of life unto life. (See 2 Corinthians 2:15–16.) So Paul calls the Philippians to be unified, to stand firm *"in one spirit, with one mind striving side by side for the faith of the gospel"* (Philippians 1:27).

Believers should expect opposition, yes. But the opposition Paul addresses at the start of his call for unity focuses on an opposition from *without*, not an opposition from *within*. With that said, Paul gives the quintessential picture of being united in Messiah.

PAUL'S CHECKLIST FOR UNITY

> *So if there is any encouragement in Christ, any comfort from love, any participation in the Spirit, any affection and sympathy, complete my joy by being of the same mind, having the same love, being in full accord and of one mind. Do nothing from selfish ambition or conceit, but in humility count others more significant than yourselves. Let each of you look not only to his own interests, but also to the interests of others. Have this mind among yourselves, which is yours in Christ Jesus.* (Philippians 2:1–5)

UNITED IN CHRIST

Paul starts with the most obvious and most essential ingredient in his recipe for true unity. That unity depends on being together *"in Christ."* Without a unity in Christ, we really possess no unity at all—just a commonality that, at best, allows us to agree on peripheral matters. But it's our unity in the Messiah that overrides every difference and demolishes every barrier that divides us.

My heart breaks when I meet genuine believers in Jesus who tell me that unity between them and my Jewish people can only be achieved by leaving a discussion of Jesus out of the equation. Their omission only reinforces the false notion that *Jesus* is to blame for the crimes that have been committed in His name! That omission isn't just evil; it drives our two peoples further apart, and it imperils my people's spiritual well-being.

Perhaps Paul, better than anyone else, understood that no genuine unity can possibly exist unless that unity finds its anchor in a personal, individual relationship with and in the Lord. Just think of the disparate and irreconcilable parties that the Lord brought together in Paul's communities and on his teams: Jews, Greeks, bond, free, male, female. How could such a unity exist? Only "*in Christ.*" Paul, the Jew, the Pharisee, the Hebrew of Hebrews, told Ephesian former pagans who had been cut off from God that now, they had been brought near by the blood of the Messiah. And because they had been reconciled to God through Christ, they were reconciled to each other, Jews and gentiles alike. *Jesus* was their peace. *He* had made them one. *He* had broken down the walls that had kept them apart. But without that foundational, personal relationship with the Lord, those barriers remained firmly in place. There could be no genuine collective unity with each other without an individual, personal unity with Christ.

The Scriptures use extremely potent images to describe the collective unity that we possess with each other solely because of the individual relationship that we enjoy with the Lord. Paul tells us that we comprise His body. How can we *not* think of the imagery that the Lord used when He described the relationship between a husband and wife—one flesh. The apostle John tells us that those who have received Him become the children of God. Without that foundational, personal relationship with Jesus, we might be companions and even closest friends, but we're not family—not until we have the same Father.

To some extent, I'm a product of the civil rights/anti-war movement of the 1960s and 1970s in the United States. We loved to sing songs about unity as we marched. We locked arms. We called each other brothers and sisters. Our burden for peace made us genuine comrades. But did that burden make us family? Not really.

Can I labor alongside those who don't know my Messiah? Of course. Can I respect, admire, and learn from them? Without any doubt. Can I love them and even sacrifice my life for them? Absolutely. But can I share a familial intimacy and unity with them, an intimacy and unity that even rises above quarrels and strong disagreements? No. Not until we're family. Not until we're one in Him.

UNITED WITH ONE MIND

Next, Paul stresses the fact that unity calls for us to have one mind. On *everything?* No. Paul makes it clear in his letter to the Romans that room for disagreement exists on many matters, such as which day we might set aside above others. But the basics of the gospel remain nonnegotiable. We can hardly itemize all those basics here. But those irrevocable, non-dilutable truths certainly include the triune nature of God: God the Father, Yeshua the Lord, and the Spirit of God, who distributes His gifts just as He wills. Those basics also include:

- The historical reality of the gospel. Yeshua died for our sins, He was buried, and He rose on the third day.
- The integrity, as well as the sole and supreme authority of the Scriptures. Yeshua's death and resurrection occurred just as Moses and the prophets foretold.
- The uniqueness of the gospel. Only Jesus saves; only the gospel is the power of God unto salvation.
- The necessity of the gospel for all people—to the Jew first and also to the gentile.
- The way we appropriate the Lord's salvation—by God's grace through faith, apart from any works.
- The exclusive mediation of Yeshua. Only the Son of God sits at the right hand of the Father, incessantly interceding for us.
- The guarantee of His second coming and therefore the need for all people to repent. Yeshua will return to judge the living and the dead.

There can be no compromise on these and other basics. When it comes to matters of life and death, unity can't be purchased at the expense of objective truth. And the gospel is a matter of life and death.

UNITED IN THE SAME LOVE

Believers are united by Who we possess, the very Spirit of God. And one of the fruits of possessing His Spirit is the ability to love, even as He loves. But it begins with God. We only love because God first loved us and gave His Son to die for our sins. And because we now love God, we love our brothers and sisters, whom He loves, even as He loves each one of us. In fact, if we're not united to our family in Yeshua by love, then there's something seriously wrong. The apostle John makes that unquestionably and uncomfortably clear. *"If anyone says, 'I love God,' and hates his brother, he is a liar; for he who does not love his brother whom he has seen cannot love God whom he has not seen"* (1 John 4:20).

But the story doesn't end there. The love that unites us to the Lord and to each other must extend to those who revile and persecute us, even to those we'd rather not love.

In the mid-1990s, we Jews for Jesus first started sending teams from Russia and Ukraine into Germany in order to reach Jewish people who were emigrating to that country from the collapsed USSR. Though we focused on bringing the gospel to our own, we never hesitated to share the good news with Germans as well. It was a joy to bring God's message of life to the children and grandchildren of people who'd sought our deaths and total destruction just a few decades before.

A remarkable, unnatural ability to love should unite us, set us apart, and send us out. And this brings us to Paul's next mark of unity.

UNITED IN ONE SPIRIT AND PURPOSE

In the nineteenth century, a British missionary to China, Charles Thomas Studd, wrote a poem that declared this riveting truth:

Only one life, "twill soon be past

Only what's done for Christ will last

Genuine believers have one single, unified purpose: to proclaim the kingdom of God. How that purpose plays out in each of our lives will vary. It all depends on how God wants to use us. But whatever the use, the purpose remains the same. It's not political, and it's not social. It's evangelistic. Though societal changes have taken place and will always occur, the purpose is not transformation; the purpose is proclamation. Peter wrote, *"But you are a chosen race, a royal priesthood, a holy nation, a people for his own possession, that you may proclaim the excellencies of him who called you out of darkness into his marvelous light*" (1 Peter 2:9). Peter, the apostle to us Jews, wrote those words primarily to his fellow Jews and own constituency—Jewish believers, scattered throughout Pontius, Galatia, Cappadocia, Asia, and Bithynia. But even so, his words certainly speak to all believers of all nationalities today. Regardless of nationality, God called us to proclaim.

Of course, Peter merely stressed what Jesus had declared before He ascended to the Father: "*Go into all the world and proclaim the gospel to the whole creation*" (Mark 16:15).

That's not a solitary pursuit. We need to serve together. The book of Ecclesiastes makes that clear enough.

> *Two are better than one, because they have a good reward for their toil. For if they fall, one will lift up his fellow. But woe to him who is alone when he falls and has not another to lift him up! Again, if two lie together, they keep warm, but how can one keep warm alone?*
>
> (Ecclesiastes 4:9–11)

We need each other, not just for the sake of a better return on our labors. We need each other for mutual strength, encouragement, and support. Without each other, we're weak, even crippled. Though the biblical text doesn't say it, I suspect that Paul and Barnabas became *something less* during the remainder of their missionary journey together after John Mark abandoned them in Pamphylia. And I suspect that Paul ran the risk of becoming something less when he and Barnabas split apart. But what Paul lacked by losing Barnabas, God graciously resupplied by providing Silas and then Timothy.

THE UNITY OF CARING MORE FOR OTHERS

Finally, Paul speaks about the unity that comes from being more concerned about others' well-being than about our own. He exhorts us to abandon our selfishness, to regard others as though they were more important, and to prioritize others' interests, not just our own. Paul, the Benjaminite, undoubtedly recalled the severe admonition that Moses gave the sons of Gad and Reuben when they wanted to place their own interests over the interests of the other tribes by staying on the east side of the Jordan. "*Shall your brothers go to the war while you sit here? Why will you discourage the heart of the people of Israel from going over into the land that the* L*ORD* *has given them?"* (Numbers 32:6–7).

Choosing to care for our brothers and sisters presumes a unity that irrevocably binds us to them. Paul ends by pointing to Yeshua as the supreme and unparalleled example of that kind of self-sacrifice for the sake of others. He humbled Himself and took on flesh in order to become one of us.

COMING BACK TO BARNABAS AND SAUL

If we apply Paul's checklist to him, the apostle to the nations, and to Barnabas, the son of encouragement, what do we find? Were Paul and Barnabas *"in Christ"*? Most certainly they were! Though we don't have a record of Barnabas's conversion experience, his inclusion among the disciples and the accounts of his labors make it clear that he belonged to the Lord. As for Paul, we have the explicit recounting of how he came to faith, both in his own words and through the retelling of the incident by Luke.

Were they *"of one mind"* about the gospel message? Of course. When Paul preached his message in synagogues like the one in Pisidian Antioch on their first missionary journey, we have no record of Barnabas taking Paul aside later on to correct him or add any nuances that Paul had failed to bring out.

Were they intent with one spirit on pursuing one purpose, the furtherance of the good news? The biblical record eliminates any question about that. No one ever labored in Messiah's cause more fervently than Paul. Barnabas certainly ran close behind.

Did they place others before themselves? The love Paul expressed in his letters and the very meaning of Barnabas's name banish any doubt.

But did they maintain the same love for each other that marked their relationship from the start? Well, that seems to be the point at which they hit a real snag. Love bears all things. Believes all things. Endures all things. Hopes all things. Love never fails.

But they did.

What happened? We don't really know, and it's always a little dangerous to second guess about what the Scriptures leave unsaid. We simply know that when it came to whether they should take John Mark with them a second time, they argued so sharply that *"they separated from each other"* (Acts 15:39).

A lifetime of mercies, companionship, and compassion, seemingly lost in a single moment of wrath.

What a great pity when we allow resolvable conflicts, arising from tempers and temperaments, to divide brothers and sisters who share a unity in every other way. What a great pity when we're less than quick to hear, slow to speak, and slow to anger. Perhaps this was the case with Barnabas and Paul when they argued over John Mark.

But I have a hunch…

> *In all things God works for the good of those who love him, who have been called.* (Romans 8:28 NIV)

I have a hunch that God planned to separate Paul and Barnabas after their initial journey, though without the rancor, just so that they could cover more ground. We know that Barnabas and John Mark returned to Cyprus, and Paul ultimately got to Rome. Whether or not Paul ever got as far west as Spain, as he'd hoped, remains a question mark. We'll have to ask him when we're all united in the kingdom after Yeshua's return.

But the expansion goes far beyond geography. In time, John Mark gave us the infallible gospel account that carries his name, while Paul's letters remain our first and only inspired textbook on systematic theology.

Did Paul and Barnabas ever reconnect? There's a hint that maybe, just maybe, they did! In 1 Corinthians 9:6, Paul asked somewhat sardonically whether only he and Barnabas had *"no right to refrain from working for a living."* True, he made no mention of Barnabas actually laboring with him. But the reference to his old companion opens up the possibility of some kind of renewed connection. And in the last letter that Paul wrote shortly before his death, he told Timothy, *"Get* [John] *Mark and bring him with you, for he is very useful to me for ministry"* (2 Timothy 4:11). Apparently, some reconciliation and reunification took place between Paul and John Mark along the way. Though we have no record of it, I'd like to think that a reconciliation and reunification took place between Paul and Barnabas as well.

That hunch leaves me with a hope. No division between genuine believers needs to remain permanent. We can always find unity if we put hands and feet to the words that Yeshua gave us in Matthew 5:23–24: *"So if you are offering your gift at the altar and there remember that your brother has something against you, leave your gift there before the altar and go. First be reconciled to your brother, and then come and offer your gift."*

DEAR FAMILY IN YESHUA,

Under the inspiration of the Holy Spirit, David wrote, *"Behold, how good and pleasant it is when brothers* [and sisters] *dwell in unity!"* (Psalm 133:1).

The call to be unified confronts us with a genuine challenge. On the one hand, we must remain true and devoted to what the Scriptures teach, even if that causes some separation. But at the same time, we must remain committed to being united just as the Lord commanded. To be honest, that's not an easy tightrope to walk! Sometimes, we compromise our biblical convictions for the sake of achieving a unity that really isn't a unity at all; it's just a search for the least common denominator. At the same time, there are those moments when we let our minor, non-biblical differences sever the unity that the love of God compels us to pursue. We say that we're being faithfully firm, but we're really just being unnecessarily stubborn, or even worse, proud. So let me end with a modest but earnest prayer. "Father, we are one, only because of our faith and trust in what You accomplished for us through the sacrifice of Your Son. May our unity be grounded in an unshakable commitment to the truth of the gospel. And may our unity be demonstrated by a love for each other that bears, believes, endures, and hopes all things. In that unity, may we bring Your good news to those who still need to hear what You have done. In Yeshua's name, we pray. Amen."

God bless you, brothers and sisters.

In Yeshua,

Avi Snyder

Isaiah 49:6

Avi Snyder serves as the European ambassador of Jews for Jesus. Connect with him at jewsforjesus.org/staff/avi-snyder.